SUZUKI CHANGED MY LIFE

Masaaki Honda M.D.

Suzuki changed my life

Masaaki Honda M.D.

SUMMY-BIRCHARD INC.

Secaucus, New Jersey

Library of Congress Cataloging in Publication Data

Honda, Masaaki, 1914-
    Suzuki changed my life.

    1. Suzuki, Shin'ichi, 1898-   I. Title
ML418.S83H6   780'.77   76-10130
ISBN 0-87487-084-4

ACKNOWLEDGEMENTS

Special thanks are due to Miss Kathy Irving, Miss Judith Heggestad, and Mr. Michael Armentrout for their assistance in proofreading and for their many helpful suggestions. And I extend my greatest appreciation to Dr. Robert Klotman and Dr. Phyllis Klotman for their help in editing.

Contents

II

Prelude

A BABY IS BORN

Twilight was creeping closer and the good earth was barren and cold. The chill wind passed through the crack in the window molding, fluttering the cotton curtain turned colorless by the sun. The mist hung low in the valley and smoke curled up from the neighboring chimney, then suddenly floated sideways as if an unseen hand were holding it down.

I was cold physically and chilled to the marrow spiritually. Everything in the past seemed fruitless and the future seemed hopeless and desolate. A month had passed since I had been afflicted with a lung disease and had returned to the house in the country where my parents were living.

After the Second World War, people in Japan had lost everything—this stroke of misfortune came equally to all. But what was not equally distributed was good and bad health, and I drew the unlucky lot.

I recalled the day when our first daughter, Yuko, was born. Junko, my wife, had suddenly complained about the pains at dawn on May 1, 1945. It did not take much time to dress, as we always slept with our clothes on in order to be ready for air raids. I helped Junko down the stairs with utmost tenderness. Once outside I pulled the cart loaded with blankets and pillows while my wife walked beside me through the narrow lane into the field leading to the hospital not far from our home. The doctor, who had diagnosed the previous day that the labor pains would begin at the earliest two days from then, was surprised but still welcomed us in good humor,

1

even though we had disturbed her slumber. At 5:25 that morning, Yuko was born, a very tiny baby with wrinkles on her face. Glancing at the rather pathetic looking little creature, the doctor feared that she might not survive. But as we could not read her mind, we did not think for even a moment that the baby might be taken back to the darkness from which she had arrived. On this same day Berlin fell and Hitler died; old and evil disappeared and at the same time newness and goodness were born. I hoped that the newborn would bring light to people. In spite of her small body, she cried with vigor, demonstrating her wish to live. Junko, whose constitution was delicate, looked tenderly at the baby sleeping at her side. She had already forgotten the hardships and sickness the baby had brought to her, and now motherly tenderness was awakening in her.

Three days later, at about ten o'clock in the evening, she was awakened by the shrill sound of the siren announcing an air raid. She quietly rose, took the baby in her arms, and went down into the basement. There she sat in the dark, holding Yuko tightly to her breast, staring at the dark wall, emotionless. The small life had given her new hope and courage.

As the days went by, Yuko gained weight, thanks to her mother's milk, which was more than adequate even without sufficient food. We were happy despite poverty though I did not know what tomorrow would bring.

The war ended abruptly. I had heard the rumor three days before it actually happened that Japan would accept the treaty offered by the Allies, but I was reluctant to believe it. On August 15 at noon, however, all the staff at the Institute of Infectious Diseases to which I belonged were called to assemble in the big hall. It was hot. We heard the proclamation of the Emperor with tears and perspiration flowing down our cheeks. This was the end. It seemed as if we had suffered the past several years in vain. On returning to my room I thought once again, yes, indeed it was the end. The mice and eggs inoculated by the influenza virus had seemed so important an hour before, but now the experiment was of no interest to me.

SUZUKI'S VOICE

I felt the coldness creeping into the room, the small barren room which held only my mattress and sleeping items. I turned the radio on. It was always a consolation to hear various programs on the air.

"Mr. Suzuki, so your opinion is that all children can develop their abilities if they have a good environment from an early age." It was the announcer.

"Yes, I am convinced that all children can develop their abilities or talents. People are apt to think that musical talent is something inherited but we all know that children throughout the world speak their mother tongue. But when we reflect on how difficult it is for adults to master foreign languages, we must acknowledge that the natural ability of children to absorb whatever comes to them must be very high. So I thought of the application to violin instead of to language, and to my own amazement I had remarkable success. Now we will have a demonstration. These children who will play today come from various family backgrounds—merchants, farmers, and medical doctors. The only similarity among them is that they all have had no music in their homes, much less a violin. We took them all as they applied, with no previous testing. I would like to make people understand talent can be developed and is not inherited." It was Mr. Suzuki.

The children began playing their violins. The tone was clean and the tempo good. It was not at all like hearing children play. I was dumbfounded to hear such a wonderful performance by such small children. I forgot the chill and the desolate room.

From the beginning of my boyhood I loved music—adored it. But I thought that music was to be performed only by those who were specially gifted. The heavenly music that we all so enjoyed certainly could not be created by ordinary people! But what had Suzuki said? If I heard correctly:

"Every child can develop his 'talent'." Then according to his understanding, talent and ability must be the same.

I reflected on my own experience in learning English. Did I possess the ability from the day of my birth? Certainly not! It was my environment that made it possible for me to understand this foreign language.

I

MY BOYHOOD IN THE COUNTRY

Until I was six years old, I lived in Okazaki, a small city in Aichi prefecture. Those were happy days for me. I was carefree and able to do what I wanted, just as any other boy in the world. My father was a merchant who sold charcoal and fuel. I was a younger son of the family. I called my mother "mommy," which came out very naturally, but I was reluctant to call my father "daddy." Something deep inside me, perhaps something instinctual, held my tongue from calling him thus.

As I said before, my life at that time was happy. In summer the nearby river was our major playground. We swam to our hearts' content. I was always in the middle of games and pranks. Much against my will I had to go to kindergarten, where I not only had to wear a white apron, but also had to keep it neat and clean. The other boys in my gang didn't have to go to kindergarten and throughout the morning they were waiting for my return. I envied their freedom and careless attitude. I hated going to kindergarten. I hated singing those childish folksongs, I hated marching hand in hand with girls and dancing those silly dances.

I always waited impatiently for the bell to ring dismissing the class. I was the first to jump up at the sound of the bell and run back home. As soon as I crossed the threshold of my house, I would cry, "Here I am; I'm back," and, flinging down the bag containing my lunchbox, would go outside again. My gang was always waiting for me, waiting eagerly for me to join them. Then came the glorious time. I enjoyed every minute I spent with my gang.

To be a leader and to sustain this position, one had to display outstanding bravery or perform special stunts. One of the games was to strike a match and see who could hold it the longest. When the flame flickered near the tip, all the other boys dropped the match rather quickly, but I endured the heat and held it almost to the end.

There was a little brook flowing through the park. Over it was a bridge with a railing about five inches wide on both sides. One day all the gang assembled on this bridge, clamoring to see who could walk on the narrow rail without falling. The distance from the railing to the ground was three feet at the edge and nearly ten feet as the bank descended. Some of the boys gallantly volunteered and stepped on the rail. But even at the edge it looked high, and as soon as they got up there they became afraid and jumped down. All the boys looked at me as if to say, "Now it's your turn." I had to walk on the rail or lose face. Once on the rail, I felt a little dizzy but without looking down I proceeded a few steps. So far, so good; it was easy and I felt gay and confident. I went another few steps to show off and even hopped on one foot. Applause and gasps of admiration arose from the group. With a triumphant look and almost bursting with pride, I balanced myself and hopped another step—but this time I had gone a little too far. I missed my footing and down I went, six feet down to the green grass on the bank. I was more frightened than hurt, but as I had sprained my ankle, I was unable to move. On hearing about the accident, my cousin came running and put me on his back. We returned home with all the gang trotting behind: I was now a hero indeed.

Time flew by very fast and at six I entered grammar school. Children came from various economic classes and different districts to this school. They were not the well-mannered, well-bred kind of children that had been in the kindergarten. They were very different, and I was happy to be with them. I had much in common with them. I also liked being noisy, and I too was full of pranks. They were all my good friends. On the first day of school, all the boys came to school with their mothers, and they all looked very sincere. After addressing the whole group the teacher asked the mothers to come to the teachers' room to talk about various details. I stood up and surveyed the whole class, studying each face. They all lowered their glances but one, a big, strong fellow, who not only withstood my glare but also stood up and stared back. I walked silently to his side and punched him in the chest. He staggered and fell back on his chair, losing all will to fight. At that moment I became the boss of the class.

Those were indeed merry days for me, except that the male teacher was not so generous as my kindergarten teacher had been. Often I was ordered to stand in the corner of the room and sometimes even asked to leave the class. This always hurt my pride, so I tried not to be caught in my pranks. Half a month had passed, and we were reading the primer. Suddenly the teacher raised his voice and called my name. I was just about to poke my friend's head when this happened, and I was chagrined that I was caught in the midst of my fun. However, instead of scolding me as I had expected, the teacher began to talk in a different tone, saying, "Honda, I hear that you are going to America in the near future and that your mother will be coming to take you there." At first I could not grasp the meaning. Instead of throwing me out of the classroom, I thought he was making fun of me in front of the whole class. But when I looked back into his eyes, I did not find any signs of a joke. Slowly I began digesting his words. But what did he really mean? America! I had heard that name. My mother had sometimes mentioned it casually in her conversation. Then I also recalled the beautiful postcard that my father had sent. I was sure my mother had told me about him, but as that did not seem important at the time, it had gone in one ear and out the other. But what had the teacher said? If I hadn't misunderstood him, he told me that *my mother was coming for me.* I had my very own mother here in this city, my mother who had been caring for me all these days, my mother who had seen me off when I left home for school that very morning. If I had another mother, who could this lady be whom I had been calling mother? Who was *she*? Or what is the meaning of "mother"? I was bewildered. My head swam and I could not make anything out of my teacher's remarks. What seemed true was that I was to visit America in the very near future. After school was over that day, I ran all the way back home, wanting to solve the mystery.

"Mother, Mother," I cried. "I heard my teacher say something I didn't understand. He said I was going to America. That's not true, is it? This is my home and I have all my friends here. I love my home and I don't want to go to America. He also said that another mother is coming for me. That isn't true. I know he was making fun of me. You are my mother and I have no other. Isn't that true, Mother?"

Mother did not speak. She just looked at me solemnly. Her face showed that she had been expecting this. She beckoned me to come sit at her side.

"My son," she began softly, "my dear son, this may be the last time I may call you this. I am not your mother. Your parents are living in the United States and I am your father's elder sister. Your real mother will be coming for you in a week to take you to America. When you were three years old, your mother left you in my care so that she could join your father in San Francisco. Since then you have been like my own son. But within three weeks we must part."

Tears were flowing down her cheeks. I was stunned. So this was the truth after all. The sun that had been shining so brightly suddenly seemed to darken. This was a little too much for a six-year-old boy to comprehend. The only thing I understood was that this lady was not my mother after all. I would be forced against my will to travel to a distant country. I understood that, and I knew instinctively that even if I resisted I would not be allowed to stay in that home.

Three days after the shock, I quit going to school. Then one warm sunny day my mother arrived on the train with my little sister Mieko, who was then two years old. We were all waiting on the platform when the big black locomotive came puffing in.

Out from the second-class coach stepped a lady wearing a dark dress and a big hat that shaded her face. In her arms she carried a little girl wearing a pink ribbon. The ribbon and the hat both seemed very exotic to my eyes and attracted other people's attention, too. My aunt stepped forward and greeted the lady, then pushed me forward, saying, "Greet your mother." Her voice sounded soft but indifferent.

I felt shy, a feeling I had never experienced until then, and I tried to hide behind my aunt's back. My mother just smiled and said nothing. I felt instinctively that she was kind and that I would feel at home with her.

She had brought many gifts, including some foods that we had never tasted before. The chocolate candy, though sweet, was somewhat bitter, and I swallowed the chunk without chewing. The butterballs were the most delicious. They were sweet and full of fragrance. I had never tasted such sweets before. If America could produce such good candy, it surely must be a wonderful country, I thought.

The following week was paradise. My aunt was extremely kind, never speaking a harsh word, no matter what I did. She also told my mother to do the same, so that I would not dislike her. I said and did what I liked without reprimand. On visiting my mother's home town I was again the idol of the village. Because I acted as though I feared nothing, they all adored me. My face reddens to this day when I recall what naughty, shameless acts I got away with during those precious days!

LEAVING JAPAN

The day finally came when we were to sail from Yokohama to San Francisco. The big liner was the S.S. *Taiyo*, a luxury steamer that had been received from Germany as part of her war reparations. Because my father was working for this steamship company, we were allowed to travel first class. Almost all of our relatives came from all over the country to see us off.

The day before our departure, we had stayed overnight in an inn in Yokohama. I was to sleep at my aunt's side for the last time. She hugged me and whispered in my ear, "You will never forget me." I promised that I never would, turning my face away from her tears in order to hide my own.

The 14,400 ton liner was large and majestic. Looking up from the wharf, I thought it was like a big, beautiful castle, more splendid than anything I had anticipated. As the gong clanged and resounded throughout the ship, well-wishers began descending the stairs, and we went up to the deck. I remember how small the people standing below looked, and I especially remember seeing my aunt touching her eyes with a handkerchief. Colorful confetti fluttered in the air, seemingly binding the hearts of people on land and on sea. It was like a pageant, a great festival, and I was excited. Again the gong clanged, signalling the final departure to the well-wishers still on board. This was the final curtain of this colorful drama.

Suddenly a jet of white steam went shooting up into the sky, accompanied by a shrill blast that pierced the air. The sound was truly terrifying, especially because we were near the big funnel. My heart jumped into my throat; suddenly I felt with all my soul and body that I was actually leaving the country where I had lived, the country with all my beloved and dear friends. I was leaving Japan and leaving my aunt and going to a strange unknown land—a land where I knew not what would await me in the future. I cried with all my might, shouting, "Mother! Mother!" to the silent figure standing below. Only the hollow sound of the blast followed. I cried out again. Again only the blast echoed in response. Then ever so slowly the ship began to creep out into the harbor, widening the dark green gap between the wharf and the ship. Confetti was still fluttering in the air.

The engine began to pound rhythmically, and white foam began to appear in the dark water below. Slowly the mighty ship left the land, with many people still crying and waving their hands, hats, and handkerchiefs.

NEW LIFE IN SAN FRANCISCO

Life on the ship was an entirely new world for me. It was like being in fairyland. There was luxury and extravagance that I had never even dreamed existed. The big dining room with its pure white linen tablecloths was especially attractive to me. The waiters and other dining room staff wore white vests and were always ready to manage our chairs and take orders. Food was always more than plentiful, and all of it tasted good. Some smells I did not like or found hard to get used to. But the best thing of all was the ice cream, which my mother always ordered for me for dessert. It melted in my mouth with heavenly sweetness.

There were many people from many different countries on the ship. Big, dark Indians with white turbans and Chinese with pigtails hanging down their backs. Their women tottered as they walked on their very small feet which had been bound. A group of Japanese wrestlers was also traveling first class. The then grand champion, Ohnishiki, was the leader of the group; he smiled when our eyes met, and he gave me a cookie. Of course this made me like him very much and from that moment on his name was firmly engraved on my brain.

The weather was fair and the wind favorable. In a week we arrived in Honolulu. Almost all the passengers went ashore, and we were the only ones left on the ship. After lunch my mother took us ashore and we rode on a streetcar that ran from the harbor to the center of the city. We got off the car at Ala Moana Park and strolled among the greenery. The air was warm and sweet with fragrance. I had a most enjoyable time licking an ice cream cone.

After we sailed from Honolulu, the sea became rough and the atmosphere on the ship lost its carefree flavor, probably due to the inclement weather. One chilly morning in early June I awoke to find the ship at a standstill and the engines silent. All was very quiet. We had arrived in San Francisco. My mother helped me put on my best suit and everything seemed to be ready. Then the door opened and a man entered. He looked down on me with emotionless, cold eyes, and said nothing. Then he turned to my sister, who was in her mother's arms; he smiled affectionately at her and said a few words. From the moment he entered the room I knew, without being told, that he was my father. I felt the cool air rising between us. I sensed immediately that this man, my father, would not tolerate my mischievous pranks. In fact, I thought that he would not tolerate my jokes and, perhaps, not even me. I certainly could not expect generosity of any sort from that cold figure of a man standing before me. As we moved out onto the deck of the ship preparing to disembark, the chill and fog crept upon me, and I felt frozen.

My new home was on Pine Street, between Laguna and Buchanan, No. 2039, on the first floor of a two-story building. Two or three days after we arrived my mother took me to a nearby park called Lafayette. Wandering through the green and flower-filled lane, we arrived on the north side of the park, which commanded a fine view of San Francisco Bay. We sat on the grass on top of the hill, enjoying the majestic view. Then, a big liner with a Japanese flag waving in the air glided smoothly in the middle of the channel, moving swiftly toward the Golden Gate. It was the S.S. *Taiyo,* which had brought me from the far Orient a few days earlier. I gasped. Within a few minutes the ship had disappeared from sight. I looked aside, trying to hide the tears flowing down my cheeks. This was the last link of the chain that had bound me to my life with dear Japan—and now it had been cut. I felt lonely, very lonely.

About two blocks east on Pine Street, there was a Catholic church, where during the summer vacation a school for small children was opened. My mother took me to this school. During the first week I just sat staring at what happened around me, neither understanding nor caring to understand what was going on. I was indifferent to the whole class. My classmates chattered in English and were indifferent toward me, absolutely ignoring my presence. The nuns with their black robes and headdresses were cool, making no effort to show special kindness to me. The only enjoyment I experienced in those days was when they served milk and cookies at ten in the morning. Sometimes it was a slice of bread with strawberry jam. This was indeed a special treat for me. It is interesting that we connect so many of our remembrances with taste and smell.

The school lasted for one month, and during that month I did not mingle with my classmates. I was unable to make even a single friend. I stuck to my own habits and did not adopt the new customs as a child usually does. I think one of the reasons was that the nuns, as well as all the children, were second- or third-generation Japanese.

On Bush Street, between Buchanan and Webster, was a Japanese school called the Kinmon-Gakuen, the "School of the Golden Gate." This school was established so that children from Japanese families could learn Japanese after they finished their regular American schooling. There was also a kindergarten, and though it was in the middle of the term, I was allowed to enter after the summer vacation.

I met my first American teacher, Miss Coffee, who taught English conversation to children. Naturally, I did not understand a single word she said and stared blankly at her face whenever she addressed me. She was always smiling and kind, so I felt very much at home in her presence. American people were kind after all; this was indeed a great relief to me.

In this school I was quite at home with the other children, and thus slowly began picking up new customs and habits. This was my new life, and I was determined to face it, like it or not.

My most eloquent means of distinguishing myself were to play pranks or to use my fists. I did both, and although my fellow classmates despised me for this roughness, I was bursting with a feeling of self-importance. So, life in the kindergarten was not at all unhappy. I had my way, using my fists, and cared not at all if I understood English. I never received any praise for these acts, only silent contempt.

I still have a photo of our group, taken before our graduation. Standing on one side of the group is the principal (whose name by coincidence was also Mr. Suzuki) and, on the other, his wife. I am in the middle with my eyes shut, sticking out my belly like a frog.

I GO TO GRAMMAR SCHOOL

A new leaf had been turned in my life. I was to enter grammar school. There were boys of all nationalities in the school district: French, Puerto Rican, Korean, Chinese, and some Japanese. The only common language was, of course, English. Like it or not, I had to speak English to communicate with my teacher and classmates.

It was difficult to understand what the teacher was saying, so I sat deaf and dumb all through the classes. This made me feel miserable, and I was gradually overwhelmed by feelings of inferiority. I even lost all my fighting spirit and became a quiet boy. This was undoubtedly the hardest change in environment I had experienced, and it hit me hard.

But as is true in all countries, the first grade lessons were very easy. Within two or three months I caught up with my classmates without much difficulty. I could then understand the teacher and my friends, provided they did not speak too quickly.

One day I had a quarrel with one of my classmates who was much bigger than I. The dispute did not last long, as I could make neither head nor tail of what he was saying. The next moment we found ourselves busy at fist fighting. I swung madly with both of my arms but missed. Then his fists landed on my nose; first the left and then the right—a straight one-two punch. Blood spurted from my nose and I lost all spirit for fighting. I was vanquished for the first time.

This event acted to intensify my feelings of inferiority. The boy told me later that to win a fight, "guts" is not enough;

skill and technique are also necessary. He had learned how to box, and whenever he had to fight, he aimed at the nose of his opponent. Bleeding was apt to discourage the spirit of his antagonist, he added. It was a good lesson.

I remember San Francisco as a city of many hills. Wherever you went, north, south, east, or west, there were steep hills. These added much to the picturesque view of the city and did not seem to hinder the city traffic at all. The cable car running up from Market Street through Powell and ending at Fisherman's Wharf was not only a tourist attraction, but was also a means of transportation. There were always a number of people hanging onto the railing of the car, especially in the morning and evening. We often sat on the sunny side of the park facing California Street, watching the cable car clanking by.

I now became good friends with the boy I had fought. His father owned a candy shop on Post Street in which he made and sold Japanese sweets and cakes. He was a smart boy and a good storyteller. I often sat in the park listening to his stories. He was good at making fiction on the spot, gathering scraps from fairy tales and other stories. When we were on good terms, he made me a hero or a prince in stories in which I was to save a beautiful princess. A warm feeling would come over me at the thought that I was to help the princess and later to woo her. But sometimes when we were not on such good terms, he made me a villain, and I felt unhappy.

Another year slipped by and I was in the second grade. I had by then completely adjusted to the new situation and did not have any trouble with the language. In fact, I fared much better than the average child. Often the teacher had a spelling contest in which the whole class joined. Half of the class stood in one line, while the other half stood facing the opponents. Then the teacher said a word, an easy one at the beginning. If one misspelled it, he had to go back to his seat. As the words became more difficult, more students were eliminated, and after thirty to forty words, only four or five of the best were left on each side. I usually made it to this group, but somehow was unable to be the last one standing.

I was now in third grade. One day I felt miserable; I was cold and my head ached. When I returned home from school, my mother, with a glance, knew that I was sick and sent me to bed. As dusk set in, I felt worse. My head was literally pounding. The light looked orange-yellow, which I thought queer, as I never before had noticed that it had color. My fever was high and for the first time I feared that I might die. Up to that day, death was something I had never even thought of. But I had witnessed many living creatures die. I knew I had personally been the cause of the deaths of many insects, fishes, and birds. Maybe I would die! I groaned. My mother came in with a wet towel and placed it on my head. I felt better and slept.

I dreamed a frightening dream. My sister was playing in the parlor when suddenly a door opened and a man came in. When I looked at his face, I felt a chill run down my spine. The man had no eyes, no nose, no mouth; he was faceless. I tried to flee, but my feet would not move. With all my might I tried, but to no avail. Then he was almost upon me. I tried to scream and woke up. I got up and sat in the dark with cold perspiration wetting my body. I was afraid to sleep again.

The next morning the fever left and I felt much better. Recovering completely from my illness, I went to school after a week's absence. The school and my classmates were just the same as when I left. But when the arithmetic class began, I felt something was wrong. I had missed something between the time of my illness and the present lesson. I sat still, not comprehending what the teacher explained.

Thus two weeks passed. One day my teacher pointed to me to solve a problem. I could not give the answer. She gave an easier one and found me stammering without an answer. The third was the same, and then she realized that I did not understand the problem at all. I stood with a red face before the whole class, overcome with shame. It was unbelievable to the teacher that I, once a brilliant student, did not understand at all. But she gradually recognized that the wound was wide and deep and, if not treated immediately, could be fatal. She quickly decided to send me to a supplementary class every day after regular school hours. This went on for a month and during the whole period, I suffered from humiliation. This, indeed, was a very good lesson for me, and even to this day, I am thankful for what this teacher did to mend the gap.

Failure in education is mostly due to overlooking the missing link or to not understanding the importance of filling the gap at an early stage. The difference in the angle of the bullet leaving the gun may be slight, but the greater the distance the bullet goes, the further it will stray from the target.

I was lucky to have such a good teacher. There must be no compromise in education. After this special training, I received very good marks in all lessons and was allowed to skip a grade the next term.

RELATIONSHIP WITH MY FATHER

The relationship with my father was not going well at all. The coolness between us at our first meeting did not change. My father left Japan when I was a year old. When my mother saw him off at Yokohama, she had me in her arms. I was not a baby who cried easily, but at that moment it seems I cried so hard that everybody was moved to tears. My father, observing this from the deck, was so moved that he later wrote to my mother, saying that that might have been the last parting, as we were still in the midst of World War I and the German cruiser *Emden* was ravaging the southern part of the Pacific. In fact, as I was his first son, he loved me dearly, and the vision of his son at the time of parting remained with him. My mother joined him later when I was three, leaving me with my aunt.

There is never again a time in one's life when he will absorb all things, good or bad, in his receptive mind, adapting to the environment, as during the ages of one to six. I had changed completely from the vision my father retained, thus discouraging and disillusioning him. Probably he expected a well-mannered, bright boy, instead of a sullen one, staring him straight in the eye. Naturally he was bitterly disappointed and resolved in his heart that he would reform me, sparing neither whip nor ruler. This made me shrink from him all the more and did not improve our relations.

The first floor of our home faced the street, but it was necessary to descend the steps leading to the back yard. On the right side of the yard was a chicken coop where our upstairs tenant kept a cock and several hens. A wooden fence about five feet high separated our garden from the neighbor's. One day I found a crack in this fence. Imagining that there might be some treasure hidden inside the crack, I thrust my hand deep into it. I was astonished to feel something smooth and oval. Of course I was not so simple as to think that my imagination would prove to be a reality. But there was something cold, hard, and smooth, big enough so that I could grasp it. A precious jewel or stone? With pounding heart, I withdrew my hand and out came the white oval into the sunshine. An egg. I was a little disappointed but thrust my hand in again. There was another and another. I was like a magician taking egg after egg from a silk top hat.

In all, there were about twenty eggs. I called my mother who was equally surprised. The excitement drew the attention of the tenants upstairs. They came down and, seeing what I had found, declared solemnly, "No wonder our hens haven't been laying eggs as they should these days. The rascals have been getting out of the cage during the night and laying eggs in a place you would never suspect." They then took the eggs, leaving only five for us. I was a little dissatisfied with this solution, but as there was no way to improve it, I bit my lip and said nothing.

Near the center of the yard was a little peach tree. It did not bear much fruit, but I enjoyed the sweet and juicy peaches immensely. One day for no special reason I began digging a hole under the roots. After digging about a foot, I suddenly found my hand dropping into a deeper hole. Maybe this was a secret hole where in ancient times a pirate might have hidden his treasure and planted the peach tree as a sign. My imagination came from reading too many stories. I searched within the hole, anticipating a pot of treasure, but in vain. Instead, I grabbed a very unpleasant object. Pulling out my hand, I found the object to be a bone of a small animal, probably a dog. I felt a little sick and, thrusting the bone back into the hole, covered it up quickly with the sand. Then I went up to my room and, after washing my hands, sat in a chair to think. I did not like the idea that a previous owner of this house had buried his pet dog and planted a peach tree in its memory. That wasn't appealing at all.

EXPERIENCE IN WORKING

I was now in the fourth grade and life was quite happy. I was no longer having any trouble with the language and was also enjoying school, as well as playing with my friends.

One sunny afternoon in June, I was sitting on our steps with a boy three years my senior who lived upstairs. The bees were busy seeking honey from the flowers planted by my father. The hummingbirds darted here and there, trying to suck the sweet juice from the flowers that attracted them.

"I am earning five bucks a month," the boy began.

I thought that was great. Five dollars a month. Gee! You could buy quite a lot with that.

"I'll tell you how. Every evening I deliver a newspaper, a French one, and it takes only about an hour, very easy as you see. About fifty copies." That's not so bad, I thought. "Do you want to try? I'll recommend you." Evidently due to lack of delivery hands, the owner of the paper had asked my friend to scout for someone who was willing to undertake the work. To me, besides earning the money, it seemed that it would be fun to ride on streetcars and then deliver papers in distant districts where I had never been.

When I asked my mother if I could take the job, she

seemed reluctant but, after consulting with my father, gave in to my earnest and repeated request. She made one condition, though, that I would not quit within three months. I was overjoyed, but when I really began to work, it was not as easy and enjoyable as I had imagined.

I lost all time for playing. After regular school, I was obliged to attend the Japanese school, Kinmon-Gakuen, where we were taught Japanese. The instruction wasn't sufficient to improve my native language and was barely enough to sustain what I had. The class lasted an hour and, afterwards, I rushed to the office. The boys filed to the printing plant and, as the papers came out, grabbed the necessary number and then went out to make deliveries. I had my route book in which the house numbers and names of the subscribers were written. As my district was way south, I had to ride a streetcar, and, to save time, I folded the papers while I rode.

Several weeks passed by. The work I did weighed heavily on my shoulders. After school, my friends shouted with glee, playing kick-the-can, hide-and-seek or blindman's buff. How my heart yearned to join them, even for a few minutes. I had to hurry to the office instead. I regretted that I had ever undertaken this job, but since I had, I was obligated to perform my duties, however reluctantly.

At the end of each month I received a check for five dollars. I had to ask my father to cash it, but when he gave me the money, it was only two dollars. He didn't explain why, and I was not at all happy to see that the amount had diminished. I believe now that my father thought it better for a boy of eight not to have five dollars in his pocket. Today I understand that my father's judgment was good after all.

One special day was a celebration for the Republic of France. I did not know what kind, but it seemed a big day. I also did not know why, on this special day, a French boy three years my senior was in the office. He seemed to be some relative of George, the boss. After receiving carfare from George, this boy followed me. I did not understand why he chose to accompany me, but he probably thought me easy to handle, as I was so small.

He sat beside me on the streetcar, chattering in a friendly tone. I was glad to have a companion to escort me on my lonely delivery route. There were many French laundry shops and some florists on my list of subscribers. At the first shop, I began to understand that the people, to show their appreciation, gave money to the delivery boy. It was usually a quarter, sometimes a dime, sometimes even a half-dollar. My escort spoke something in his native language and, on receiving the money, pocketed it. Of course, I knew that this was meant for me, and when I complained, he told me that he was just collecting for my sake and would give all the money to me in the end. My list of subscribers numbered nearly forty, and I knew that at least half of them had given something, the total of which would amount to about five dollars.

When we finished the last delivery, the French boy gave me two quarters. I was very surprised and disappointed, so I told him that the amount was at least ten times what he had given me. Then his attitude changed. Scowling, he snapped that the money he had given me was all that had been collected and that I was insulting him. He was big and he towered over me. I knew I could neither fight him nor win the dispute.

The next day George asked me how much I collected, and when he found out that I had received only fifty cents, he was very surprised. I told him the details and, hearing them, he faced the boy, who was standing nearby, and spoke to him. But the boy said something very rapidly in French and, after listening, George looked at me and only shrugged his shoulders. I still pity the boy for his deed, even to this day.

One day we had a holiday from school, the first day I had to myself, and I enjoyed the leisure. I went fishing in the Bay with my friends. There was a crack between wharves, and we went down on the planks near the water. There were quite a number of big fish swimming, looking hungry, but, contrary to their looks, all they did was smell the bait and turn away. What we caught were small, inedible fish. We stayed for a considerable time and, when we came up, I was surprised to see the sun setting in the far west. I knew I was late for the paper. I hurried home and, leaving the fishing lines, ran to the office. There were no boys; only George was there, biting his nails, anxiously waiting for my arrival.

Looking down at me, he said nothing, and gave me a quarter instead of the dime for carfare. When I returned home, it was late at night, and I was terribly tired. I went to bed without supper and during the night had a high fever, which kept me in bed for the following three days. The next day my father phoned George that I was quitting the job.

I had worked for six months and understood what it meant to earn money.

BOOK READING

There was a man named Thomas Okuno, who boarded at my home. He was a little over twenty years old, and was a student in the dental school of the University of California. His hobbies seemed somehow connected with mechanics, and at this particular period he was constructing a crystal radio. When I first had the earphones on my head and the sound of music came floating from the air, I thought it was like magic.

One day Thomas gave me a set of books called "The Junior Classics" published by P. F. Collier & Son. One of the ten volumes was missing, but when I placed the nine on my desk, I was thrilled and full of joy. It was a beautiful clothbound set and I treasure it to this day. In my free time I plunged into the books.

Volume 1 was "Fairy and Wonder Tales." It contained "Tales of the American Indians," "Tales from India," "Tales from the Norseland," and, in fact, tales from almost all the world over; then came "Some Old Favorites," the great majority from Grimm and Andersen; and lastly, "The Fables of Aesop." Volume 2 was entitled "Folk Tales and Myths," Volume 3 "Tales from Greece and Rome," and so on. In fact, the set covered nearly everything a boy would enjoy, and I absorbed most of my knowledge of history and literature from these volumes.

The teacher who was in charge of our class seemed to like poetry very much. At the beginning she recited such simple poems as "Who Has Seen the Wind" by Christina Rossetti, or Robert Louis Stevenson's "The Swing" or "The Lamplighter." As she was a very good reader, we enjoyed this very much, imagining the rustle of the wind or how it must feel to go up in the air. One day to her delight I brought one of my books, Volume 10, devoted to poetry. From this book she began selecting more difficult poems, like "Elegy Written in a Country Churchyard" by Gray, or "Daffodils" by Wordsworth, "The Charge of the Light Brigade" by Tennyson, or "Paul Revere's Ride" by Longfellow, "Horatius at the Bridge" by Macaulay, or "Lady Clare" by Tennyson. Of course, I did not understand all the meaning, but the beautiful verses melted into my heart, and I did not easily forget them.

Sometimes I grew tired of reading my books. There was a public library several blocks from my house. Imagine my surprise and delight when I found that I could borrow two books for a whole week, free. I felt as though I was wandering in the woods of limitless treasure hidden among the shelves.

Until midnight, I indulged in reading all kinds of stories, from *The Wizard of Oz* to *Tarzan*. Week after week, month after month, and year after year, I frequented the old library until I had read almost all the books that suited my taste. Schoolwork was not at all difficult for me then. I did not do much homework but was always ranked at the top of or second in my class.

One afternoon a friend of our teacher visited the class, probably because she had something important to say. Mrs. Trowbridge, our teacher, went out to see her. While they were speaking in the corridor, some of my classmates and I sneaked away from our seats to observe what was going on. Mrs. Trowbridge caught sight of us, and we scampered back to our seats, trying to look innocent. She was a strict teacher and disliked such behavior. After seeing her friend off and coming back to the classroom, she stood with arms crossed, looking very stern.

"Those who looked out, stand up," she said in a piercing voice. Silence. Nobody stood up. "Do you hear me? Those who looked out, stand up." I stood up. I was alone. "Why did you leave your seat?" I was a little scared, but looking her in the eye answered, "I was curious." I lowered my head anticipating her sharp reproach. A silence. Then, pointing at me, she cried, "Honest boy!" I was stunned. Instead of being scolded as I had anticipated, I was praised. I felt it was inconsistent to be called honest when in my heart I knew I was not.

MUSIC LESSONS

Our music lesson was an hour a week, which I thought was not enough. I liked to sing very much, and the piece I especially loved was one by Stephen Foster. One day the teacher asked each student to sing the song he liked the best. When my turn came, I sang "Massa's in the Cold, Cold Ground." I thought I sang well, but when I finished my classmates all laughed. I knew I couldn't carry the high parts very well and that some parts were a little out of tune, but I was sure it wasn't as bad as they made it out to be. My pride was hurt, and since then I have hesitated to sing before an audience. I was convinced that I had no talent in music.

My mother was taking piano lessons, and every Saturday morning an elderly American music teacher with a dignified mustache came to our home. Usually he came about ten o'clock, and I sat in the niche between the piano and the wall to hear the lesson. The lesson began with little pieces like "May Song," "On the River," and so on. I loved to hear these pieces and, although my mother played very badly, I sat listening throughout the lesson. I never thought of asking my mother if I could take lessons; and she didn't mention the possibility. Lessons seemed far beyond my grasp. I thought that studying music was difficult, and that instruments like the piano were only for adults.

Ever since I had come to San Francisco, I went to Sunday School. The school was located on the ground floor of Christ

Church on Post Street. The first song I learned was "Jesus Loves Me, This I Know." My mother told me to ask my teacher if he would write it in English, which he did on the following Sunday. Since I couldn't read it well, my father recited it for me word for word until I learned the song by heart, although because he had to repeat it often, he scolded me for my bad memory.

From ten o'clock on there was a class for older boys and girls. I sometimes lingered to join this class because I liked the hymns they sang better than the ones we younger children learned. Ours were simple, easy songs, while theirs were real hymns which I liked much better.

After Sunday School, my father usually gave me a dime and told me to go to the movies. There were several theatres on Fillmore Street; admission to the cheapest one was five cents. I loved the Westerns, where the cowboys fought Indians or sometimes quarreled among themselves; at the end the strong or the right always won out. A group of musicians played pieces to accompany the scene. It was enchanting, and I loved best the sweet tone of the violin. As far as the scenery was concerned, I liked the Rockies more than the desert or the prairie.

The most impressive, unforgettable film was *Peter Pan,* played by Betty Bronson. Her slim figure appeared in my dreams, and I actually fell in love with her. When I became older, I loved to see melodramas full of romance. As my classmates still preferred "Wild West" pictures, I hid my feelings.

Many of my friends were members of the Japanese Y.M.C.A., and I envied their activities in sports and games. At last I persuaded my mother to allow me to join and pay the three-dollar annual fee. I became a member of the Bear Cubs, the youngest group of members. Every Saturday morning at ten o'clock the Cubs held a meeting. I was surprised to see a boy who was not at all popular in school sitting in the chair as president, banging the gavel. He spoke and acted with authority.

In the downtown section, there was another, bigger Y.M.C.A., in which the members were mostly Americans. We were allowed to use the indoor swimming pool in this building from seven to eight Saturday mornings. I could hardly wait for this day, and I arose at six when all the household were still asleep. I jumped out of bed, put on my clothes, and went out into the street. My friends who lived in the neighborhood would wait outside, usually with their roller skates on. We skated to Laguna, turned right where the hill was not so steep as on Buchanan, then rolled down to Bush Street. Arriving early, we waited for the steel shutter overlooking the pool to open. A few American members were swimming with easy strokes. As soon as the gate was opened, we rushed down the corridor, stripped off our clothes and, running through the shower, jumped into the cold water. After twenty to thirty minutes, there were more boys huddling together in the warm shower than in the pool. Those who were still in the water shivered with purple lips. I will never forget the first day I went to this pool. Of course I could not swim at all, but paddled wildly, churning the water. After struggling for more than thirty minutes, however, I was able to swim about five or six yards. It was much easier the next time and I could swim a considerable distance. If you once learn something through your body, like swimming or riding a bicycle, you are not apt to forget it easily. Within a month I became a good swimmer, surpassing all my colleagues.

I was now in the sixth grade, after being allowed to skip another grade. Naturally I felt not a little proud to be allowed to move to a higher class. But there were disadvantages. In the first place, you lost all your former friends and needed to adjust to new ones. We had been together and had formed a sort of group. Especially when one is older, it is more difficult to be accepted by a group than when one is younger. Also it is more difficult to catch up with one's lessons in the higher grades. But somehow I managed to do so within two months.

It was near Christmas, and the teacher ordered the class to draw a poster. The best three would be displayed in the city hall. The title was "Light for the Poor." Most of the pictures that the pupils drew were of poor people living in humble huts, while relief workers distributed goods. Much to my surprise my teacher selected mine as one of the three to be displayed. My picture was a very simple one, a radio speaker announcing the words "Light for the Poor."

After that the attitude of my classmates toward me changed. I now sat in my chair with a more comfortable feeling of confidence. The best remedy to heal an inferiority complex is to give a child something he can be proud of—a little limelight or praise to bring out his confidence. Then the wagon will move easily.

One beautiful Saturday, a warm and sunny day, I went with two of my friends to Ocean Beach. In my pocket were two quarters that my mother had given me, and I felt rich. We took a streetcar from Sutter Street. The fare was five cents. When we arrived at the beach, the sea was blue and the air pure. After looking at some seals near the Cliff House, we strolled down the beach. There were many stores selling candy, ice cream, and hot dogs. For lunch we bought a hot dog and a bottle of Coke, and baked apples for dessert. It was a luxurious treat. Leaving a dime in my pocket for the carfare home, I rode on the merry-go-round and other rides.

The roller coaster was especially thrilling. When it slowly rose, you could see the whole view—the ocean, foaming against the rocks, colorful stalls, and the tiny merry-go-round way down below. You swelled with a feeling of greatness to be up so high. But the next moment when the car went down, your heart jumped into your mouth. The speed, the incredible speed, far more than you anticipated, was terrifying. Oh! it was such fun. Being contented, we now played on the sunny beach: running high jump, broad jump, stunts like walking on our hands or turning somersaults.

The time flew, and we noticed that the sun was setting. The beach, which had been so bright and sunny, was now a little hazy and lonesome looking. It was time for us to go home. We knew that by taking the streetcar we could return by dusk. I thrust my hand in my pocket to make sure the dime was there. I did not feel the small coin, which I expected to find in the right pocket. Of course it must be there. No! I could not touch the friendly milled edge. My friends looking at my startled face knew that I could not find the coin. "Maybe you put it in your back pocket." Without replying, I searched the right, then the left. No coin. Now I knew that during my somersaults it had slipped out of my pocket. The miserable feeling that I must walk home alone came surging up. I looked at my friends helplessly. A moment of silence; the boys were thinking. Slowly the elder spoke. "We can't desert him in his time of need. Let's all walk. Now let's buy some hot dogs with our money and eat on our way back." Slowly as I walked, I chewed and swallowed the fragments of bread and sausage they shared with me, feeling the warmth of my friends' hearts and of the hot dog.

I GO BACK TO JAPAN

A new year dawned, 1925, with a veil hiding the bright hue and glory or perhaps sorrow of the coming year. Toward the end of the previous year, I often overheard conversations between my parents which hinted that we were to return to Japan. I gathered from their words that, due to bad management, T.K.K., the steamship company where my father worked, was near bankruptcy and was to be sold to N.Y.K. Shipping Company. Preferring not to stay with the new company, my father decided to return to Japan.

As I was now twelve years old, it was important for me to receive my education in Japan if I were to live as a Japanese. Often in our lives, we need some motive to make a decision to change the easy pace of our daily routine. To move means to leave the familiar comforts and to jump into an entirely different situation, which might be either a success or a failure. My Japanese education provided a strong motive for my parents to return to Japan.

The ship we took back home was by coincidence the same S.S. *Taiyo* on which my mother and I had come to America six years before. That was her maiden voyage, and now this was her last under the flag of T.K.K. The departure of the big ship was more colorful than ever. As it pulled out from the wharf into the deep sea, I enjoyed standing on the deck, breathing the fresh salty air. As the ship passed the Golden Gate, rapidly gaining speed, I stood emotionless on the deck, looking at the fast fading hills of North Beach. Suddenly I realized that I was now leaving this fair land, this country where I had developed my dreams— leaving the city of the Golden Gate where I had so many friends and memories, maybe forever. I felt a surge of sorrow coming up and the tears began flowing, dimming the far-off land.

The voyage back home was delightful. I was at just the right age to enjoy it, especially since I did not have such luxury at home. In those days, one of my favorite fruits was the banana. As it was rather expensive, I never could have enough; but in Honolulu someone gave me a whole branch of ripe yellow bananas. After leaving the port, I peeled one with eager haste and almost swallowed it whole. It was so delicious that I ate another. This kept on until I finished nearly half a dozen. But somehow the last one wasn't good at all. Maybe it wasn't ripe; so I tried another. As I began munching and proceeded to swallow, I felt sick to my stomach, and although I tried, I could not proceed any further. From that day on the mere smell of a banana made me nauseated, and, much to my dismay, I had to throw all the rest into the ocean. This taught me another lesson, that I should not crave something even though I liked it very much; also, that there is always a limit to one's desire, be it food or material goods.

BACK IN JAPAN

On the day of our arrival in Yokohama, I got up early, dressed myself, and went up to the deck. It was still dark but quite a number of people were on the deck, walking back and forth, speaking excitedly and pointing to the dark distant land that rose above the sea. "Boshu," they cried. I understood it to be the name of some place in Japan but, of course, could not identify it. The sea was calm and the ship sped along the coast. I was excited. So this was Japan, the country where we were to live—the land where my future lay, the place where I had lived in my early childhood, although the memory had faded.

Suddenly someone shouted, pointing in the direction the ship was facing. Mount Fuji! Its silhouette rose in the west, towering over the other mountains. Beautiful in its symmetric form, the top glowed pink, catching the first rays of the rising sun. More people came on deck to see the glorious sight. Even though the gong rang for breakfast, few went to the dining room. A buzz of excitement quickly infected the ship.

The big vessel was now ready to touch land. I walked down to E deck where the door would be opened and the gangplank would connect the ship to land. I could see many people looking eagerly toward our boat, shouting something. The first person who attracted my attention was a policeman who had a sword at his waist. Policemen in the States did not wear swords but instead had clubs dangling at their sides, swinging as they walked.

The next moment people rushed inside the ship, and I was lost in the whirl. While I was standing blankly next to the entrance of the elevator, a woman of about forty, clad in a Japanese kimono, came to my side, hugged me, and asked, "Do you remember me?"

I replied, "Yes," thinking to myself that it was my aunt. But to my surprise, she did not carry the conversation further but turned away coolly to greet my parents. I knew instantly that I had made a mistake. Then another lady came and embraced me affectionately.

"Do you remember me?" she whispered in my ear. This time I instinctively knew that this was my aunt.

"No!" The word slipped out against my will.

"Ah, you forgot me. You lived with me for a long time in the past. You promised that you would not forget me. Don't you remember your aunt?"

"No." The word again slipped out against my will. Hearing this, my aunt silently shed tears. I felt bad; still I did not speak.

Afterwards, my aunt often said in front of our relatives that I was cold-hearted to forget her, who had so loved and taken care of me in my childhood. I kept silent. That night I stayed at a friend's home in Tokyo. The house was on the outskirts of quiet Ueno Park. At times, the sound of a piano floated through the air from a music school nearby. For a week we shifted from one house to another and at last moved to a new house in Azabu. I overheard my father telling my mother that he liked the place because the location was so quiet. No wonder it was quiet. Beyond the backyard fence was a graveyard.

Although the days were busy, I sometimes got homesick for the hills and the cable cars in San Francisco. The melancholy trumpet of the peddler selling *tofu* especially made my heart ache. I looked with wonder at the ease with which my parents adapted themselves to the new circumstances.

The *tofu*-seller was one of many peddlers visiting our home. *Tofu* is kept in a wooden casket filled with water. It is so soft that without water it would break into pieces. I learned later that it was made out of soya bean juice, formed into shape, and hardened with lye. It is white and tasteless. But I liked it very much, eating it with soya sauce or cooked in sukiyaki. Some other interesting peddlers were the fish mongers. They also brought their goods in wooden caskets, hung from ropes over rods which they carried on their shoulders. They moved briskly from one door to another and the load actually squeaked. This made the purchaser think that the fish were fresh. It was wonderful to see how swiftly and skillfully the men cut the fish into pieces.

Our home was located in the residential quarter, not far from a street where there were many small shops. The streets were twisted and narrow with no sidewalks. One never knew where a street led; often it was to a dead end. In front of my home was a small lane where children played in the evening before supper. Some of their games were the same as those we had played in San Francisco, like tag, hide-and-seek, or even hopscotch. We quickly became acquainted and in a short time were good friends. In fact, life was not bad after all.

A month had passed since we returned to Japan, and now I had to go to school. One sunny day in May, my father took me to the public school nearby. The principal, a solemn-looking man in his early forties, greeted us warmly. My father produced the papers I had received from the Kinmon-Gakuen certifying that I had finished the fifth grade. It seemed that documents from an American school were not necessary. I was sorry that they did not heed these reports, as I had received good marks. The principal and my father shook hands, and it was concluded that I should be allowed to enter the sixth grade.

I was more interested in the sounds outside than in the monotonous conversation between my father and the grave-looking principal. There were shouts and cheers from the playground. Looking out, I saw many students, boys and girls, sitting on the ground, cheering for their fellow class-mates who were running races. They all wore white uniforms with caps, some red and others white. Liking sports very much, I focused my eyes on the races.

Suddenly my father beckoned me and, much against my will, I had to go. Now I liked the Japanese school very much, thinking these meets would be held often. Later I found out that this was a special event held to commemorate Navy Day. There were no more such colorful events after I began going to school, and the atmosphere was as gray and dreary as the building.

The lessons in the sixth grade were difficult. I could carry on daily conversations easily with my classmates but what went on in the classroom was almost incomprehensible to me. I had been in sixth grade in the San Francisco grammar school and received good marks, but here in Japan, I understood neither arithmetic nor history, not even the Japanese language.

I could read the *kana,* which is similar to the alphabet, but with *kanji,* or Chinese characters, I was lost. Thus, in trying to read a whole chapter, I could not make out the meaning. My idea of arithmetic was that this subject was universal. But, although the figures were the same, the contents were quite different. Especially to solve an applied problem, I needed a knowledge of Japanese. This I did not have, so I gave up.

History was my favorite subject. In the American school we learned from the viewpoint of the United States. For instance, in the year 1776, the Declaration of Independence was proclaimed. What happened in England that year, in France, in other countries? What we learned here was from the Japanese viewpoint. Japanese history went back before that of America, way before the Pilgrims or even before Columbus. I learned the history of Japan in comparison with that of the rest of the world. And the stories were always in favor of Japan. Sometimes they were different from what I had been taught in the States. I wanted to cry out that what was told us was wrong but stopped, reflecting that the history of Japan must be different from that of the United States, just like arithmetic. After all, it seemed only a story.

Calligraphy was another subject that bewildered me. I had never held a brush pen before in my life. There were three kinds of brushes: one for thick writing, the second for medium, and the third for thin. The stem was made of bamboo the size of a pencil, and the brush, of badger's hair. It was not so difficult to write with the thin brush, as only the tip was dipped in india ink, so the brush remained stiff and could thus sustain some pressure. But writing with the thick one was intolerable. The brush had to be crushed, losing all its stiffness. Dipping it in a sufficient amount of ink, you then had to write with a loose arm on a clean white sheet of Japanese paper. This meant that the elbow must not be held on the table and the arm had to move with strong and swift movements. With my arm loose, I felt that I had no control of my wrist and hand. I tried to write carefully but the brush ran beyond the point where I expected to write; instead of making a line, the brush collapsed and I made only a black dot. This was very difficult. You could put your will to the end of the bamboo, but from there to the tip of the brush, there seemed to be a vacuum. To write a beautiful strong letter, you have to make your will penetrate through this vacuum.

Japanese ink is made by collecting soot which consists of carbon and is not erasable. The carbon is compressed into a rectangle; and to use it, the rectangle of carbon is rubbed on a special stone plate called *suzuri* and mixed with water, which makes a fluid. Good ink has a fragrance and is treasured by the owner for more than a hundred years. The best ones come from China. The ink used in schools is a cheap ink contained in a bottle.

Again, I liked the subject of music best. In school they taught songs from books, beginning with volume one. We used volume six. I loved the melancholy melodies and the verses which expressed the seasons and scenery in Japan. I could not carry the high key of songs in the American school, but I hoped that maybe the music in Japan would be different. At least in America the names of the keys were fixed: c, d, e, f, g; but here, it was do, re, mi, fa. But when I found that my voice faltered on high E, I was so discouraged I lost all confidence.

The school uniform the boys wore was the kind that was closed at the neck with five brass buttons. I wore my civilian clothes from the States and I envied the boys their stylish clothes, especially their raincoats, which had attached hoods. The boys made fun of my separate hood, calling me a fireman. I ran back home, cap in hand, soaked to the skin, but was damp more in my heart.

There were many temples in this part of Azabu and in the back of the temple there was usually a graveyard. Facing the front street was a big graveyard hidden by a hedge, and surrounded by many kinds of trees. One summer day with some of my cronies, I went over the fence with a long bamboo stick to catch cicadas on the trees. On the tip of the stick there was a sticky lime. If we touched the body of an insect, it was caught. There were several species of cicadas in this area. Those with clear transparent wings were treasured more than those of somber color. It is only the males that have the characteristic sound of their species. Usually they perch high up in the branches, so we had to climb up onto a bough to catch them.

On this particular tree, I found several insects clustered together and singing to their hearts' content. Mostly they were those with the beautiful wings, looking very enchanting. They were high up, and in order to catch them I had to climb the tree with the bamboo stick in my mouth. Way up there was a slim branch, and holding my whole weight with my left hand on this bough, I took the pole in my right hand, thrusting it upward; miraculously I caught the whole bunch of these screaming insects.

I was overjoyed and, raising the pole high in the air, gave a cry of triumph to the gang below. Then the bough made an unpleasant groan and broke, and down I fell, ten feet, down to the ground. Later, my mother told me that I was indeed lucky to have landed on the soil rather than the hard gravestone, which might have killed me. Still, the height was enough to break my right foot. There I lay helplessly on the ground, stunned, pale with fright and pain. I felt as though I was dreaming a bad dream. But this was reality, not a nightmare.

When my parents received the news, they came rushing to the place where I was lying. My father carried me on his shoulder to the hospital nearby. My dangling foot hurt as he walked, and I groaned. My father scolded me for making such mischief. I felt miserable, biting my lip and holding back the tears.

That night my right foot ached so much that I moaned and groaned all through the night. My foot was on fire and my body burned along with it. It was indeed a long, long night and I did not sleep at all. Two days later I was more comfortable, as my foot was now in a cast. My father brought me one volume of Junior Classics from home, and it was a big consolation. When the doctor saw me reading English, which seemed quite difficult to him, he exclaimed in admiration: "Since you are so clever as to read such difficult material, you surely can endure the pain."

I thought his logic was ridiculous but held my tongue, since I was at his mercy. I recovered after three months and went back to school, starting with the new term in September.

Winter came. The trees became barren and the days grew shorter. The atmosphere in the school became more gray than ever. It lost all color in sound and in mood. In Japan at that time, there was a big barrier between grammar school and middle school, and there was intense competition to get into a good school. Each individual had to struggle and prepare to do his utmost to enter what was supposed to be a good middle school.

Those who were to proceed to the middle school stayed until dark for supplementary lessons. I stayed in the class, understanding almost nothing. Because I had been out of school for three months, I was hopelessly lost. I failed to pass the entrance examination and my parents had the idea of putting me in another grammar school.

One day my mother took me to a public school nearby. The principal with a solemn face told my mother that there was a rule preventing a boy from entering the sixth grade again after he had already graduated. My mother talked to the principal about my special status and at last he agreed to make an exception.

Now I was again in the sixth grade. And as I had boasted and looked down upon the fifth graders in the former school, I knew that these classmates were all a year younger than myself. I felt humility biting my soul, and when I saw that I was faring no better than I had the previous year, I was again overcome by feelings of inferiority. Looking back on this, I now think my parents were partly to blame. I should have entered the fifth grade at the outset instead of the sixth. It is much easier to climb up from below than to stay repeatedly on the difficult step. But still, I had made some progress during the past year and the subjects were easier here than in the former school.

About half a mile from our new home, there was an inlet of Tokyo Bay. The water was neither clean nor deep, and it was destined to be reclaimed in the near future. I, with two of my friends, one who was two years my senior and already in middle school, went often to this inlet to fish and swim. This older boy was a member of a group of juvenile delinquents, and he was proud of his bad acts. He was friendly to me and taught me many things, some evil. We bought lugworm as bait at the store and fished in the quiet sea. It was he who taught me the best way to make a hook and line. It was indeed great fun to catch those fish, some of which were too small to eat.

One day we went into a shop to buy some hooks. "Hello," we called. No answer. We sat on a chair and called again, more loudly this time. Still no answer. Suddenly the boy looked around with a piercing glance. The next moment, quick as lightning, he opened the case and stole several envelopes of hooks. He put them in his pocket and went out of the shop with a quick step. I followed him, my mouth feeling very dry. But though he did evil deeds, he never pressed me to follow his way; nor had I any intention of copying him.

One hot Saturday afternoon in late June, we got home early from school, and my friends came for me. We were to go fishing and swimming. We shouldered our rods and went down the steep hill to the Shinagawa Station; then, turning right, we walked to the sea.

We borrowed a boat and went down the coast. The sun was shining and the sea was calm. We were happy fishing and swimming. I was now able to swim an almost limitless distance without getting tired. Leaving the boat to drift, we swam to a small island miles out in the sea. It was great fun.

Suddenly we noticed a speck of black cloud in the western horizon. It became bigger and bigger with terrifying speed. The sky which had been so blue and sunny now changed into murky darkness. As reckless as we were, we knew that a storm, and quite a dangerous one, was coming. We rowed back with all our might but saw that we were not gaining much. The tide and the wind were strong. It was now a full gale and the waves leaped over us with furious anger. My friends looked alarmed, but I was not afraid, having confidence in my ability to swim if worse came to worst. We were gaining inch by inch, slowly but steadily. Through the howling wind, we heard a cry for help nearby. Turning around, we noticed another boat with two college students raising their hands, screaming for help at the top of their voices. In spite of our own danger, we rowed to their rescue. Throwing the rope and then binding our boat to theirs, we began rowing back again. To tow their boat against the wind and tide seemed almost impossible, but when the two youths saw that those who had come to their rescue were merely three boys much younger than themselves, they regained their courage and began to row. Fear had paralyzed their muscles.

In a short time we were all safely back on shore. They shook our hands and hurriedly disappeared, probably feeling ashamed to be rescued by such youngsters. Twilight had settled and the wind disappeared as quickly as it came. The sky was clear again, and the sun was setting in the west. From the east the moon rose—a full moon, round, big, and red.

It was a beautiful evening. We trudged back, joyfully humming a song. We did not know what made us so happy, but we all acknowledged within ourselves that we had accomplished something special and that made our spirits rise.

It was utterly dark when I returned home. Then I noticed my mother waiting at the entrance. She knew that I had gone to the inlet and, when I had not come back, not even after dark, she was so worried that she waited outside all that time. She smiled to see me, and, taking my hands, led me into the house, saying how worried she had been all through the afternoon.

I BECOME ILL

Another new year came, and all my classmates were again busy preparing for the entrance examination. This school did not have a special class for the preparation, but those who could afford it went to a private supplementary school. I did not go, so I was free from the restless feeling of those who would proceed to the upper school.

It snowed heavily during the night, the world was crystal white, and the frost on the trees was beautiful. Though the weather was fine, the temperature was quite low. After school several of my classmates proposed to have a snow fight. We went to a field near my home and divided into two groups. At first the fight was languid, but gradually moved into full swing. I was fighting at the front of our group, when suddenly I felt a terrible blow in my right eye. Stunned, I dropped to my knees, holding my right eye, which had suddenly and painfully swelled. All the boys stopped the game and made a circle, looking down on me. The boy who threw the snowball was baseball champion of the school, and he molded the snow as hard as a baseball, throwing with all his might. I think he had had some kind of grudge against me. The fight ended and I went home with a sightless, swollen black eye and an icy chill down my spine. I went to bed early that evening with a high fever, which I thought was caused by the blow.

The next day the fever was still running high. And so it was the next and the next and the next. My parents became worried and asked the nearby doctor to make a call. The doctor, a good-looking man in his early forties, came to our house and, looking carefully at me, diagnosed my ailment as a cold. Three days passed and the fever was still running high. Another doctor was called. He examined me carefully, and his diagnosis was pleurisy. He said that the right side of my chest was infected and some fluid had accumulated. He confirmed that if I were to stay in bed for two or three months, I would recover. Another week and the fever still had not gone down. My father's friend recommended another physician who was a famous specialist in respiratory diseases. After a routine examination, he drew out a syringe and thrust it into my chest. The pain ran through my body, but I did not cry out. He withdrew a fair amount of cloudy liquid with the syringe. He shook his head and said in a solemn tone, "There is no doubt that this boy is having pleuritis exudativa, and I think the best thing is to have him in the hospital."

I had heard the name of this disease before but, as the doctor added that I must be taken into the hospital, I thought it must be a serious disease. Even though I could not make out in what way pleurisy was more serious than pneumonia, or jaundice, or any other disease, I still felt proud that my illness was something with an important name and significant enough for me to go to the hospital.

I was taken to the Red Cross Hospital in Tokyo. The hospital was located in Takagicho near Shibuya and was a very old building on a vast area of land. In it were many small rooms on corridors. The room I was to occupy was of considerable size and contained six beds. All the beds were occupied by patients, mostly in their early twenties, who were suffering from the same disease. I was the youngest, next to a boy who was two or three years my senior.

My Japanese had by this time made such progress that I was now able to read magazines. I especially liked a monthly magazine for boys. As soon as it came out every month, I devoured the contents, inhaling with pure joy the smell of the ink. I had to keep myself from reading the whole issue at once, so as to leave some pleasure for later. In the hospital I had plenty of time and, now that my fever had gone down and the pain was gone, could enjoy the magazine at my leisure. The Japanese language, which had been so difficult a year ago, was not at all difficult now, and I could easily read any of the articles in the magazine.

One day one of the patients lent me a thick book, saying

he had never enjoyed stories like these before. The title of the book was *The Count of Monte Cristo* by Alexandre Dumas. I was reluctant to begin such a thick book, as I had never read a whole novel before. At first it was difficult to trace the roles of the characters, but, as the story moved on, I became so interested that I could not even spare the time to eat. I was so involved in the book, devouring it day and night, that my fever rose a little.

Three months in the hospital were not at all bad. In fact, I even enjoyed my stay. All my roommates were kind and, as they had to have absolute bed rest, they could only express their feelings, emotions, and philosophy in conversation. Though I did not always join in their talks, I learned a lot. They were always interested in each other's symptoms. Often, when a member of the family visited them, bringing up some problem, they discussed it and consoled each other. I remember the Japanese proverb, "Those who have the same disease sympathize with each other."

I left the hospital in June, not entirely cured. Of course, I could not foresee to what extent this illness would affect my future destiny. Neither did I know the real cause of the illness. In the United States, there was almost no tuberculosis. During my six years in California, I was not exposed to the germ and thus had no immunity. When I returned to Japan, the germ had slowly invaded my lungs and done the mischief. If I had received the vaccination of B.C.G. (Bacillus of Calmette and Guérin), a bovine strain of tuberculosis with a low degree of virulence which gives relative immunity and with which every child in Japan today must be inoculated, I probably would not have developed this disease. Thus, the crack (scar) had been made in my body which would last to the day of my death.

To this day, I have suffered from this malady, which at the time of onset seemed bad, but in the end turned out to be beneficial. At that time, I did not know the proverb: "A crack received in youth which does not break immediately may never break," but luckily it applied to me.

Of course, I did not have any idea of immunology or knowledge of immunity. But reflecting on my own experience, I began thinking what the words really meant, not only in the physical sense but also in the philosophical. We all possess some immunity, which we receive from our mothers at birth. Naturally, the quality and quantity of an individual's immunity depends on what he inherits from his mother. Most of this immunity diminishes three or four months after birth. As the immunity decreases, it is necessary to give inoculations to boost or reinforce it. When a vaccine for a special disease is inoculated, it works as an antigen, causing an antibody to develop which will result in immunity. There is a specificity between antigen and antibody which means that the body is immune only to a special disease. For instance, if typhoid vaccine is given, the body will develop immunity only to typhoid, and if influenza vaccine is inoculated, the antibody specific to influenza develops. Recently, combined vaccines, like those for diphtheria, tetanus, and whooping cough, have been developed. With one shot, the body is immunized to these three diseases.

Now once the immunity is made, it will prevent the development of disease when the germs enter the body. It works automatically day and night without the person knowing it is working. This immunity is made artificially or, in a sense, acquired after birth, boosting what the body originally had.

The function of immunity is wonderful. If this phenomenon could be applied to a child's mentality, it should inhibit evil entering his mind. For instance, if a child is brought up in a good environment and exposed only to good from a tender age, then if evil happens to enter, the senses will work to neutralize or even to counteract this antigen. At least the mind would be so uneasy that it could not tolerate the evil taking root within it.

Before Red China, there were many false silver coins in China. When we entered a shop to have money exchanged, the boy in charge bit it, then clanged it on the counter. Instantly he could distinguish the fake from the real. The story is that the owner of the stall would raise the boy from early childhood to handle only real coins and never allow him to touch a counterfeit. Thus sensitivity for the truth will develop, and when the false appears it will be recognized almost instinctively. The most important role of education is to immunize a child so that he cannot tolerate evil, ugliness, and cruelty.

I RETURN HOME FROM THE HOSPITAL

As I have related, after three months in the hospital, I returned home but not entirely recovered. The doctors were reluctant to let me out of the hospital, as I still had some inflammation in the right lung, although the fluid had been absorbed. If I had left the hospital fully recovered, my future life would have been changed completely. At least I would not have suffered from this disease against which I am now fully immunized. One of the reasons for my coming home was the problem of expense. The cost of the hospital and medical fees was not low, and the amount paid by my parents every ten days put a considerable strain on their finances.

Back home there were no restrictions such as there were in the hospital, but I missed the attention of the nurse as well as my fellow roommates. I stayed in bed for the first week, but at the beginning of the second week, I began running around the house with my brother and sister. Naturally this had an effect, and again I developed a fever which kept me in bed for some time. My mother now kept a sharp eye on my behavior.

The rainy season began. Every morning, day after day, the rain fell silently from the dark sky. Even when it did not rain, the clouds hung low, curtaining the blue sky.

It was not raining on one special day. I had finished my breakfast and was in bed thinking of the past when my youngest brother, who was three, came up the stairs to say good morning. He could now climb up the steps all by himself and was beginning to talk. In short he was very cute. He toddled past my bed to the windowsill, which was quite low compared to those in Western style homes. Looking out onto the street, he said something. The next moment, I noticed everything was very quiet. I did not know what had happened till my mother came rushing into the room, calling the baby's name.

"Do you know where Makio is?" she asked in breathless tones.

"He was here just a moment ago. Isn't he here?"

I suddenly recalled a peculiar sound before everything became quiet. A chill ran down my spine and a cold feeling clutched my heart.

With a quavering voice my mother replied, "Is that so?" and ran downstairs.

Outside in the street I could now hear many voices.

"The child fell from the window."

"Is he dead? He doesn't move at all."

Another voice: "He's alive, he's breathing. Take him to the hospital at once. Where's the ambulance?"

My heart throbbed and I yearned to look out the window, but I stayed in bed, neither moving my body or hands. Slowly I had to admit to myself that my brother might die. Tears came flowing down my cheek. The small boy who was so full of life a moment ago now lay cold, probably on his way to the hospital. Maybe his heart had stopped beating by this time. I hid my face under the blanket and wept silently.

Late in the night my parents came back home from the hospital. From their conversation I understood that my brother was in a coma, still unconscious and in very critical condition. The doctor's diagnosis was that there was a 90 percent chance the child would die, and if he survived, his brain would be damaged and he would be retarded.

Later when my brother returned completely healed, my father told a friend who visited us, "When I heard the doctor's diagnosis, I was very angry and told the doctor that it is the nature of parents to take anything a doctor says very seriously. To say that the odds were 90 percent that our boy would die, and that even if he survived he would be mentally retarded, was like a death sentence. You should be careful of the words you speak to patients or to parents." After I became a doctor, I did not forget my father's words.

After three days in a coma, my brother began to recover and eventually healed completely with no trace of injury of any kind. I myself did not progress, for I would take one step forward, then one step back. The reason was I did not stay in bed as I was ordered. But at last my temperature went down to normal and I felt wholly recovered.

Summer came and a friend recommended a resort in Boshu where we could rent a little home by the seaside. Arrangements were made, and we were waiting for the day to start. I was happy to think that I could live by the seaside, far from the dinginess, grime, and heat of the city. I imagined myself strolling on the white sand, while the waves washed onto the beach. I could see the blue sky, the blue sea, the white gulls flying lazily in the sky, and the sails of yachts and fishing boats far off the coast. I could even smell the salty, crisp air.

The night before our departure, everything was packed and we were ready to go. I could hardly sleep that night. But when morning came, it was raining. I heard my father talking to my mother: "It's raining and I think we should not go today."

I heard my mother say something, but I knew she never strongly resisted my father. The trip was first postponed and then cancelled. I never saw the blue sea nor the white sails.

I ENTER MIDDLE SCHOOL

It was especially hot that summer. The concrete pavement, which absorbed the sun during the day, reflected its heat even at night, and it was difficult to sleep. At last the long summer came to an end and the breeze in the morning became cool.

My schooling was now a great concern to my parents. I

had missed the whole first term, and there was little possibility that any middle school would allow me to enter the second term, which would begin in September. I myself was not at all concerned about school. I enjoyed my daily life without any study and wasn't in a big hurry to go back to school.

One day early in September, my father told me, "Tomorrow we will go to take the entrance examination of Akasaka middle school. I have phoned all the schools within the Tokyo district, and the only school that will allow students to enter this term is Akasaka. Though the school is not ranked as a good one, it's better to go there than to miss another year." I had heard the name of this school. Some of my classmates who did not do well in their school work had passed the examination and gone there.

Early next morning we presented ourselves to the school official and were told to wait in the reception room. A dignified middle-aged man with a lame right foot appeared and greeted us smilingly. He asked me an easy question about a definition in mathematics. I answered correctly. Next he brought out an English reader. He opened the first page which began like this: "Winter is over, spring has come." It was so easy I had to smile. Then he asked me to read the last page of the book, which was also easy. He closed the book with a bang and said, "You have passed the entrance examination and you can join the B class of the first grade tomorrow."

Even though I had missed the whole first term, which had begun in April, the lessons in middle school were not so difficult as they had been in grammar school. First, there were several English lessons in which I excelled and this gave me confidence in other subjects. In English I received the admiration of both my teachers and classmates. Being an American returned boy was no longer a handicap, and I was now in a favored position. My reading ability in Japanese had also increased; the language and the literature were no longer as difficult as they had been. At the end of the second term in December, I was ranked seventy-fifth out of one hundred and fifty in the whole first grade.

Because the boys commuted from all over Tokyo, I met many different types from different homes. The majority came from the lower middle class, and some came from poor families. The classrooms were without heat. Located in the middle of Tokyo, the school had a very small playground, but I enjoyed playing baseball there regardless of its size. Classes lasted for an hour with a ten-minute recess, during which we went outside. On cold mornings, we clustered in the sunshine, moving about to warm ourselves and keep cheerful.

The second grade of middle school was the happiest time of my schooling in Japan. Then Japanese was not at all difficult and I was healthy all through the year. Other years I often had to stay home because of a high fever.

After the second term of the third grade, we began receiving supplementary lessons to prepare us for entrance to high school, and again school life became colorless. The only bright days came when I was in the fifth and last year of middle school.

It was bright and sunny on a particular day in May. Some of my classmates were standing around, talking of going somewhere. I overheard them speaking the name of Mrs. Cunningham. I approached one of the boys and asked, "Who is this lady you are talking about?"

The boy replied, "Oh, she is an American lady who lives in Yotsuya, and every Wednesday afternoon she teaches a Bible class for middle school boys."

"Can I go?" I asked eagerly, regretting that I did not know earlier about such a wonderful affair.

"Why, of course," he answered. "We are just about to go. Come with us if you like."

Of course I liked, and then and there I visited Mrs. W. D. Cunningham in her home in Yotsuya, about thirty minutes' walk from our school. Mrs. Cunningham's home was located in a very quiet area. There was a small park across a narrow street from her house. Entering her gate there was a green lawn and a flower bed on the left side of the walk. Several rattan chairs were on a comfortable porch. It was an American home such as I had not seen for a long time.

Hearing the noise and clamor, a foreign lady came out smiling. She was in her late fifties or maybe early sixties, of medium height and a bit stout. Her hair was gray with white streaks. I felt instinctively that she was kindhearted. When I introduced myself, she looked surprised to hear a boy speaking English.

A table and several chairs were placed on the lawn. As the weather was good, the lesson took place in the garden. The class began with a prayer. Since I could understand her words perfectly, I joined in the amen. Raising her head, she looked at me and smiled.

Then a lesson in English began. It was a very simple conversation, like, "What's your name?" or "Where do you live?" More than six years had passed since I had heard English spoken by an American, but it came back easily. I could understand every detail and wondered why my classmates could not comprehend such easy conversation. They stammered, stumbled, and scratched their heads. Then Mrs. Cunningham (the boys called her Mother) would look at me and smile, saying, "I think you can answer this question."

The day was beautiful and I enjoyed the atmosphere very much. I was proud and so relaxed I even looked at the pretty daisies and marigolds in the flower bed. You feel so confident when you know that you have an ability which others do not have. Yes, that was a happy day.

I went to church the next Sunday. It was a small green church next to Mother's home. At nine the Bible class began. This was mostly for the middle group, and I saw some of my classmates. Mrs. Cunningham read the Bible and a college student interpreted. As I knew all the stories and understood all her lectures, I noticed several mistakes in the translation.

From this Sunday on I was a diligent student, going both to English class and to the Sunday Bible school. Later Mrs. Cunningham told me to attend the regular church service at ten. Though I did not much enjoy the sermon given by the

Japanese priest, I did so to make Mother Cunningham happy. One afternoon after school, an English teacher called me to his room. "I have just received information from Waseda University that they are having an English speaking contest on June 21. I think you should take part in this contest. There is still a month and you have plenty of time to prepare." I thought for a moment. It was easy for the teacher to say that I had a month to prepare, but considering that I had to write a speech, then practice reciting it, there wasn't much time. Still the idea appealed to me. The contest seemed a very good opportunity to test my English.

"Yes, I think I will enter the contest," I replied.

That night I racked my brain to write the speech. It was not at all as easy as I had first thought, and I could not even think of a title. I left the title for the time being and tried to think of a subject for my speech. No good idea came to me. I became tired and lay down and looked up at the ceiling. I could feel the pulse beating in my temples. I must, I must; I will. Yes, I will; there must be a way. I began writing:

"When given a certain project, we think it seems easy to proceed. But in reality it is not so easy. You must have a will, a strong desire to overcome adversity; once you begin, it is not so difficult. From a distance, you think the road must be blocked, but when you approach that point, you can find a way. To accomplish something worthwhile, you must always have a strong will and a strong body. After you have proceeded to a certain point, you will be encouraged to go further. In fact, you can develop some motivation which will enable you to go still further."

My speech took about six minutes. After finishing, I pondered again for a title. "Where there is a will, there is a way," seemed too simple. Again I racked my brain. You have to be strong. Yes, you have to be strong to do something. That was the title: "Be strong."

After finishing my manuscript, I brought it to Mother Cunningham. She corrected all the mistakes and a week later, I stood before her to recite my speech for the first time. I held the manuscript in my hand and during the speech often looked at it. Mrs. Cunningham interrupted me in the middle: "That will not do. You have to memorize your speech and not look at the manuscript. You can never put your feelings into your speech unless you have it all well-memorized without a single mistake."

This was another shock. I had observed that when Japanese politicians gave a speech, they consulted a paper. Teachers always looked at their papers, too. I never dreamed that I must totally memorize my speech, but if this was necessary, then I must. On the way home I began learning the speech, and in another week had memorized the whole piece. But standing before Mother, I found that my memorization was not sufficient. When I forgot one word, the whole sentence failed me.

"This will not do. You have to memorize it well. Understand, you will be excited on the stage and this can happen to any person. The important thing is to memorize so well that you will not fail under any conditions."

During the next week, I tackled the speech in real earnest. I memorized it so well that I could now even begin in the middle or any other place. I found that if you memorized well you could then brush up on your pronunciation and could concentrate on your feelings. To memorize is important but to memorize well is more important and this can develop real ability. Now I stood with confidence before Mrs. Cunningham. She polished my pronunciation and I was able to proceed immediately with the next sentence.

Before the day of the contest she said, "You have done very well and I am sure you can win. Even if you don't, you have developed yourself, which is much better than any prize in the world." I understood her words and thanked her from the bottom of my heart.

The next day was Saturday, the day of the contest. My teacher and I left the school a little early and, after getting off the streetcar, approached the hall. We were expecting to see a crowd and placards announcing the contest. But in front of the auditorium everything was quiet and empty. We felt very queer. Maybe we had come too early. We entered the hall. Not a single person was there, except a man sweeping the corridor. The teacher approached him and said, "I understand that there will be an English speaking contest held in this hall this afternoon."

I waited for his answer with a lump in my throat. Without even looking up, he answered casually, "Nothing of the kind today. Maybe it was last Saturday." A great disappointment filled my heart. I felt my legs shaking. So it was all over.

When I returned home, I flung myself on the bed. Tears flowed down my cheeks. All my effort, everything I had done was in vain. Oh, if I could only appear on the stage and deliver the speech to the audience, I would not care if I won or not. I could not choke back my sobs.

At supper my father, observing my red eyes and hearing what had happened, said, "Don't be a sissy. It's only a contest. Nothing for a man to lament."

I bit my lip and kept quiet.

But during the next day or two, the feeling of mortification melted and I forgot the bitterness.

A week passed. I had finished my last lesson for Saturday. Suddenly I was called by my English teacher. "Honda, I just received a phone call from Waseda University telling me that the contest is being held today. They asked whether you could come. It's noon now and there's an hour left. I think you can make it."

There had been some mistake or misunderstanding. I was panic-stricken. I had already put the whole affair out of mind and hadn't even recited a sentence all week. The teacher talked casually, not understanding what I was suffering.

"Yes, I think I will go."

"You'd better hurry up. I'm not going with you this time," and with this he left me.

Contrary to the week before, there was a big placard posted in front of the hall and there was bustle and din all over. As the contest was to begin in five minutes, the hall was almost full. My head swam and my heart began pounding at the thought that I was going to make a speech to this big crowd without any preparation.

When I entered the room next to the hall, about twelve students, boys and girls, all with their teachers or parents, stared at my lonesome figure. I slipped quietly to the corner seat. I did not receive a program and thus did not know when I was to deliver the speech. My turn came rather early, fourth from the beginning. When I heard my name called, again my heart jumped into my mouth. I felt as though everything had been blanked out of my mind. There was applause. I had to face the audience, like it or not. My manuscript was at home. If I stumbled, I would be out of the contest.

"Mr. Chairman, Ladies and Gentlemen."

I began slowly. Suddenly my confidence returned. I felt at ease and began delivering the speech clearly and fluently. I remembered all the details, even recalling the advice of Mrs. Cunningham to emphasize certain places and to pause in other places. All my practice and endeavor was not in vain.

The last speech was over. Silence fell as the judge, a dignified foreign gentleman, began, "Every student has done his best. It was indeed difficult to judge the winner, but after consultation, the judges have decided that the first prize goes to Mr. Chikaraishi, the second to Miss Tanaka, and the third to Mr. Nakajima."

I felt a surge of disappointment. I was leaving to return home when a college student called me to join the party which was to be held in the back room. At the party I learned that I had won fourth place. The best five were to deliver their speeches over the radio in a national broadcast two weeks later. After the broadcast I received a golden pencil on which the station's initials were engraved. I treasured this pencil for a very long time.

I ENTER MEDICAL SCHOOL

I passed the entrance examination for medical school, which I had long yearned to enter. The competition was strong—ten applicants to one opening—but luckily I passed. After commuting to school for a month or so, however, I discovered the school was not at all as exciting as I had expected. Every day was full of study and work, and there was no color or brightness in the school life.

Each Sunday I went to church. Even though young and rather a newcomer, I was nominated president of the whole Bible class. This tickled my pride. I enjoyed interpreting for the English Bible class. Within six months, I developed my ability considerably in interpreting English. Even when Mother Cunningham gave a very long lecture, I could follow it easily. My confidence increased. I took pride in my ability and was always happy and ready to translate any English speech delivered by a foreigner. The more I used my ability, the more it developed.

It was a cloudy and cold Sunday. Mother Cunningham had asked me to accompany her to visit one of her students in a tuberculosis sanatorium. After church we had lunch in the dining room. It was always a joy to have dinner with my foreign friends. Roast or fried chicken was served, which I loved.

It was a long ride to the Kiyose hospital. Six men, ranging in age from eighteen to thirty, were in bed in a special ward. The windows were open and a cold draft passed through the dismal room.

I stood by while Mother Cunningham spoke to the men. I was conscious of my health and my bosom swelled with pride that, contrary to these poor fellows, I was strong and healthy. After returning home that evening, I told my father about the visit to the hospital. He replied, "You'd better be careful about visiting that hospital. You might get infected."

I did not answer but thought in my heart how unsympathetic he was. Besides, now that I was so healthy, I had no fear of infection.

I went to take a bath that evening. In the hot water I stroked my arm and observed its smooth youthfulness. I was so happy to feel that I was healthy. Just then I felt something queer in my chest—a very unpleasant sensation. I coughed. Something sour came out. I spat in the sink. It was red. Bright red. I could not believe my eyes. There was no mistaking that it was blood. I felt a chill running down my spine. Consumption developing in a day. Although I was only a junior in medical school, I had enough common sense to know that this was impossible. But then where did this blood come from? Maybe a slight injury in my throat. I tried to believe this, but deep in my heart I knew that it came from the lungs. The hemoptysis lasted for two weeks. For a day or two, I did not take it seriously and moved about. But every time I moved that unpleasant bubble-like sound began and there was bleeding. Then I acknowledged that I must have complete rest or it would not stop. It was indeed agony to lie so quiet. My body ached all over, but within four or five days I got used to it and did not suffer so much. The bleeding stopped for four days and I thought it was over. I sat up in bed. My head felt heavy. I never realized that I was carrying such a heavy load.

The world looked so bright and beautiful. But suddenly I heard that sound again, and I quickly lay down again. The milk had been spilt. I knew I had to begin from the first, suffering and waiting patiently for another week. Tears began to flow down my cheeks. My mother tried to comfort me, but I cried bitterly, "What have I done to suffer so much? Unlike other boys, I have followed a clean life. I've never tried to be mean to others and I've gone to church. Why must I suffer so much? What have I done to be so heavily punished?" I pulled the covers over my head and sobbed.

Next day I received a card from Mrs. Cunningham. On it was printed a verse from the Bible: "Let not your heart be troubled, my peace I give unto thee."

Then I knew that I had been proud in my heart. Peace came over me and I was willing to endure anything that might come.

After two months of rest, I went to school again. The opinions of the doctors differed. One said I had to rest for at least a year, and another said I could go to school on condition that I would take utmost care and never overtire myself. The latter was a professor in my school, so I gladly followed his advice.

I had another attack when I was in the third year, but I overcame it and graduated with good marks.

MY WORK IN THE INSTITUTE BEGINS

I spent a year as an intern at St. Luke's International Hospital, then I applied for duty as a ship's surgeon, thinking that the pure air of the ocean would do me good. During a month on standby I commuted every day from my home to the branch office of N.Y.K. in Yokohama. This was indeed a gay time. I had money in my pocket as never before, ate lunch at fancy restaurants and strolled in Yamashita Park nearby. My bosom swelled looking at the big liners, fancying myself a surgeon on those luxury ships. But my experience turned out to be quite different from my expectations.

One day I received an order to embark on the S.S. *Genoa,* a steamer chartered by the Japanese Army for military transportation. There was no choice but to go. The ship left the port of Hiroshima for China, loaded with soldiers and arms. Much against my will, I had to cruise up and down the Yangtze River and the coast of China under dangerous conditions, risking my health as well as my life. After a year, utterly exhausted, I appealed to the military authority and was allowed to disembark due to my bad health.

After a month's rest, I was on a freighter bound for the United States. What a great difference there was between the atmosphere of China and the blue sea of the South Pacific.

After three years of life at sea, I felt healthy and wanted to carry on my studies. On my return I applied to the hospital where I had done my internship. Since there was a shortage of doctors in this hospital, the chief doctor gladly welcomed

me to his hospital as a staff member. My life in this hospital
was very happy.

But I had another ambition: to have a career in the Institute of Infectious Diseases. This Institute was attached to
Tokyo University and ranked the highest in Japan. To become a staff member was most difficult, even for graduates
of Tokyo University and even more so for graduates of a private school, as I was. My father, who knew Professor Kojima,
the chief of staff, had contacted him about me. One very
cold windy night, I went out to phone him—we didn't have
a telephone in our home—about the possibility of studying
in his Institute. I expected a refusal, but instead Professor
Kojima directed me to come to his house immediately. Returning home, I told my mother of his summons. She said,
"I am not keen about your going out in this bad weather.
You have been rejoicing that you were accepted by St. Luke's
Hospital. Why don't you phone Dr. Kojima and tell him that
you are going to work in that hospital? I don't like the dismal
atmosphere of the Institute."

"Well, Mother, I have promised Dr. Kojima that I will go
to see him. I have to keep my word. I can decide after talking
with him."

Dr. Kojima's home was in Den-enchofu, not far from my
home. I took a car and arrived at his home within thirty minutes. When I rang the bell, a maid appeared and ushered me
into the parlor. I sat rigidly on a chair, waiting for his appearance. He was in the casual Japanese kimono.

"Glad to meet you," he began. "So you want to work in
our Institute. All right, I have a position for you. One of my
staff has been invited to Indonesia and you can take his place.
Your study will be of the influenza virus. Come to the Institute next Monday."

He did not allow me to say a word. That is how I began
studying in the Institute of Infectious Diseases of Tokyo
University.

The entrance to the Institute was on Shirokane Street. A
big gate of steel lattices shut it off from the public. Next to

the gate was a small building with guards who kept out intruders. As there was a clinic annex to the Institute, many patients visited this place. I could not understand how these guards distinguished thieves from patients. Perhaps the mere presence of the guard scared away those who had no legitimate reason for entering. Or maybe they were there only to give information to the patients. In front of the brown brick building was a vast lawn and a tall, majestic Himalaya cedar. The building was three stories high, topped by a tower with a big clock. It had all the dignity and authority befitting the leading institute in the country with an international reputation.

But inside the building, all was dark and dirty, and the smell of animals permeated the air. I knocked at Dr. Kojima's room and entered. A man standing in the middle of the room stared at me. I introduced myself and asked if Professor Kojima was there. Without smiling, he told me to follow him. His attitude was unfriendly and I could not engage him in conversation or ask questions. He was about my age but his hair was quite white. We went down to the ground floor. Without knocking, we entered a rather small, dark room. A man wearing a gown stood up as we entered. "This is Dr. Honda. He will be in this room," the first man said to him quietly. Then he turned to me and handed me a thick book. The title was *Handbook of Bacteriology*. "Read this," he said and, without another word, left the room.

Later when Dr. Kojima arrived, he summoned me to his room. "You are to investigate influenza virus." As I had many questions, I cleared my throat. But he didn't look at me and dismissed me with a wave of his hand. Thus my investigation of influenza virus began.

I MEET JUNKO SAKURADA

It was autumn. The sky was high and blue. One could tell by the soft, gentle breeze that summer was over. The leaves of the ginkgo tree had not yet changed their color but their fluttering showed signs that their prime was past. This is Nature. Time never stops, always moving steadily, like the hands of an unseen clock.

Half a year had passed, and I was quite familiar with my routine. I had mastered all the techniques necessary for the research of influenza virus. I had read many articles and bibliographies concerning influenza virus, not only in Japanese but in English as well.

Professor Kojima did not instruct me in any way; neither did he give me any direction. During the past months, I had been meditating on what subject I should investigate for my first work. I suddenly hit on the idea that there must be some relation between vitamins and viruses. People who are undernourished easily fall prey to infection. Vitamins, naturally, have an important role in nutrition. Probably vitamins have some effect in preventing or healing influenza. I had not read any report in this field. Thus my theme was determined. The title was "Effect of Various Vitamins on Influenza Virus."

Because there was a shortage of drugs it was difficult to get good vitamin products. But through the cooperation of chemical and food companies, I ordered and received considerable quantities of good quality vitamins A, B, C, D, and E.

The tests were immediately carried out, mainly in two ways: first the preventive effectiveness of various vitamins, second the healing effects.

A number of mice were fed or given various vitamins subcutaneously, while the control group was fed without vitamins. After two weeks, influenza virus was inoculated intranasally to all these mice. The virus was diluted ten, hundred, thousand, ten thousand, million, and ten million times.

If any special vitamins had an effect of preventing the development of influenza, this could be easily checked by autopsy on the animals. The same kind of experiments were carried out to find what had a healing effect. In the latter test, vitamins were to be given after the inoculations. I had been preparing for this experiment all through the hot season and was ready to begin by early autumn.

It was September 18, 1942, and the day was beautiful. A speck of clear blue sky could be seen high above from my underground laboratory. That day I was excited about my hypothesis and wanted very much to discuss it with someone. I picked up the phone and called Dr. Sakurada, but he was not in his office. Dr. Sakurada was a year my senior in the medical school. I had met him when I first went to the dining room six months ago. He was studying in the First Laboratory under Professor Hosoya. As we had graduated from the same school, we became close friends and every noon after lunch we went out for a walk. He lived with his mother and eighteen-year-old sister. I recalled that he had said his sister was taking vocal lessons from a foreign teacher, Mrs. Netke Loebe.

Since Dr. Sakurada had invited me to visit him in his home, I decided to go there. His home was not difficult to find; it was much bigger and finer looking than I had imagined. He had never told me he operated a clinic, but there was a brass plate on the door and a sign: "Physician and Pediatrician, Office Hours 6 to 9 p.m." I realized that he saw patients after he came home from the Institute.

Through the glass entrance door I could see a shaggy old dog lying on the floor. He looked feeble and meek, so I knew that he probably would not even growl. I rang the bell. No answer. I rang again, a little stronger.

"Who's there?" It was Sakurada's voice.

"It's me, Honda."

"Well, well, welcome to my house, come on in. I'm fixing my motorcycle and my hands are dirty. Come into the parlor and make yourself at home. I'll join you in a few minutes."

It was not difficult at all to find my way to the parlor. I seated myself comfortably on the sofa and, picking up a magazine, began turning pages lazily. A knock and the door opened.

I raised my eyes expecting Dr. Sakurada. Instead there was a smiling girl of medium height with short curls. She was beautiful. I looked straight into her sparkling eyes. She looked startled under my gaze, but without lowering her eyes bowed slightly and sat down gracefully on the sofa nearby.

"My brother suddenly had a sick call and went out to visit the patient."

Her voice was enchanting, not too high, not too low. It came floating through the air.

"I think I saw you on the stage Saturday night. You were a member of the chorus, standing third from the left," I spoke slowly.

"Oh, yes! So you were there? I now recall my brother telling me about a doctor who loved music. So it was you, Dr. Honda."

I smiled and she smiled back. We felt at ease and the conversation, mostly about music, began to flow.

A pause came and we were silent.

"Will you please sing me a song?" I asked abruptly. Without showing any sign of shyness, she walked over to the piano and placed some music on the rack. She began to sing in a clear voice:

Leise flehen meine Lieder durch die Nacht zu dir;

I was expecting to hear some old folk songs or other simple music, but no! Here was a fully trained voice, singing classical music with control and beauty. To my astonishment she also played her own accompaniment:

In den stillen Hain hernieder, Liebchen, komm zu mir!

It was, of course, Schubert's "Serenade," which I liked so much. I listened, completely enchanted:

Flüsternd schlanke Wipfel rauschen in des Mondes Licht.

Her German diction was clear and could easily be understood. Here was the kind of girl I had been waiting for all my life. I had found her at last.

Days flew by, four days since I had met her. I was in my laboratory sitting before my desk with a glass cylinder containing three mice. I shifted the mice to a smaller cylinder containing ether. After being anesthetized, each mouse was inoculated with influenza virus. Having finished the work, I carried the cylinder to the shelf in the corridor. I accidentally turned my head and glanced toward the stairs. There was someone colorful walking through the dark corridor, illuminating the whole passage. It didn't take long to identify Junko Sakurada, dressed in a bright Japanese kimono, her long sleeves fluttering. I could not believe my eyes. I welcomed her into my room and gave her a seat. We talked for more than an hour. Her appointment with Mrs. Netke Loebe was at eleven and as she had arrived a little early, she happened to drop in. That was her excuse for visiting. I walked with her to Mrs. Netke's home, which was not far from the Institute. Seeing her disappear, I walked slowly back to my room. The leaves on the trees were turning color under the bright sun.

Her smile, her colorful clothes, her whole figure were vividly stamped on my mind. Though I sat in my chair, I could not continue my work and just stared blankly up at the blue sky.

That night I wrote a letter to her confessing my love. I folded the letter carefully, pressed it softly to my lips, and mailed it the next morning.

Nearly a week passed without answer. I continued with my experiment. One morning I heard a knock on the door. I was surprised to find Junko waiting outside. She beckoned me to come. In a second I was beside her, shutting the door of the lab with a bang.

"I am going to Mrs. Netke," she said softly.

I tucked my white gown under my arm and walked beside her through the Institute, past the stall where horses and cows were kept. The day was beautiful and the sky high and clear with specks of clouds moving slowly. She stopped suddenly and, facing me, said in a soft voice, "Here is my answer."

She handed me a white envelope and quickly left my side.

Slowly I turned back and with thumping heart opened the envelope. "The person I have waited for so long has suddenly appeared. It is more than mere destiny. An ivy seeks something to cling to, and we need air to live. What I need is love, love as deep and wide as the ocean. Looking up at the fleecy white clouds floating in the sky and often thinking of the loneliness and fragility of life, I was waiting for his arrival. His love must be broad and he must also have the heart to yearn for the beauty of nature and art. I kept telling my heart that no such person exists. Then suddenly he arrived, clad in white and blue, clean and pure. He is a fantasy and also a reality, strong as a ray of the sun and tender as moonlight."

I stopped in my path and the earth seemed to be glowing.

WE GET MARRIED

With new energy and zeal I plunged myself into my investigations. The result was rewarding. Of the various vitamins I used, C seemed to have the effect of preventing and curing influenza. Vitamin A also showed some effect in preventing the disease. Junko called me often on the phone and we spent many happy hours together, discussing music and life. When I walked with her, distance and time seemed to fade away.

Professor Kojima instructed me to report my work in a symposium held at the Institute. As our Institute was ranked at the top in the study of infectious diseases in Japan, a report carried great authority. I delivered my talk with confidence, and afterwards, during a short discussion, was able to convince all of the accuracy of my results. To be allowed to give a report within a year after joining the Institute was indeed extraordinary. I was thankful to Professor Kojima for his generosity.

Two months later my report was printed in the Journal of the Institute and I wrote the following dedication on the front page: "To Junko Sakurada, with love, the effect I have made, and glory that comes from this work."

Winter arrived bringing bitter cold weather. Fuel was scarce and so was food. We had to be content with what we had. In spite of all the adversity that war brought, I was happy. The world seemed to rotate around me and everything was just fine.

One warm February day when I came back from the Institute, there was a letter in a white envelope on the desk. I knew instinctively that it was from Junko. My face clouded as I began reading with a sickening feeling, and my mouth went dry. "I have torn my heart to write you, but my conscience orders me to do so. During the past months, I have been happily basking in your warm love, not thinking much of the future. But since I have visited your home and met your parents, I realize that I am not suited to be your wife. Your home requires a bride who is obedient in a traditional way. Your mother expects a daughter-in-law who concentrates on household arts, such as cooking and sewing, not one who excels in music or art. I can read it in her eyes. If we were to marry, tragedy would come to us all and my dreams would be destroyed. Though it be hard, I think it is better to part."

I stood still. The letter trembled in my hand. What she said I knew was true. Instead of facing the problem, I had been avoiding it. But the time had come when we had to discuss the obstacles which she so clearly expressed.

I sat for more than an hour, staring out of the window. Then I walked downstairs and called Junko on the phone. "I received your letter," I began.

"Yes," she said in a sad voice.

"I must see you and talk."

"I think we'd better not meet again."

A despairing feeling surged up. "We must talk and try to find an answer to our problems. I will be waiting for you on the platform of Gotanda Station at five-thirty. Please!"

At the station I waited impatiently, searching for her figure among the crowds that poured out of the coaches. Five-thirty. Five-thirty-five. She had not yet arrived. I waited another five minutes with sinking heart. Five-forty, then the familiar figure came into sight. She was wearing a red coat and red hat. I walked casually to her side. Although she noticed me, she did not speak. We walked slowly to a private car, got on board, and some minutes later got off at Senzokuike Station.

Dusk was falling and the lake was dark. Everything was quiet. People hurried to their homes; only fools would take a walk by the lake in such cold weather.

We walked in silence, first by the shrine and then to the lake. I felt that words could not express our feelings. Finally Junko stopped and looked at the light reflected on the calm water.

"I know there are many difficulties but we can try—" I began. She did not respond.

"I think we should try," I began again. Silence.

Then in her clear, well-controlled voice she began to sing Schubert's "Ave Maria."

I knew that she was suffering as I was. The only response she could give was to ask: "Ave Maria, please help me, please accept my prayer," tears flowing down her cheeks.

That night I could not sleep. I tossed and tossed. Finally a little before dawn I slept and dreamed that I was walking alone in the dark. I was so miserable and lonely, I felt like crying. Awakening, I understood that I could not live without her. I got up and, without breakfast, went to her house instead of going to the Institute. Dr. Sakurada had already gone, and her mother was sitting alone in the living room. I asked for Junko and she called her to the room. Glancing at her face, I knew that she too had not slept.

"I would like to talk to both of you," I began quietly. Junko was casting her eyes down, not looking at me, but I knew she was listening intently.

"Before proceeding, let me say that I fervently wish to marry Junko, and I promise with all my heart to make her happy."

I watched Junko as I spoke, and with these words I noticed a slight blush pass over her face like a ripple on the surface of calm water aroused by a gentle breeze. I continued:

"There are many men and women on this earth, almost as many as stars in the sky or waves in the ocean, but to meet and love an ideal person is destined by fate or God. I have met the ideal woman for me, and I know we love and understand each other. Though I am aware that without love, there cannot be a happy home, still I admit that there must be more than love to make a happy home. Each home has its traditions, customs, and way of living. Preserving the good in this tradition and absorbing the advantages of another home will develop a new life to higher standards. If we were so meek as to follow blindly our parents' instruction, we would live 90 percent of the time as our parents did (there never is 100 percent). And if this were so, culture would simply decline by generations.

"I know well the faults of my parents and, consequently, what Junko is afraid of. I will strive with all my might to make our life better than theirs. A successful marriage or life is measured by the fruits it produces. Even if outwardly the young couple seem to lead a happy life, if they degrade each other, their marriage is a failure. On the contrary even if they quarrel and will not compromise on the low level, if they still seek truth and better themselves, though slowly, I think the marriage is a success and they will have a happy future, and as a consequence bring good to society."

Junko's eyes shone and she nodded her head at my words.

During this emotional period of my life I did not neglect my investigations. My main project at the time was to make an influenza vaccine. A very high percentage of virus could easily be obtained from the lung of an infected mouse but, as it was difficult to eliminate the vast amount of protein it contained, the best quality was made from virus inoculated into egg embryos. The disadvantage was that only a small portion of fluid could be obtained from these eggs.

The next test was to determine the efficiency of inactivated vaccine. The result of this vaccine showed equal immunity. The next step therefore was to find what chemical substances were best for inactivating the virus. Indeed, there were many, and the following year I made a number of reports along these lines.

One rainy day Junko and I were walking from the Institute up the hill of Dogenzaka. The cold rain fell quietly but we didn't care. The leaves of the trees had fallen and winter was rapidly approaching.

It began to pour. We took shelter under the roof of a house, huddling together. The beat of the rain became steady and fast. We were not at all concerned or troubled. It seemed as if we never had enough time to talk of all our thoughts.

Up to this time I had never mentioned the date of our marriage. It was something I wanted Junko to decide, and I was willing to wait until she was ready.

We looked at the rain. A silence fell between us. Maybe it was an angel resting her wings on the bough between our hearts.

"Shall we be married next spring?" She spoke casually. It was so sudden I could not believe my ears. Maybe she was joking. "Let's get married next spring," she repeated.

Now I understood her words, and my heart leapt with joy.

We were married the next year, March 21, 1944, and all the houses in Japan hoisted flags. It was a national holiday.

The sweet atmosphere of the honeymoon did not last long. Japan was fighting a hopeless war and rushing to destruction. I had finished my last report, "Co-work of Influenza Virus with Various Bacteria." All these reports were submitted in partial fulfillment of my doctorate at Tokyo University. In three years I had completed my work and applied. This was indeed a very rare case.

But I was wasting away, getting thinner every day.

Yuko was born May 1, 1945, the day Hitler committed suicide and Berlin fell. The war ended August 15 that same year.

A year passed and I was tired. Every day in the late afternoon, I ran a fever. Taking aspirin I kept up with my work. Then suddenly I had an attack—the same old bleeding from the lung. This time it did not stop so easily and I suffered for two weeks.

One day Junko returned home with a gloomy face. She had visited a famous physician who had diagnosed my case. I asked the result but her mouth was tight. I coaxed her, saying that as I was a doctor, I knew everything and was also prepared to withstand any prognosis.

She did not state it clearly, but what I surmised was that I was doomed, and even if I did live it would be for no more than two or three years. It didn't shock me, but it did help me to make up my mind to resign my position and take a rest in the country.

I RECOVER

The pure air and good food did wonders for my health. I had been back in the country living with my parents for six months but was already putting on weight and running no fever at all. I led my life with strict regularity, eating at the same time, resting, and walking each day. I read a lot and also had time to write and meditate. Here was no noise of the city. Everything was quiet and clean. The winter was very cold, but the rest preserved my energies and by spring I was much improved.

Some of the neighbors, hearing that I was a medical doctor, came to my home for consultation. They were very glad to receive my treatment, and I made up my mind to open a small clinic at my home. Junko wrote me a heated letter of protest, saying I would kill myself. I answered that this would not add any physical stress and would stimulate my spirit. She finally agreed and brought Yuko to the country. My parents moved to Tokyo and in a way we exchanged homes. This was convenient, as the shortage of homes was acute in Tokyo, as well as in all parts of Japan.

A year passed. I was getting so strong that even in the most severe cold, I could make sick calls by bicycle even several miles away.

The feeling that I was helping others and playing an important role in society boosted my self confidence. This spiritual stimulation made me much better even though I did not rest as I should. I forgot that I was sick, and led a normal life.

One sunny day in June, I was returning through the mountain roads from the station. It was a shortcut and the road, besides being dusty, wound up and down hill. While I was slowly climbing the hill, a man overtook me and bade me good-day. It was Mr. Kondo, the principal of the nearby grammar school.

"Dr. Honda, have you ever heard of Mr. Shinichi Suzuki?" he asked.

After pondering the name, I replied, "Yes. Once I heard him speak on the radio and his words impressed me deeply. He demonstrated his idea by having small children play the violin. Then he insisted that talent is not inherited but could be developed. In other words he expressed the thought that every child in the world can and should be educated."

"Yes, that's right. We are going to form a class using Suzuki's method. Mr. Yamamura from Nagoya will come once a week to teach violin. We need at least twenty children to begin. Can your daughter join the class?"

"I think it is wonderful, and I am sure we would like to have Yuko join the class. I will talk with my wife tonight and give you an answer within a few days."

That night I spoke to Junko about Mr. Suzuki's school, telling her what impact his words over the radio had made on me.

"Well, I was thinking of having Yuko study piano. Violin is something of which I have no knowledge and it seems so difficult."

Observing her hesitation, I insisted, "I agree with you that Yuko should study piano. But as there isn't a suitable instructor, why not have her begin with violin? She can shift to piano in the future if she wants. The important thing is to begin, and I think this is a wonderful opportunity. We never even thought of her beginning at such an early age as four."

We agreed to apply for the class, and that was the first step in my acquaintance with Talent Education.

Yuko was a quiet, reticent child. Probably it was the environment of our home that made her this way. Because I was sick, she had been living with only her mother for the past two years and naturally saw very few outsiders. When a stranger came she clung to her mother's skirt and burst into tears. She was also delicate and in some ways stubborn.

When she first began to walk, I bought her a pair of green shoes. She loved these shoes dearly and every day when I took her out for a walk, she raised her arms and sang "Ah," with joy. Within a month or two, the color faded and the shoes became dirty. One day I painted them blue and they looked as good as new. I expected her to rejoice over the new shoes, but when she saw them, she began sobbing. My feelings were a little hurt and, ignoring her resistance, I put the shoes on her feet. Instead of walking joyfully as I expected, she stamped her feet and began crying as though her feet were on fire. I had to take her shoes off and use benzine on them to remove the blue paint. But somehow she never enjoyed wearing those shoes again.

I had made up my mind to raise Yuko with strict discipline. One day I bought some wooden blocks which had the Japanese alphabet printed on one side. She enjoyed playing with the blocks, building houses and bridges, but when she was tired of playing, she left them scattered on the floor. I sat down beside her and ordered her to put the blocks back into the box. She ignored my order and did not lift a finger. I showed her how to put them in the box, then scattered them again and told her to put them back. She understood what I wanted, but just stood still and seemed to think it was not necessary to obey. I ordered her a third time and she still refused. Losing patience, I put her in the closet until she promised me she would do what I told her.

Reflecting later, I think the problem was mine. Yuko was enjoying herself very much with the toys, creating various things, but putting them back in the box was not part of the fun. Her resistance became stubbornness when she found me sitting beside her, ordering her with a stern look to put the blocks in the box. It was just like the old fable. The harder I blew, the tighter she wrapped her cloak around herself. In my ignorance, I was stimulating the girl to develop the ability to resist.

II

YUKO'S FIRST LESSON

We were informed that lessons were to be once a week, at Dr. Yato's home. Dr. Yato was a dentist and his office was on the second floor of an old building. The living room adjoining his office waiting room was where the class met.

Junko told me what happened at Yuko's first lesson. Violins had already been ordered in different sizes and, as Yuko was among the smallest, her violin was one-sixteenth size. Mr. Yamamura began the lesson. All the children stood before the teacher in two lines. Mr. Yamamura spoke to the children.

"Now let's begin. The first lesson is to bow. When you come to the class for a lesson, you must always bow your head. This is very important because you have to learn good manners. Now, when I say one, two, three, let's all bow together. 'One, two, three.'"

All heads went down but one. It was Yuko's.

"I noticed that one child did not understand me. Now, again, when I say one, two, three, let's bow our heads. 'One, two, three!'" Again one head was sticking up, while all others went down. Perceiving this, my wife told me she was so ashamed she felt like hiding under the table.

So Yuko's first lesson began.

One of the most unusual ideas in Suzuki's method is to teach a well-known melody from the beginning. The very first piece is "Twinkle, Twinkle, Little Star." This piece has six variations; instead of using a long bow, in the orthodox method, children are taught detached sixteenth notes with short bow in the first variation.

It is difficult for beginners even to hold the violin under the chin. The teacher instructs the child to hold his left shoulder with his right hand, then to move his face forty-five degrees to the left, and place the violin under his chin. Now he is given the bow. He plays the very first note on open string A, or the second string: *ta-ka, ta-ka, ta, ta, ta-ka, ta-ka, ta, ta.*

After children master this pattern on the A string, they are taught to cross the bow to the E, or first string. The first stage may be the most difficult. After mastering the first variation, the children proceed to the second and to the third: in this way they learn all six. The "Twinkle" variations are not only the major theme of the *Suzuki Violin School,* but also include almost all the basic techniques required in playing violin. Even when children are far advanced, they are always encouraged to practice the "Twinkle" variations.

It took two months for Yuko to master "Twinkle," and she had great difficulty. Her arm just didn't move, and her hand found it difficult to place the right note.

FIRST MEETING WITH SUZUKI

In September, Mr. Suzuki came to Toyota for the first time to have a special lesson with the children. Each child played the piece that he was studying, and Mr. Suzuki sat nearby with his violin, listening and often plucking a string.

He was always smiling and his friendly attitude made the children like him very much and their mothers feel relaxed. Mr. Yamamura sat nearby and nodded assent to each bit of counsel Mr. Suzuki gave to an individual child.

Yuko played "Lightly Row," and she played quite well. She stood straight and rigid, without a smile even when Mr. Suzuki joked. After she finished, Mr. Suzuki praised her.

At the end of the lesson, all the children lined up to play in unison. Some could barely hold the instrument and some stooped. Some children swung their bodies while they played. Mr. Suzuki corrected the posture of each child and all eyes could recognize the change. It was like magic. A half-day's lesson, and all the children had made good progress—everyone on the program was happy.

That night a reception was held in a nearby inn. I had already greeted Mr. Suzuki in the afternoon, but as it was during the lesson, I knew he did not recognize me. Mr. Yamamura introduced us.

Instantly I felt his warm personality and liked him. He has something which attracts people's affection, even at the first meeting. "Mr. Suzuki, I heard you speak on the radio last year. You said that all children, provided they have no brain defect, could be developed. You said talent is something not inherited but developed by circumstance. Since then, these words have been ringing in my mind. I have been waiting for this day to meet you and hear your words personally, and I am indeed very happy. May I ask how you happened to develop this idea?" He thought for a moment, and then began speaking slowly.

"That is a long story but, as it is very important, I should tell all to you." He took out a cigarette, lit it, and after a few puffs began:

"I was born in the city of Nagoya in 1898. My father, Masakichi Suzuki, was a samisen [Japanese string instrument] maker. When he was young he met a teacher who owned a violin. When he first heard the tone of this violin, he was bewitched by its beautiful sound. He begged to borrow it for a night and studied its construction carefully. After many failures, he made his first violin in 1888.

"Then he built a violin factory that began producing the famed Suzuki violins. My father wanted me to help him in this profession so he sent me to a commercial school. After graduating from the school, I felt that if I were to follow this profession, I must learn to make a good violin. In order to produce a good violin, I thought it necessary to play the violin. So I began taking lessons from Mrs. Ko Ando when I was eighteen years old.

"Unfortunately I developed lung trouble, so my father sent me to Okitsua in Shizuoka Prefecture to rest. In the same inn where I stayed was a man named Mr. Yanagida. We became close friends and later he introduced me to Prince Yoshichika Tokugawa, who was the lord of Owari province." We all knew of the famous Tokugawa. His ancestor, the great Lord Ieyasu Tokugawa, had seized power; he and his family ruled Japan for three hundred years. Ieyasu built a large castle in Tokyo, then called Edo. Because the Tokugawas were afraid that Christians would invade Japan and take power, Ieyasu forbade the spread of this religion and later closed Japan to Western civilization.

"I visited Prince Tokugawa at his large estate. As we both were from Nagoya, we got along very well. A few years later the prince told me that he was going on a trip around the world. I had always wanted to study in Germany, but I knew my father was not keen on the idea. I spoke to Prince Tokugawa about my dream but also added that my father probably would not consent to my going. With a twinkle in his eyes, Prince Tokugawa said, 'I will tell your father that you should travel with me to see the world. I am sure he would not object and, once we are in Europe, you can stay in Germany and study violin as long as you like. My father gave me ten thousand yen, which is more than enough.'

"Just as the prince predicted, I stayed in Germany, where I studied violin under Professor Klingler. Though living in a foreign country, I did not have any difficulty with violin study, but I did have great difficulty with the language. I could not understand what people said nor could I express my desires in words. I did not think that I was a dunce—I had been a bright student in school—but with German, I was like a retarded child.

"Suddenly I observed that every German child at the age of three or four spoke and understood German very easily. This had a great impact on me. When I was in Japan and heard small children speak their mother tongue, I didn't think this was anything special. But considering how difficult

it was for an adult to learn a foreign language, a child's potentiality for learning must be very high. Since children can acquire languages so easily, they must have a wonderful potential, much more than we adults ever dreamed. After I returned
to Japan, I began to apply this idea in teaching violin to children."

His story was very interesting and, though he spoke casually, he stressed the point that all children can develop their
abilities regardless of heredity.

When I mentioned that I was a medical doctor and, as such,
believed in hereditary factors, he responded, "Of course I am
not denying these factors. I would like to put it this way.
Probably the hereditary factor is the speed with which we
adapt to circumstances or grasp something in our minds."

The first concert was held in November, nearly six months
after the class began. The concert took place in a kindergarten
in Toyota.

The program began with the small children playing
"Twinkle, Twinkle." Yuko played "Lightly Row," and I
thought she played well. The older children who had begun
with her had advanced to Volume 3, which seemed amazing.
Even some children who were the same age as Yuko had progressed beyond her. One four-year-old boy played Menuetto
by Boccherini. It made us a little unhappy to know that
Yuko was lagging behind these children.

I recalled Mr. Suzuki saying that there is a difference of
speed in adapting to circumstances. Maybe she was naturally
slow. She was not very good in singing, either. Every time she
sang out of tune, my wife would glance at me with a look of
reproach, hinting that the fault was on my side. The last per-
former was Isako Yamamura, the twelve-year-old daughter of
the instructor. Her piece was Concerto in A Minor by Vivaldi.

I was speechless at her playing. With a small bow she made
the melody flow strongly, then gently. Her bowing technique
had wonderful ease. I listened enchanted. I wondered if Yuko
could ever acquire such skill.

WE VISIT MATSUMOTO

The new year of 1950 dawned and we were quite happy. Our second daughter, Mayako, had been born two years before. She was light in complexion and, compared to Yuko, was quiet and seldom cried. Yuko always made a fuss when she thought we were going out. Even when we tried to sneak out, she was always quick to notice. Mayako slept well, usually taking her nap in the sunroom on the second floor. As we would go out we would look up to the second floor and see her standing up, waving good-bye.

Junko and I were making plans to visit Mr. Suzuki in Matsumoto in the coming spring. This would be a big trip for our family. We decided to make the visit in April since the weather in Matsumoto is very severe in winter.

Our party of five included Junko's mother. We took a train from Nagoya which, after three hours, began puffing up the mountain. It was interesting to see that the line of cherry trees was in full bloom in Nagoya but had only tight buds as the train ascended.

There was a river running parallel to the railroad, flowing swiftly down toward the Pacific. We were traveling in this district for the first time, so we all enjoyed the scenery very much. We arrived at Matsumoto at dusk and then took a small tramcar to Asama Hot Spring, where I had reserved a room at the Aioi-kan Inn. The inn was way up on the hill, a rather old but comfortable looking building. The hot spring was warm and refreshing and the two girls, especially Mayako, enjoyed it very much.

I called Mr. Suzuki to inform him of our arrival, asking if I could visit him that night. I remember his voice, with its special accent, saying: "We are having a lecture at the music school building and Mr. Takasaki, the vice-president of Talent Education, is to talk. Won't you come to the school?"

I promised to be there later and hung up, feeling a little discouraged that I could not speak to him personally.

After supper I went to the school. The hall was full, and

Mr. Takasaki had just begun his lecture. He was a little over sixty, ruddy-faced, and balding. He smiled as he talked, adding gestures to make the audience laugh. His speech had no interest for me because I was impatient to speak to Mr. Suzuki. At last he came out and I introduced myself. His eyes focused on my face but did not seem to recognize me. "I am Dr. Honda from Aichi Prefecture. We have traveled all day to meet you. May I speak to you tonight?" "I am sorry I have no time tonight. Can you come tomorrow morning at eleven?" Of course I could. Because I didn't know my way back to the station, he escorted me there. I was deeply touched by his kindness.

The next morning we all went to Mr. Suzuki's home in Ohyanagi-machi. It was an old but well-kept building and quite attractive. Mr. Suzuki was waiting for us and, as we talked, Mr. Takasaki came in to say good-bye. I was introduced to him and we chatted about the weather and other insignificant things. During the conversation I noticed that Mr. Suzuki was a chain-smoker. I had smoked until I was thirty, then gave up smoking completely. After I stopped smoking, I became healthier and I realized that the habit of smoking was deleterious.

"Mr. Suzuki," I began, "I notice you are a heavy smoker. I advise you to drop that habit. It will bring you nothing but harm." Mr. Suzuki just smiled and said nothing. Later, when I met Mr. Takasaki in Tokyo, he remembered my audacious words.

Mr. Suzuki reserved the whole afternoon for us. He was then living with his younger sister, Mrs. Hina Aikawa, who had lost her husband and had come from Nagoya with her son. An orphaned boy named Koji Toyota also lived with him.

"When Koji was three years old, he was one of my first students. He lost both his father and mother during the war. After the war I found him helping his uncle in Toyohashi. I took him into my home and since then he has been living with us. At first we were concerned with his manners, but I told my sister and nephew not to reproach him but to show him a good example by our deeds. Now he is developing his ability in violin. I will have him play a piece for you."

Koji, a boy of sixteen, came into the room and greeted us. "What will you play for Dr. Honda, maybe the Concerto by Beethoven?"

At this suggestion, Koji tuned his violin and began playing. His tone was beautiful and his posture almost perfect. We listened, deeply absorbed in the music.

"Koji is now learning French and also English from Mrs. Sekiya. He is writing his diary in English. Will you bring your diary and let Dr. Honda look at it?" Koji went up to his room, brought back the book, and handed it to me shyly.

The words he used were simple but they were beautifully written with very few grammatical errors or misspellings. I was surprised to see a boy who had begun studying English so late write such a good diary.

Meanwhile Mrs. Aikawa was busy on the phone, calling to ask some children to play for me. Soon three appeared with their violins. They looked small but were probably ten years old. Mr. Suzuki introduced them as Hiroka Yamada, Yoko Oike, and Tomika Shida. The girls began playing the Concerto in G Minor by Vivaldi. These girls were the most advanced in Suzuki's class, and they played astonishingly well.

We left Matsumoto early next morning. It had indeed been a fruitful visit. On the train back, I was in deep meditation— the scenery did not attract me anymore. Again I was convinced that I had observed something very important for the education and development of human potential, probably going beyond the field of violin playing. I had always dreamed of doing something for others, and now the dream had materialized. I made up my mind that I would help spread Mr. Suzuki's idea, not only in Japan, but throughout the world.

ECUMENICAL WORK CAMP, 1951

The year 1951 was very important. In a way it decided the direction of my future life. Life in the country was easygoing and we were happy. I recovered my health, and even the sick calls at night did not bother me anymore. As there were few medical doctors in this district, besides internal medicine, I had to do some surgery.

One day an emergency call came from the next village. There had been a bad accident in a mine. The place was too far to go by bicycle and, looking up at the clock, I noticed that there was only five minutes before the train left Sanage Station in the next village. Since it took fifteen minutes at least by bicycle to get there, it seemed impossible for me to catch the train. The next one wouldn't arrive for an hour. I called the stationmaster and told him about the case and pleaded with him to hold the train. He held the train ten minutes after the scheduled time of departure, an extraordinary feat in Japan.

Many people talking in loud voices gathered at the site of the accident. But I could not see the patient among them. Noticing my arrival, a man who seemed to be the boss approached me and began to explain in a hurried tone: "The patient is down in the pit, 300 feet below. He has received an electric shock and cannot move. Will you please go down on this lift?" The dark pit and the lift looked very uninviting, but I had no choice.

After the descent we still had to walk about fifty feet. The walls and the ceiling were dripping with moisture. A drop fell onto my neck, and I felt very uncomfortable. The man was lying face down on the wet floor. He was stripped to the waist and soaking wet. After turning him over, I saw that his pupils did not show any reflex. He was dead.

"I am sorry, there's nothing I can do," I told the boss. "But how did this happen? Do you have high voltage electricity in this pit?"

"No, it's only for the light and the voltage is the same as

in our home. He touched the light to fix it and received a shock." Looking carefully, I could not perceive any injury to his right hand or left foot. If high voltage had passed through, there would have been a burn in these places. I recalled the body of a boy who was shocked to death by touching a source of high voltage. He touched the wire with his right hand and the current passed through his body, emerging from his left toe. I recalled another case, that of an electrical engineer who, while fixing a wire on a pole, received a shock. It was the same voltage that killed the boy. The engineer was unconscious but survived after my treatment. Now why did he survive, while the boy died, when both had received the same amount of current? Does electricity produce immunity?

That didn't seem possible. But the electrical engineer had been used to touching electricity. Perhaps by being frequently exposed to electricity, he developed something which changed his constitution. This often happens in medicine. For instance, if a man receives a lethal dose of morphine, it will kill him. On the other hand, if he is given a small dose, then increased amounts little by little, he will eventually withstand the usually lethal dose. This can be considered as a change of constitution, or, in a way, immunization.

The body of the mine worker was wet, thus sensitive to electricity, and a hundred volts was sufficient to kill him.

If the physical constitution can change like this, there is a great possibility that the brain can also change. If the brain could be developed so as to absorb good and not tolerate evil, then we must find the way to stimulate the brain towards this end. Compared to knowledge of the function and physiology of the body, studies of the brain and mind are very insufficient.

Many interesting medical cases like this exist in the country, but the opportunity to carry out the research they suggest is indeed poor. There is a saying in Japan that a million-dollar actor needs a stage worthy of his price. If he acts on a poorly equipped stage, he will find it difficult to perform and eventually will become a country actor. I began to realize that continuing to live in the country would not develop my own potential. As I had fulfilled my purpose for living in the country, I made up my mind to move. Fortunately, my father, after leaving the country, was back in his original real-estate business in Tokyo. I wrote him a letter about my desire to live somewhere near Tokyo. The city of Odawara, situated about a hundred miles south of Tokyo, with good climate and location, was my first choice. In April I took my family to Tokyo. Yuko was five, Mayako three. They wore the new pink dresses that Junko had made them. We took a fast train from Nagoya and I bought special reserved seats, a great luxury. We felt rich and happy. The day after our arrival in Tokyo, I asked my father to go with us in search of a suitable place. We saw many lots and homes but there was none that suited our needs and tastes.

The cherry blossoms in Odawara Park were in full bloom. My father, Junko, and I had lunch together under the trees. Though we did not find a suitable house, it was a happy moment—the three of us healthy and cooperating in one project.

After returning to the country, I learned from Mr. Deal, an American Lutheran missionary who lived in Nagoya, that the Ecumenical Work Camp, which had been in operation for the past two years, was considering a summer project in Sanage.

Receiving the news, I resolved to invite the camp to Sanage village. The project for the camp would be to construct a playground for the children in the Christian nursery, called Garden of Canaan. I immediately wrote a letter to the Ecumenical Camp headquarters informing them of our need to have help in this district, where the influence of Buddhism is so strong. Consequently, Sanage was nominated as one of the candidates, and in late April a united team of American-Japanese missionaries came to conduct an inspection.

When they arrived in Sanage, I took the whole team to the town hall, where I introduced them to the mayor. He was a Buddhist and was not at all keen on having a Christian influence in his village. Nevertheless I convinced him of the importance of the project.

A month later I received a letter informing me that Sanage, along with two other cities, was chosen for the camp. In the letter was an invitation to participate in a meeting held to prepare the camp, informing me also that as there were no funds I should come to Tokyo at my own expense. The meeting was held in the small city of Itsukaichi, an hour's ride from Tokyo. It took me thirty minutes to walk up the hill to the Youth Home where we were to meet and lodge. Discussions of the work camp project, mostly of how to feed and house the campers coming from various countries, lasted all day. The campers were to pay their transportation and some of their expenses; headquarters would provide food shipped from the U.S. I understood that my first responsibility was to find suitable lodging for about thirty male and female campers.

After staying a night in the Youth House, I returned to my parents' home in Tokyo. My younger brother, Hideo, told me that he had heard from a colleague who lived in Fujisawa, a city 35 miles south of Tokyo, that there was a suitable estate near the terminal of the Odakyu Line in Katase Fujisawa.

Next day we visited the estate. It was surrounded by pines and I thought it was much better than the one in Odawara which we had seen a month before. Unfortunately the land was not for sale. On the way back, I noticed the sign in another real-estate office. A man in his middle forties was sitting at a desk when we opened the door. I told him that I was looking for an estate in this vicinity. He drew a map from the desk and, pointing at it, explained that a suitable piece of land had just been put up for sale. The site was near another private railway, Enoden, which runs from Fujisawa to Kamakura. The location of the lot was very near the Kugenuma Station. The land belonged to a rich family who could no longer afford to pay the taxes and it was being divided into smaller lots. The price was 1500 yen per "tsubo," which is equivalent to a six-foot square. Looking at the map I decided to buy a corner lot; it was 150 tsubo, just the size I wanted. The price was reasonable and the location good. Mr. Yoshinaga, the agent, took us to the site. I selected the same lot which I thought was best on the map. It was too good to be true.

The next day I brought my deposit money to Mr. Yoshinaga. He looked up from his desk and smiled. I knew he had taken a liking to me, probably more because of my profession than for myself.

"I want to buy that corner lot," I began.

He thought a moment, then said, "There's an estate just across the street from the lot you propose to buy. I think you are aware that your lot faces south and is on a hill. It will cost a considerable amount of money to level. Your backyard gets no sun and will be cold in the winter. This new lot is larger, 210 tsubo, and it's level, as the owner has been using it for a tennis court. Besides the price per tsubo is cheaper, 1300 yen. If you are interested, I can take you to the site."

The land was beautiful, rectangular and in good condition. The neighborhood was quiet, with many big pines. As a residential quarter, it was perfect. I did not care if the place was good for my clinic; I had fallen in love with the whole area. It took only three minutes to walk from it to Kugenuma Station. Next to the property was a white Lutheran church, small and pretty, with a tiny belfry arch and a cross on the roof.

The land was owned by a wealthy man living in a big mansion on the hill nearby. When I visited him later he was sitting on a veranda surrounded by beautiful tropical flowers. His wife was in the garden, sitting on a swing with her friends. The air was sweet with the fragrance of flowers and the breeze, cool. I thought if there was a paradise on earth, this place was certainly it.

Junko was overjoyed to hear of our good fortune. We talked about destiny, thinking that if I had not attended the meeting about the camp, I surely could not have obtained this land. Serving others seems not only to bring spiritual happiness but also practical gain.

Now we had to borrow some money as our funds were far

from sufficient to build a house. The government had a public corporation that loaned funds for purchasing land and building houses. I applied for such a loan, filling out many papers. I was told that there were many applications, outnumbering the candidates three to one, and that lots would be drawn to choose those who could borrow. My number was thirty-nine.

During these procedures I made a contract with a construction company to build our house, thinking, of course, that I would win the lottery to obtain a loan.

The period of the work camp was one month, starting July 23. I was now as busy as ever, preparing to receive the campers. The nations they represented were the United States, the Philippines, Hong Kong, and Japan. In all there were twenty-four students from various colleges and universities. The most important problem was to find a suitable dormitory. The Sanage Middle School seemed the best choice, so I went to the mayor and asked him to lend us the school building. He consented in my presence but later called to say that the village council was opposed. I was angry, thinking that some religious prejudice was behind the decision.

Now I was in trouble. Thinking hard, I recalled the Agricultural High School, which was established by the Prefecture. I knew the principal, Mr. Tsuzuki, well. He was my patient. I visited his school and asked about the possibility of borrowing the dormitories. He said that he would need to obtain permission from the government, but he did not think this would be difficult. Then he showed me a dormitory which wasn't being used at that time, since most of the students were commuting. It was in poor condition but with repairs could be used. I estimated the cost of repairs and needed equipment to be 50,000 yen, and wondered where to get the money.

After saying good-bye to Mr. Tsuzuke and dragging my bicycle down the long path to the entrance, I racked my brain about where I could get 50,000 yen. That night I called Mr. Deal and asked whether he could accompany me to meet the governor. His answer was very friendly, saying that he would be free in the afternoon and would meet me at Nagoya Station with his car.

The governor's waiting room was full, but the secretary, noticing Mr. Deal, put us at the top of the list. Things went fine and the governor promised to pay all expenses for the repairs.

Next we went to the head office of Nagoya Railway Company. This company operates the train that runs through our district. I met the manager and told him about our project and about the students coming at their own expense from various countries to help restore Japan. I asked him whether his railroad would issue free passes from Sanage to Mifune Station, where the project was to be located, and he consented.

The next visit was to the Mainichi Newspaper. I asked the editor to cover the news and also requested the use of their room to meet campers on their arrival at Nagoya. He also agreed. The day was a success. When I thanked Mr. Deal for his cooperation, he said he had merely acted as chauffeur, but I appreciated his presence very much and was convinced that his smile made things easy.

The next problem was to collect sufficient bedding and blankets. I asked the Village Women's Association to help. This caused quite a discussion about whether their association should help any special religion.

I replied that, although the campers were all Christians, their object was to help people, regardless of religion. They continued to dispute among themselves, and I was very discouraged. I asked, "Are these students not coming to help your village, sacrificing their summer vacation, spending their own money? I am ashamed to admit that the women of this village are reluctant to help." I felt like shouting but kept my temper and continued quietly, "Well, if I cannot get your help, I must approach the Women's Association of Toyota City."

Then a woman in her mid-forties stood up and said in a

firm voice, "Dr. Honda, that would be a shame for us. I am willing to lend our bedding." Others followed her lead, and when the meeting was over I had more than enough.

My next concern was food. Though the instructions I received said that the campers would do their own cooking, my opinion was that, after their day's heavy labor, tasty, nourishing food should be ready for them. I needed to find a man who would volunteer to help with the cooking. One day I received a phone call from Mr. Goro Inoue, a big landowner. He invited me to have dinner with him the next night. His home was on a large estate. After talking about the camp, we began dinner. Various dishes were served and all were good. Near the end a short man with grey hair came in the room smiling and sat down to eat with us.

"I forgot to introduce you. This is Mr. Honjo and he did all the cooking. He was . . ." Mr. Honjo raised his hand and stopped further conversation. We shook hands and sipped sake. Mr. Inoue said to Mr. Honjo, "You don't mind if I tell things about you, do you? Dr. Honda needs information about you." Mr. Honjo just smiled and did not show any sign of disapproval this time.

"We were in the same school, from Gakushuin to Tokyo University. Of course he is my senior and was a classmate of the present Emperor. He is of noble blood and a former viscount. After the war, he lost not only his title but everything he owned. During the prime of his life, he often went hunting and fishing. It is the traditional rule to cook what you catch and so, cooking became his hobby. Every time he ate in a good restaurant, he asked the cook the secret of the seasoning. Usually cooks will not tell others their way of cooking but, as he was a viscount, they told him all their secrets of seasoning. Thus he became an expert in any cooking form— Japanese, Chinese, and French. He can even bake cookies and make candies. Last week I happened to meet him in Nagoya and told him about the camp. He is willing to cooperate. How do you like his cooking?"

This was the story of how Mr. Honjo became our cook for

the camp. All the campers arrived at Nagoya Station on July 15, 1951. Some came from Tokyo, others from Kyoto district. As soon as a group arrived, we took them to the lobby of the Mainichi Newspaper Building. By five o'clock they had all arrived and were introduced to each other. Nagoya Railway provided us with a free bus to Sanage.

Mr. Honjo, Junko, and members of the Women's Association busily prepared supper. They used huge kettles to boil the rice. As this was their first experience in cooking in such large quantities, the first batch of rice was a failure; it was soft and paste-like. Mr. Honjo ordered it thrown away. The shortage of food was still acute, so Junko and the other ladies hesitated to throw away the precious food. But Mr. Honjo was adamant. Perhaps because this was the first supper, he did not want to lose face and dignity.

There was much excitement in the village on the part of those who were preparing to welcome the campers. I had asked the mayor to donate some money for expenses, and the village council gave a considerable sum. To express our thanks I had invited the mayor and all the council members to the welcome dinner. Mr. Honjo and his assistants were busy all day preparing for the feast. The main course was beef stew with rice. No wonder the rice was so important. We arrived at the school at six-thirty, and the campers went to their rooms to wash their hands and change clothes. The big hall was furnished as a dining room. All the councilmen, having lined up, glanced at each other uneasily. They did not know what to expect. I told them that each should serve himself. The custom of self-service was not yet popular, but they all took cups and saucers in their hands and moved awkwardly to the table. They had always been honored guests and were used to being waited on. This was their first lesson in self-service.

Next day all the campers started their new work. All wore clean jeans and shirts and each had a shovel or pick in his hands. The girls wore large straw hats or tied colorful bandannas around their heads. They were a merry group indeed.

Canaan nursery was not far from Mifune Station. The future playground was overgrown with weeds and the ground was uneven. They began attacking their project with energy, a little too vigorously for the beginning. I left them to go back home to my clinical work.

At noon I again went to the school and waited for them at the entrance. One by one dropped in exhaustion. What a sorry sight. They changed from clean, fresh youths to a dirty, perspiring, gloomy bunch, lying on their backs, tired and worn out. Working and sweating under the hot sun, instead of sitting in a cool classroom, handling picks instead of pens, was not as easy as they thought. This was back-breaking work, and there was nothing romantic about the project.

Within a week they had changed completely: their hands hardened with calluses and their skin tanned by the sun and wind. They had changed from green, intelligent youths to sturdy, hardy workers.

The project proceeded smoothly, and at night we had several meetings with the village folk and the Women's Association and Youth Organization. The campers from the United States, the Philippines, and Hong Kong introduced their countries' customs, and ways of living. One night they even performed dramatic skits, making their own costumes. They were good actors and actresses, performing their parts wonderfully without rehearsal. I was surprised to see they were so able in these fields.

As the weeks passed, my physical condition showed signs of strain. Although I enjoyed life with the campers, I also had my clinical work to do, which was getting heavier. I broke out in a rash due to fatigue. Sometimes my mouth was so swollen I had difficulty eating.

During the strenuous work, we provided the campers with recreation, taking them to see pottery and making of Noritake china, and to a zoo in Nagoya. One day we all hiked to Sanage Mountain. The day was fine and the breeze was cool in the mountains. We had fun climbing and when we started back, twilight had begun to set in. We all rode home on the back of a truck, sitting against each other and making ourselves as comfortable as possible. Stars came out on the horizon, and we began to sing camp songs. Then silence fell and, though the road was bumpy, all felt very romantic, driving under the starlit sky.

Days flew by, and the time soon came for the campers to go back to their homes. The night before the departure, everybody became very sentimental. They all had come to an unknown country, worked for the same project, made friends with each other and with the village people. Their accomplishments might not be so extraordinary, but they lit the light of love in other people's hearts and in their own. They learned many things and would remember the hard days they endured for the sake of other people. They would never forget their days in Sanage, and surely they acquired something that would be bread for their souls all through their lives.

WE BUILD OUR HOME IN FUJISAWA

When I stood in the middle of the hall after the last camper had left for home, I had mixed feelings of sorrow and relief. The place had been full of life and noise. Now everything was quiet, and the only sign of life was the leaves fluttering outside the window. I recalled the famous haiku by Basho, *"Natsu kusa-ya, tsuwamono domo no yume no ato"* ("the site where the warrior dreamt is overrun with summer grass").

A few days later I received a letter from my contractor saying that he had laid the cornerstone of our home in Kugenuma, Fujisawa City. In Japan it is customary to have a ceremony when the frame of the house is completed. The ceremony, usually conducted by a Shinto priest, consists of prayers to gods, asking them to protect the workers from accident. After the ceremony, carpenters and all who are engaged in the construction work make a feast under the roof, drinking sake. I wrote a letter to the contractor, telling him I could not attend but to proceed with the feast, the expense of which I would pay later.

The day after this ceremony, I arrived at my lot and there, in the midst of the field, was the skeleton of my future home, two stories high, standing under the blue sky. I inspected the materials and found to my satisfaction that they were quite good. The contract called for payment of one-third of the whole expense as soon as the roof was on. I had spent almost all the funds I possessed, and I was concerned about the possibility of borrowing money from the bank. If luck failed us, I would indeed be in serious trouble.

I returned home with a heavy heart, and, when I entered, my wife gave me a card. I knew instantly that this lottery card had come to determine our destiny. On it was printed, "The numbers are those divisible by three." I jumped with joy and hugged Junko. Our number, thirty-nine, could of course be divided by three. It was a great relief to know that we could borrow the money to build our house.

In Japan, to own land and to build your own home is a dream. I was indeed lucky that I could buy a suitable lot and have a new house. We now drew plans and designed the house, arguing over details here and there.

We had been living in a very rural, inconvenient situation, so we wanted our new home to have all modern up-to-date appliances. We went to Nagoya to buy a gas range with an oven, which was just out on the market.

Mr. Honjo's idea was that the entrance to the house should be covered with special stones to give it a touch of elegance. After the camp, he stayed with us most of the time, teaching Junko how to cook. His culinary knowledge was vast, from simple everyday dishes to fancy Western cooking. His private life was a story in itself. He was laughing when he told me that Shochiku, one of the major movie producers, made a movie of his story. "I never received any royalties," he added. His dream was to manage a fine restaurant in the Shonan area; I promised that after I was established, I would help him to realize this dream.

Winter came and still the only garment he had was a summer shirt and trousers. Seeing him shivering, I gave him some of my suits and overcoats. He was once a viscount, wealthy and famous. Now he was alone, almost penniless, shivering in his summer clothes and living in a hut without electricity.

Our contractor informed us that our house would be completed by the end of November. After consulting with Junko, I decided to move on December 1. We sent our household goods and luggage by freight. The home where we had lived for four years seemed desolate with all the furniture gone. The night before our departure we stayed with Mr. Inoue.

The next morning we were all up at five. It was very cold, and the stars were still shining brightly as we walked to the station over the frosty ground. The lobby of the station and the platform were crowded with people to see us off. My heart swelled to see that people had gotten up so early and had come so far to see us. We shook hands and said good-bye and thank you.

I wrote Mr. Honjo, who was now living with his friend in Okazaki, that we would pass that station at 7:30 a.m. I got off the coach and saw him standing there, a lonely figure in the cold, crisp morning air, wearing my heavy overcoat. He saw me and moved to my side quickly.

"I will be waiting for you to come to Kugenuma." I slapped his shoulder and shook his hand.

He smiled and said nothing. His face was sad and I could never forget the way he looked. That was the last I saw of him. A year later, I received a letter from Mr. Inoue informing me of his death. I wrote back immediately, "If my instinct is right, I think he committed suicide."

A few days later an answer came: "You are right, he drowned himself in a dam, in the mountains." I can still see his lonely figure on the platform.

When we arrived at Fujisawa station, dusk was falling and people stared at our family struggling with so much luggage. Yuko was carrying her violin in one hand, a big doll in the other. We were all tired from our long trip but happy to be in our new city. The future destiny of our family was in Kugenuma, and I prayed it would be happy.

The furniture and heavy luggage came the next day and our new life began. I had no friends or acquaintances in this city. My friend who had lived in Kugenuma told me that because homes in this section of the city where we lived were on large parcels of land, the population was small. He predicted that it would be difficult to succeed as a medical doctor. This indeed was a harsh prophecy for my future, and although I was happy to live in such a beautiful area, I could not help feeling moments of anxiety. We had used almost all our money and our bank account was very low.

The climate was much milder in this district than in Aichi Prefecture and, although it was somewhat chilly in the morning, the thermometer seldom fell below zero centigrade. It took seven minutes to get to the beach from our home. The street led straight to the beach of Sagami Bay, among the pine trees. The water was blue and clear. On the left there was a small island, Enoshima, and, on the right, far on the horizon, snow-capped, majestic Mt. Fuji.

I often took my two daughters for a walk to Enoshima, a good thirty minutes along the beach. There was a long bridge spanning the shallow water to the island. The bridge led to a narrow street, with all kinds of shops on either side and vendors crying and gesturing potential customers into their stores. At the end of the street a long flight of steps led to the Enoshima Shrine. And, of course, there was a red Torii, which always symbolizes the shrine. Past the shrine, up more steep steps, heaving and puffing, we arrived at the summit, on which there was a high tower. There was a lift to the top of the tower, which commanded an enchanting view of the green hills of the mainland, the blue water of the sea rippling and changing colors each moment, and Mt. Fuji in the distance. Looking straight down we could see tiny figures of men and women. A steep ladder led to a room with a big lens. This tower was also a lighthouse, shedding its light far out over the dark bay.

Beyond the lighthouse was another street with many shops, at the end of which steep steps led down a precipice to the waterfront. The sea was deep at this point, crystal blue changing to indigo. White foam churned, attacking and biting the big rocks. We walked across a very narrow wooden bridge connecting the gap between these rocks that led to the entrance of a big cave. This cave, made by the wind and water, grew bigger and deeper each year. We paid some money and received a candle, then bent down and walked, straining our eyes unaccustomed to the dark, and protecting the flickering flame from being blown out. As we went further, the ceiling became lower and we had to creep. At the end, there was a small shrine to the god of mercy. The atmosphere was both awesome and eerie. Indeed it was great fun to go to the island and I went there often, which was evidence that my medical work was not flourishing.

On Christmas Eve, I went to the church and sat on a chair. Behind the altar was a big cross made of plain white wood. I felt very humble and prayed in my heart for guidance and help in this new place and way of life.

The violin teacher in Fujisawa was Mr. Nakamura. The class was held in a room belonging to Misono Girls' High School. It took nearly thirty minutes to get to this school from Fujisawa station. The classroom was barren and cold, the only warmth coming from a small pot containing charcoal. Here Yuko began to take lessons from Mr. Nakamura as soon as we were settled. She had progressed to Gavotte by Bach in Volume 3. While we were waiting, a small girl about Yuko's age passed by with a friendly smile. She was Aiko Komori, the most advanced pupil in the whole class.

We got up at dawn on the New Year, and I took my two daughters to Enoshima and climbed to the top of the tower. The horizon was tinged with pink, then deepened into red. The whole sky reflected the color, and suddenly a bright red crescent peeped out from the horizon. Within a moment it floated up and became a red ball. Mt. Fuji was tinged with the reflection and glowed, changing from pink to dark purple. I stood holding my breath with the beauty, praying in my heart that this would be a good omen for my future life.

The girls were stamping their feet, blowing on their hands to warm themselves.

Yuko was ready to go to grammar school in April. Besides a public school there were two private schools: one, a Catholic girls' school, the other, coeducational. It was difficult for Junko and me to decide where to send Yuko. There were advantages and disadvantages to both schools, but considering the importance of coeducation we selected the latter. She passed the entrance test easily.

Yuko was now playing Bourrée by Bach. One of the salient characteristics of Suzuki's method is the sequence of pieces. Even in Volume One, Minuets 1, 2, and 3 by Bach are set in the middle, and the book ends with Gavotte by Gossec. This piece is quite difficult and is even played by professional artists in concert. Mr. Suzuki always stresses that children must master each piece before proceeding to the next one. With this approach, the pupil will develop sufficient technique to master the new, more difficult piece. Otherwise, it is like constructing a building on a loose foundation. The further you go, the more difficult it will be, and both mother and child will feel as though they are facing insurmountable obstacles.

I BECOME DIRECTOR

One day in April I received a call from Mr. Suzuki. He invited me to dine with him at the Coq d'or, a French restaurant in Tokyo. I was delighted, not only because I had never eaten in such a fancy restaurant, but because Mr. Suzuki himself invited me. During the dinner, which I enjoyed immensely, he asked me to be one of the directors of the Talent Education Institute, a non-profit organization. When he asked me whether I would accept, I almost choked on the food. Would I accept? Of course! Never in my life was I so excited. Here was an ideal chance for me to help the movement, legally and with authority. Junko also was happy to hear of this offer. In accepting, I resolved to help Mr. Suzuki spread his ideas throughout the world.

Next month the first board meeting was called and various problems were discussed. There were two very important subjects on the agenda: first, the need to define "talent" in relation to its use in the name Talent Education, and second, the need to set up motivating goals.

The word "talent" is generally thought to mean superior mental endowment or a particular faculty or gift, including mental ability in general. Our concept of "talent," however, is that it is the same as "ability," which means there is a possibility of cultivating and developing various abilities within any human being to a very high degree.

The fundamental ideology of Talent Education is based on the assumption that originally all humans are born with high potential for self-development. This idea was suggested to Mr. Suzuki by observing the phenomenon of children learning their mother tongue. Every child in the world has this wonderful ability, and it is developed by environment. What they receive from their parents at birth is not language itself but the ability to learn and speak language. Provided a baby has no physical defect, each is born with this ability.

Talent Education applies not only to knowledge or technical skill but also to morality, character, and appreciation of beauty. We know that these human attributes are acquired through education and circumstances. Our movement does not aim to develop so-called prodigies, nor does it intend to emphasize early formal education; rather it is *total human education.* Thus, while our use of "talent" does not agree with the general meaning of the word, since there is no other suitable expression, we chose the name Talent Education.

The subject of motivation is also very important, not only to the board, but also to instructors, parents, and pupils. Mr. Suzuki has been publishing the *Suzuki Violin School* instruction books, and now all volumes through Vol. 10 (Concerto No. 4 by Mozart) have been completed. We all know there is no limit to achievement in the arts nor in the development of human character. But as our object is not necessarily to make musicians, it is important to have some kind of ending point.

If we set progressive goals during the whole learning process, it would be easier for parents or children to work for one goal and then proceed to the next.

Talent or ability according to our idea does not only mean speed of learning. It should be evaluated by development of skill, understanding, and musical sensitivity. And of course we do not consider that a diploma shows that these have been achieved. During the process of learning, many factors should be considered to help develop motivation in those who learn as well as in those who teach. One of the most important ways to motivate people is to have them accomplish something. A feeling of success is apt to lead to increased motivation, and from this motivation further success will follow. Thus we decided to apply a graduation system in our movement. This system has another merit. Sometimes, relations between parents and teachers do not go well. When parents are not satisfied with the character or the ability of the teacher, they change teachers, often causing embarrassment on both sides. It would be easier for everyone if the change came after graduation. Dropping out occurs for various reasons, though usually the fault is not with the child, but with parents or instructors. Should a child drop out after he has graduated from the elementary class, even this diploma will give him some satisfaction.

We divided the ten volumes of *Suzuki Violin School* into four steps. The diploma for the elementary step is given after Volume 3, the second after Volume 5, the third (high school) after Volume 7, and the fourth (college) after Volume 10. We decided to have the first graduation ceremony October 25, 1952, in Tokyo.

Meanwhile Yuko was having trouble with the new instructor, or maybe it was the instructor who was having trouble. Though all the instructors taught the so-called Suzuki Method, each one adapted it somewhat according to his own ideas. Most of the teachers had learned violin from other schools; they joined the movement because they approved the concept. Children always copy their teachers. It is interesting to see children from different instructors lined up on the stage to play. One can easily identify which child is the pupil of which instructor by his posture. Not only posture, but also the manner in which he holds the bow and the bow arm. Naturally, the teacher likes to mold the newcomer to his style. This often leads to confusion on the part of the child and the mother. The veteran teacher will not try to correct form in a short period, but inexperienced instructors often try to make corrections too quickly.

Abilities develop by using and repeating what has been learned. Thus it is more difficult to remold those pupils who have studied hard and practiced long than it is the lazy ones. A child who has been obediently following the teacher's instructions will be upset and confused if another instructor suddenly tells him to do things differently.

A good instructor will not emphasize a pupil's faults. He will use positive reinforcement rather than negative. The pupil will be encouraged and, as the good points develop, the bad habits will slowly diminish. It takes some time to develop a habit and it takes twice as long to erase it. Motivation is most important in developing ability. Motivation comes from a feeling of satisfaction after accomplishing something, such as playing a special piece successfully. Finding fault and giving no encouragement will lead to a sense of failure, causing a loss of motivation. Not providing motivation is like plucking out all the good buds. Even if the flowers come out, they will often be without color or fragrance.

When Yuko joined the new class in Fujisawa, the atmosphere seemed to change. In my opinion the class was not doing what Talent Education should. There were no meetings or gatherings among mothers and instructor. One afternoon, after a coffee break, I moved the chairs around the instructor and asked the mothers to gather and have a discussion. The atmosphere became awkward.

Besides this meeting, I proposed many changes, hinting that if changes were not made, the approach would become a mere violin instruction rather than the Suzuki Method.

It was customary for mothers to take turns at bringing tea and cakes or sandwiches to the class. Little by little, the tendency towards competition arose among the mothers and they started bringing luxurious and expensive delicacies. Of course, I had no objection to this during the coffee break but was not keen at the idea of the instructor eating in front of the children.

One day Junko came home with a pale face. During the tea, the lady in charge accused her openly, saying that the friendly atmosphere of the class had been destroyed by a newcomer. This made me very angry and I telephoned to ask what she meant by this. Grasping the phone, I thought again. Angry words would not make matters better. Maybe I was too hasty in introducing something new. The best remedy might be to form a new class and develop it in an ideal way. This would not hurt anybody and would bring new development.

The bylaw on forming a new branch says that three conditions must be met: 1) recommendation by a neighbor class; 2) twenty-five charter members; 3) approval by the board of directors. I began working with the kindergarten attached to the Lutheran Church. After securing permission from the teacher, I gave a talk about Talent Education at a P.T.A. meeting. Quite a number of children enrolled, and the church gave me permission to use their building as a classroom. Again fortune smiled on me. One of the instructors, Mrs. Mariko Hara, who lived near my home in Kugenuma, commuted to Tokyo to teach. She was willing to take the new assignment and everything was set. The Fujisawa class gave its recommendation, and I received approval from the board of directors. Yuko changed classes and so did a few other children. We moved along fine and everybody was happy.

One day Mrs. Hara told me that she was expecting a baby and requested a leave. Now I had to find a temporary teacher. I again contacted Mr. Suzuki, asking for a substitute. His answer was that he would send three interns, and each would teach three months in succession. I was glad to receive young instructors who had learned directly from Mr. Suzuki. But, contrary to my expectations, this plan did not work out. Later when I found that Mrs. Hara was unable to return to teaching even after her baby's birth, I had to find another good instructor.

THE FIRST GRADUATION

The date of the first graduation was set for October 25. We began preparing for the ceremony as soon as the summer was over. First, the names of the graduates had to be listed. The total number of students graduating was 195. Because many were arriving the night before graduation, we needed to make hotel reservations for them. At the time of the students' arrival, we divided the staff into three groups and sent each group to one of the three large stations in Tokyo to welcome the children and bring them to the hotels. Later, the other directors and I visited each of these hotels to see that the students were comfortably settled.

To our amazement, some of the families did not arrive at their hotels. We received a bill from the manager and later had to pay cancellation fees. We discovered that, though these people had asked for reservations, they had changed their minds and stayed at the homes of friends or relatives without notifying anyone. We decided that we would never again take any responsibility for providing lodging in Tokyo.

The Kyoritsu Hall was full. Mr. Suzuki introduced me to a dignified man, Mr. Tokugawa. This gentleman was the person who took Mr. Suzuki to Germany.

The curtain rose and the ceremony began. After congratulatory remarks from Mr. Suzuki, I read the names of all the graduates. Each stood proudly at his seat when his name was called.

After the ceremony, all the graduates joined in playing a concert on the stage. Though we had had local concerts in different districts, this was the first time the children had played such difficult music together on the stage. The audience was thrilled to hear the beautiful tone and witness such a wonderful performance.

After the concert, we who had worked so hard to make the arrangements were indeed happy with its success. With Mr. Suzuki in the center we talked about having the second ceremony in Tokyo next year.

A NEW TURN

One of my first tasks in 1953 was to find the best teacher for the class in Kugenuma. At the beginning of the movement, in order to spread the idea on a wider scale, Mr. Suzuki felt the need of assistants. Many violin teachers volunteered to help him. After receiving some training, they began teaching in various parts of Japan. At this time there were about eighty instructors in all.

Soon the number of branches increased to about one hundred. Developing a good class in one district stimulated other classes, thus boosting the level of the whole area. With the growth, the need for instructors was acute. Graduates of the college course, finishing Volume 10, had the privilege of applying for positions as instructors. After two years' training in Matsumoto, they received diplomas as assistant instructors. Mr. Suzuki gives lectures and demonstrations for Talent Education teachers at an annual seminar, held for the purpose of improving instruction.

Selecting a good teacher is particularly important in Talent Education. Though the main purpose is not to train concert artists, still the teacher's ability to play is a consideration. Unless there is a good technical foundation, the potential development cannot be fully realized. Of course, this development is not always fast. It could be slow but steady. A good instructor must acknowledge individual differences in children and never hurry or induce competition.

In Japan there is a custom of breeding nightingales for their beautiful song. People go to the woods to catch the young birds and, bringing them home, take them to the teacher bird to be taught how to sing. The future singing of the bird depends upon the selection of the teacher. If the teacher is good, the "student" will be a good singer, regardless of his heredity; the opposite also holds true. I wanted an instructor who had studied directly with Mr. Suzuki and also had demonstrated good results in teaching. Mr. Hidegoro Ito, one of the two vice-presidents, recommended Mr. Teisaburo Okumura. Mr. Okumura was among the first to join Talent Education. Besides teaching small children in Matsumoto, he had been giving lessons to others in the teacher-training program. I wrote him a letter inviting him to visit us in Fujisawa. He did so, and I tried to convince him that he would be happy teaching here. Receiving permission from Mr. Suzuki, Mr. Okumura made up his mind to move to Fujisawa.

My next problem was to find a home for Mr. Okumura. The shortage of housing was still acute, and I asked all the members to cooperate. At last we found a suitable house not far from the church. While the house was under repair, we borrowed the second floor of the laundry shop. Mr. Okumura came alone and began teaching. Keiko, the three-year-old daughter of the owner, was attracted by the music upstairs. Every day when the lesson began, she climbed the stairs and sat at the top, listening to the music attentively. Later she joined the class and much later attended a music college to follow a professional career. If Mr. Okumura hadn't been invited to Fujisawa, this might never have happened. Indeed, man is the son of his environment.

MAYAKO HAS AN ACCIDENT

The meeting of the board of directors was scheduled for February 27, when Mr. Suzuki was to give a special lesson at Kugenuma. I made arrangements for the meeting at the Kaihin Hotel in Enoshima.

The day was cloudy and cold. The lesson was being held at the Lutheran Church. As the warmth came only from two small coal stoves, the children sat shivering on the wooden bench. Late in the afternoon, snow came fluttering from the sky, lightly at first, then gradually gathering force until there was a real storm. When the lesson ended at five o'clock, the whole landscape was completely white.

We had tea in our home, then started for Enoshima, taking the streetcar from Kugenuma station. From Enoshima station, it was only a ten-minute walk to the hotel, but in the deep snow which had piled up in such a short time, we stumbled for nearly a half hour. By six in the evening, all the directors, including Mr. Takasaki and Mr. Ito, the vice-presidents, arrived, fighting their way through the storm.

The main subject was the method of disseminating ideas and strengthening the organization. We didn't get to bed until nearly 2:00 a.m. The meeting was adjourned at ten the next morning and everyone went back home.

The storm was over and the sun shone brightly, making everything sparkle like diamonds. Mt. Fuji showed its majestic figure in the west, clad in a robe of white. The sea was calm and blue. Indeed the world seemed to have changed within a day.

Returning home exhausted, I lay down on my bed, completely forgetting that I was to take Junko, Yuko, and Mayako to Tokyo. Junko reproached me, saying that they had been waiting for me to get ready. I didn't feel well but, understanding their desire, I got up.

We got off the train at Tokyo station and walked toward the Maruzen department store. Waiting for the signal to turn green so we could cross the broad street, I took Yuko's hand while Junko took Mayako's. While we were in the middle of the crossing, the signal turned red and we were obliged to stop. I thought, of course, that Junko had Mayako's hand, but suddenly I saw something red dart in front of me. It was Mayako. While Junko was rearranging her handbag, Mayako freed herself and ran in front of us. She was probably trying to show that she could cross the street alone.

"Look out!" I raised my voice in despair. But it was too

late. Many cars started when the light changed and, in front of our horrified eyes, Mayako was hit by a taxi. She was thrown about five feet in front of the car and lay motionless, crumpled on the damp street. I rushed to her side and picked her up in my arms. She was unconscious and limp. At that instant I thought the world had stopped moving. Everything was suddenly quiet. All the cars stopped. I stood blankly looking down on the pale face of my dear three-year-old daughter. It was like a waking nightmare. Junko came to my side and cried sorrowfully:

"Mayako, Mayako, forgive me, I should not have asked to come today."

A policeman came and we were hurried in a car to the emergency hospital.

All this happened in a very short time, but to me it seemed that hours had passed. Rushing into the consultation room, I put Mayako gently on the bed. The doctor in charge examined her. There was no internal bleeding. The light reflex in her eyes was positive. I sighed in relief. She was alive! The doctor ordered a syringe and gave her a shot. Her face twitched and color flushed her pale cheeks.

"Mayako, Mayako." Junko knelt down beside the bed and called her name softly. The next moment, Mayako opened her eyes.

"I think she is all right. Let her rest awhile and then you can take her home," the doctor said calmly. I went outside where Yuko was sitting alone in the dark corridor. She was clasping her small hands in prayer. Tears filled my eyes and overflowed. We rested for two hours in the office of Dr. Seki-guchi, a dentist, whose house was nearby. He was a director of Talent Education and had just returned from the meeting the night before. Mayako was very quiet during the following day and had no appetite. She was still weak and pale, but slowly recovered. I thank God that her life was spared.

THE FIRST NATIONAL CONCERT

Yuko was making good progress. She always sat in front, listening attentively. Her tone was improving and, as the children lined up, this was easily observed by all instructors and parents. Our second daughter Mayako was also receiving violin lessons, and though she was gifted in facility, she did not have the perseverance or concentration of her sister.

Two or three times each year, the classes in Shonan District arranged special lessons with Mr. Suzuki as instructor. The lessons were usually held in the hall of the kindergarten or sometimes in a hotel.

Fujisawa, Kamakura, Zushi, Odawara, and Mishima were the five cities in Shonan District that had such classes. The classes took turns in sponsoring this special lesson. This was to give each class a chance to observe Mr. Suzuki's lessons. The parents also had the opportunity of meeting each other, making friends and exchanging opinions, usually after the lesson. All had a chance to hear advanced students and also to observe the wonderful results of Mr. Suzuki's teaching. For instance, a girl about ten years old while playing the Vivaldi Concerto in A Minor was swinging her body sideways like a pendulum. Of course everybody noticed her movements and wondered how Mr. Suzuki would correct her. He simply took out his violin and, kneeling beside the girl, began playing so that the frog of his bow pointed toward the neck of her violin. Naturally, if the girl moved her body, her violin would collide with Mr. Suzuki's, so her movements stopped. We were surprised to observe such instant results accomplished with such wit and humor.

The second graduation ceremony was to be held at the hall of Aoyama Gakuin University on October 28. This time, we did not encounter any difficulties. The number of children graduating was 363. After the ceremony I proposed to the board that we have a concert on a wider scale, in which every child, whether graduating or not, could join.

The next important matter was to introduce the Suzuki

idea and method to the United States. Mr. Kenji Mochizuki, who was studying theology at Oberlin College, wrote his impressions for our magazine. He had attended the first graduation ceremony in Tokyo and, as he had studied violin himself, was amazed at the level of ability of the children. He was especially astonished by the bowing. The swift vertical action of the right arm was different from orthodox bowing. Also the philosophy that *all* children can develop themselves attracted him very much, and, in his essay, he expressed a strong desire to introduce the Suzuki movement in the United States. This, of course, coincided with my idea, and I arranged to send him a tape of one hundred children playing the Bach Double Concerto. Some weeks later, I received a letter telling me that the people in his college did not believe what they had heard. One hundred children playing the Bach Double? Unbelievable, impossible! If this was true, it was the miracle of the century. It had to be seen to be believed. Therefore, he asked if he could make a motion picture of the children.

I was quite surprised to receive this letter, thinking that the tape was sufficient for people to understand. To make a movie was beyond our ability. Such a project would have to be undertaken by a professional production company, and that was beyond the means of our organization.

The two problems of making the film and allowing wider participation in the concerts were discussed at the board meeting. It was decided that I was to take charge of making the movie. Since we had no funds, I was to approach some motion picture company.

Like all geniuses, Mr. Suzuki is sometimes impractical. His ideas are far-ranging and dynamic. He once said: "As I am always studying and making progress, Suzuki of tomorrow is different from Suzuki of today." This flexibility, though admirable, is sometimes difficult in the everyday problems of administration. I tried to think of someone who could help us with these problems and be an advisor to Mr. Suzuki. Mr. Tokugawa seemed ideal in all respects. He has prestige, a wide view and is influential in politics, business, and culture.

I decided to visit Mr. Tokugawa at his home. His estate once covered many acres, but after the war more than half of it was sold. The building was old and on the entrance was a big board on which was printed "Tokugawa Biological Institute." In front of the building was a square, man-made pond with a queer fan twirling water in the middle. The water was green and not transparent.

When I rang the bell, Mr. Tokugawa himself came out and, seeing me looking at the pond, smiled and said, "That's chlorella. Our Institute is studying it to see if we can make food from it."

He took me inside and showed me a dark greenish powder. "From this powder we make bread. Here is some. Try it." I put a piece in my mouth. It had a weed-like smell and the taste was not good.

After sitting in the parlor, I began, "Mr. Tokugawa, I want to thank you for attending the graduation ceremony and congratulating the children for their hard work. You know our organization is expanding and we need an advisor. Since you have influence with many people, I was wondering whether there is any possibility of asking you to be our honorary president."

Without hesitation he answered, "Yes, I think I can help, and I will be honorary president. It's like a hat, but after all I think it better to have a hat on your head than no hat at all."

His eyes twinkled. I was surprised to receive such a quick response. Usually in Japan, a man of importance will avoid answering instantly. He will usually say, "I understand your proposal. I will think it over." He would probably be afraid of losing dignity by answering too quickly. Mr. Tokugawa was different—no wonder he was popular.

Now, as the important problem was settled, we began conversing on various topics. I said, "Mr. Tokugawa, after World War II, you probably lost a great part of your wealth and your title. This is a foolish question, but which life was better, the life before the war when you had power and wealth or now?"

He indulged in thought for a moment. He did not answer my question but began telling the story of his life. "I was born in the family of Lord Matsudaira, the fifth son of famous Shungaku Matsudaira of Echizen Province. My mother was very strict in raising her children. Contrary to the common custom, we were educated to endure hardship. A lord should enjoy things after the people and suffer before the people. We were not even allowed to wear *tabi* (a kind of stocking) in winter. When people read stories or look at movies, they are apt to think life in the castle was very extravagant, full of colorful events, but this is not true. Boys were raised to endure every kind of hardship and develop themselves physically and spiritually to be future lords. In those feudal days, the lord had all the might and power; thus his responsibilities were also heavy. If the country had a foolish lord, it did not thrive but fell to destruction.

"When I grew up, I was adopted by the Tokugawa family of Owari Province. As you know there are three clans of Tokugawas besides the Shogun or dynasty. The Tokugawa of Owari were the the wealthiest, and I had fame, wealth, and everything else a man desires. Even in those days, we owned several cars and our house was full of servants. At any kind of party or meeting, I always sat in the seat of honor. People, including geisha girls, always praised and flattered everything I did. Getting older, I became skeptical, wondering whether these words were for me, for my position, or for my money.

"After the war I donated all my goods and treasures to a museum in Nagoya. When I take a walk on the Ginza these days, people do not recognize me and I feel at ease. I own no cars and my transportation is by taxi, tramcar, or on foot. This is very good for my health. Though I lost or gave away everything, in a way I am much richer. I can now believe in people and work for the good of humanity. I think there is no greater ambition than this: to deny and crave nothing for yourself."

The room was getting dark. The furniture, which in the past must have been magnificent, was shabby and the color of the curtains was fading. But, in spite of the shabbiness of the room, Mr. Tokugawa's face glowed, showing satisfaction with his present life. After all, it isn't material things that make one's life happy.

MAKING THE FILM

Now I had to work in earnest to find a sponsor or raise funds for the film. I wrote many letters to foundations in the U.S. I received an answer from the Rockefeller Foundation saying that one of the directors was coming to Japan. I made an appointment to meet him on his arrival at the Imperial Hotel. I explained the importance of introducing the movement through the film. He understood perfectly but replied that he was in no position to donate funds for this project.

Then I read in the newspapers that Mr. Johnson, president of the Association of Film Companies in the U.S., was visiting Japan. All the major companies, like Warner Brothers, 20th Century Fox, Paramount, are members of this association. I contacted Mrs. Ohgimi, the secretary, and asked her to arrange a meeting with Mr. Johnson. After a week, I called to ask Mrs. Ohgimi about the result. Her answer was, "Though Mr. Johnson understands your project, the association is not in position to make films. Besides," she added, "there are many things in this world of greater interest that many people would like to have filmed. I doubt if professional people will be interested in shooting your project."

Though disappointed, I understood later that what she said was true. Mrs. Ohgimi, an Englishwoman, was the wife of a diplomat serving in the Japanese Embassy in Caracas. I had met him in Venezuela fifteen years before.

I was getting a little impatient. Even with my amateur knowledge, I knew that to complete a picture requires at least half a year. I decided to appeal to Dai-ei, a Japanese film company. I asked Mr. Yoshichika Tokugawa if he would accompany me and he willingly consented to go. After making an appointment with the general manager of the company, we went to the head office of Dai-ei in Tokyo. Mrs. Hirata, one of the members of Talent Education, also accompanied us.

I explained to the manager the importance of making this film about a cultural movement that originated in Japan. He listened patiently. If Mr. Tokugawa had not been with me, the manager probably would have interrupted me. "Yes, I understand the importance but the policy of our company is not to make children's films. We never make any profit with children's films."

I knew that he was mistaken, but I kept quiet. There was no use discussing the matter with him. Later Dai-ei Motion Picture Company made a film named "We Have Once Passed This Road." It was a story of a small girl learning violin, and the Vienna Choir Boys acted in some scenes. I never found out if Dai-ei made or lost money on this picture.

A friend told me about Shinri-ken Motion Picture Company, a small film company in Tokyo that made documentaries. On a cold dreary day I visited their office, a dark room, dirty and smoky, located on the second floor of a building in Tsukiji, Tokyo. I waited in a small room without taking off my coat. It was cold. A man came in and introduced himself as the manager of the company. I asked him how much it would cost to shoot the last part of the concert. Of course, we would want to include the five hundred children playing the Bach Double Concerto. He called his assistant and began calculating. A crane, many lights, and several cameras would be necessary to shoot from different angles.

"Maybe you'd better go back to your desk, calculate, then show me the figures," I said.

A few minutes later, he came back and gave me a paper on which was written 300,000 yen.

I called Mr. Suzuki and asked whether our finances were sufficient to pay this amount. I knew well that our balance sheet was in the red, but it was still my strong belief that to shoot this concert was of the utmost importance. Mr. Suzuki agreed with me.

In 1955, the preparations for the annual concert took more than twice the time and energy as the graduation ceremony. We had to find a hall large enough to accommodate more than 1500 children. The best place was the Tokyo Municipal Gymnasium. The location was very convenient, right in front of Sendagaya Station. The gymnasium is on the edge of the big Meiji outer garden. Nearby are baseball fields, swimming pools, and a stadium. The place and the surroundings were highly suitable for our concert.

Mr. Tokugawa took the responsibility of inviting the Imperial Household. We were very surprised and honored to receive information that the Crown Prince, Princess Chichibu, Prince and Princess Takamatsu, and several grandchildren of the Emperor would attend.

One of the important tasks was to raise funds. As this concert was sponsored by our organization, every member was required to pay a certain amount. Besides these funds, we needed to solicit program advertising from various companies. I volunteered to undertake the unpleasant task of obtaining advertisements. Visiting various department stores and other leading business firms in Tokyo, I was successful in acquiring a substantial number of commitments.

The next task was to extend invitations to the diplomats in Japan. I visited the American Embassy several times and also cultural centers both in Tokyo and in Yokohama. It was also essential to solicit cooperation of the Japanese and foreign press, as well as radio and TV stations, for publicity. A press reception was held in Tokyo Kai-kan, one of the fanciest restaurants. Several delegates came and were given individual briefings.

As the children were coming from all over Japan and had never met each other, much less played together, forming groups and lining up the children was very important. This work was left in the hands of the instructors. Since the gymnasium is very wide, it might be difficult for the children to hear the piano. To avoid the difficulty, speakers picking up the piano were placed every six feet. All instructors in Tokyo cooperated in the work, and everything seemed to be ready before the day of the concert.

It rained heavily the night before, but fortunately it cleared up in the morning on this special day of March 27. The air was crisp, and I shivered with cold and excitement. The doors were to be opened at 10 a.m., but I noticed many small children, with their violins, hurrying from the station to the gymnasium quite early. Inside the building, there already was a buzz of excitement; instructors were shouting and hurrying to and fro. It seemed as though everything was in disorder and confusion. What we had so carefully planned seemed to be melting like ice.

I stood in the center and tried to concentrate. Within a few moments I got back my self-possession. After all, we had done our utmost in the preparation. The only thing left was to have confidence in the children. Just then Mr. Suzuki came into the hall. Looking around, he exclaimed, "Dr. Honda, what's this? There is no order. It's impossible to have a concert in this atmosphere."

I led Mr. Suzuki aside and said, "Please sit down and ease your mind. Everything is completed and there is nothing to worry about."

At noon the noise came to a peak. Small children were scurrying in all directions, calling their mothers. Microphones were shrieking names of lost children. Everything was in turmoil. But when the bell began to ring, a miracle happened. Everything became very quiet.

The graduation ceremony began in a quiet and dignified atmosphere. Everything moved along fine, except for one event near the end when flowers were to be presented to Mr. Suzuki. We had entirely forgotten to prepare for this. Over the microphone came the announcement "The next event is the presentation of flowers." We looked at each other blankly. Suddenly Mr. Junichi Ito, one of the directors, grabbed the vase on the desk, pulled out the flowers, and handed them to a child, who presented them to Mr. Suzuki.

The first national concert began at two o'clock, and all the royal guests were present. It was an overwhelming success. Judging from an article written by Mr. Ragner Smedsland, Finnish Minister, "Everyone who was present at the concert in the Tokyo sports hall must have found it an eloquent testimony of the possibility to bring to light and develop children's talent at a tender age."

The sound film of the concert was taken by Shinri-ken and this became most valuable in introducing Talent Education in the United States several years later. Since then the national concert and graduation ceremony have been carried out every March, usually in Tokyo.

FIRST PERFORMANCE
BEFORE A FOREIGN AUDIENCE

One Sunday after church Mr. Richard Meyer, the American pastor, came up to me and asked whether some children could play the violin for a meeting of Lutheran missionaries in Tokyo. He had already asked a boy to play the piano. I gladly consented and selected four girls and a boy. Of course Yuko and her friend Aiko were among the group.

The night of the meeting we all sat at the same table and a gentleman with a boy of five or six years sat next to me. He introduced himself as Mr. Toyohei Nojima and the boy with him as his son Minoru. Minoru was taking piano lessons from Mrs. Keiko Endo in Kugenuma Fujisawa, commuting from Yokosuka City. "What is your son going to play tonight?" "Turkish Rondo by Mozart," he replied. I was surprised to hear that such a small boy could play this difficult piece.

He was to play first on the program. He sat on the chair with his feet dangling, unable to touch the pedal. His technique was wonderful and the applause was enthusiastic. Several years later Minoru Nojima became a leading concert pianist in this country. Then our children played the Concerto in A Minor by Vivaldi and some small pieces. Again there was loud applause. When we were about to leave, an American gentleman approached and said quietly, "What amazing children. I have never heard such beautiful performances by small children. I hope you can come to the United States someday. Approach Ed Sullivan in case you come. He has a TV program which is very popular."

It was the first time I heard the name of Ed Sullivan, and I never even dreamed that some years later I would meet him.

THE FILM IS SENT TO THE U.S.

The financial situation of Talent Education was getting worse every year. There seemed to be two reasons: first, education is not a business and will not bring a profit. In the long run, of course, education is the best investment, not only for a nation, but also for human beings in general. Still, in the present age, some financial stability is important to carry out a project. Second, Mr. Suzuki is more an artist-educator than a businessman.

We had asked Shinri-ken to shoot the film, and, though the whole film took only thirty minutes, I thought it covered most of the necessary territory. To make a copy would cost another 100,000 yen. Of course we did not have the money and, as no company was willing to buy the picture, I thought it might as well be stored in the warehouse for the time being.

In the spring of 1958, I received a letter from Mr. Kenji Mochizuki, asking for the film. The Ohio String Teachers Association was to have a conference at Oberlin College and his urgent desire was to show the film at this meeting.

Again I racked my brains for a way to raise the money. I knew it was impossible for the organization to pay this amount. I thought of Mr. Shiro Endo, owner of a small steel company. He lived nearby in Kugenuma, and his second son was taking violin lessons. Because his hobby was raising roses, people called him Mr. Rose Endo. He had gone with me to solicit advertising for the national concert program, so he knew our situation well. One day I asked him if he could lend us 100,000 yen, promising that as soon as the organization had enough money accumulated, he would be repaid. Without a second thought, he willingly consented to lend us the sum, and that was how we were able to have a copy of the film made to send to Mr. Mochizuki.

Mr. Clifford Cook, then an associate professor at Oberlin Conservatory of Music, arranged for a room and a projector. As this was a 35 mm film, quite a bit of preparation was necessary to put it on the screen. It was shown after the conference, and a number of people saw it. Expectations were not high because people did not know the content. Otherwise, a large crowd would have filled the hall. But those who saw it were utterly amazed. Here in the Far East a miracle was performed. If it weren't on screen and with sound they would not have believed it to be true.

Several weeks later I received a letter from Mr. John Kendall, then a professor of strings at Muskingum College, New Concord, Ohio, expressing the surprise he encountered in looking at the picture and informing me of his desire to visit Japan, provided some foundation would offer him a grant.

The second national concert was held in Nagoya City in 1956. This was the first and last time the ceremony was held outside of Tokyo.

MY DAUGHTERS' EDUCATION

Yuko, under the instruction of Mr. Teisaburo Okumura, was making wonderful progress. Now she was the top student in the whole class. She was a very good encouraging example to those whose progress in the beginning was slow. She had easily conquered the Vivaldi Concerto in A Minor, which once seemed a lofty peak, and she was quickly gaining velocity as well as developing sensitivity.

We bought recordings by famous artists for her. Often she listened to these before she began a new piece. And after the piece had been memorized, she would again listen to the records.

You can fully concentrate your energy on technique once you have memorized the entire piece. Contrary to opinion, memorization is not difficult for children. The secret is, like all truths, simple. First, children are taught to memorize a short piece. Then another is added. After these two have been completely memorized, another is added. In other words, after A is memorized, B is added, then C. The children are taught to repeat from A to C, and only after they completely memorize these three is D added. In the first stage, the children find it difficult to memorize but the ability gradually develops and memorizing becomes easier.

One of the differences between the human brain and a computer is that if the program in a computer is erased, it is gone forever, but in the brain, though the input seems to be gone, what has been learned is in reality stored in the memory. I have a friend who lived in China during his early years, but when he returned to Japan at the age of six, he completely forgot Chinese. Upon graduating from the University, he was employed by a trading company. After a few years of internship, he was sent to Peking. Within three years he spoke Chinese with such fluency that people thought he was a native.

Yuko next finished the A Minor Concerto by Bach and received a high school course diploma. In 1958 she graduated from the college course, finishing the Violin Concerto No. 4 by Mozart. She was twelve years of age and surpassed all of her classmates.

Fundamentally, the Talent Education philosophy is not to make musicians. It is to develop character through music. Music has all the advantages for developing one's sensitivity. By studying the violin, one develops not only the ability to play but also to memorize. As a result, those who want to follow a professional career usually go to a conservatory.

Now, as Yuko had completed the college course, we had to think of her future career. One way was for her to enter some music conservatory and, for this reason, she withdrew from Mr. Okumura's class and began studying with a professor at Tokyo Music Academy.

She was now playing Concerto in E Minor by Mendelssohn. I well remember the first day we took her to the professor.

While Yuko was playing Mendelssohn, he moved around her, his arms folded, observing her keenly. At the end he criticized her sharply, though not in an unfriendly tone. His teaching method was orthodox, requiring much practice on etudes and scales.

Yuko studied for two years with the professor. These lessons were indeed good for her to brush up on her technique, but she also lost many things, particularly musical sensitivity. Her playing lacked musical feeling and seemed very mechanical. She herself recognized this and one day asked whether she could study with Mr. Suzuki again. Two years before, when studying with Mr. Okumura, she commuted to Matsumoto and received lessons from Mr. Suzuki. It was difficult for a girl of ten to ride the train for more than six hours to distant Matsumoto. She stayed there with Mrs. Hina Aikawa, sister of Mr. Suzuki, who took tender care of her. Within a year, however, Mrs. Aikawa developed a very serious illness and had to be hospitalized. Yuko was unable to continue staying in her home; this was one of the reasons she stopped going to Matsumoto for lessons.

One day Junko took her to Tokyo to receive a special lesson from Mr. Suzuki. Listening to her play, Mr. Suzuki advised her to use the strength of her shoulder and gave several more suggestions. He also played some pieces with her.

That night Yuko came to me and said, "Father, I wish to study with Mr. Suzuki again. I do not care even if this changes my future career. The most important thing is the music, which I lost during the past year. Besides I am now old enough to commute to Matsumoto." From then on, every weekend she traveled to Matsumoto, and she now stayed in a hotel.

On June 24, 1959, John Kendall arrived in Tokyo. He was the first American string teacher to come to Japan to study Talent Education. It was interesting to know how he evaluated our movement. The following are extracts from his reports:

Mr. Suzuki insists that the primary purpose of Talent Education is not to train artists, but to give all children the opportunity to develop the amazing potential which is illustrated in their ability to learn their mother tongue. The teaching begins immediately with rhythms on open string—four détaché sixteenth notes and two staccato eighths in the middle of the bow. In fact, the teacher may tape two spots on the bow, so that the child can check visually.

In this intense "ear training" approach recordings play a vital role, but even more important is the role of the mother. She is expected to attend . . .

Another noteworthy aspect of Mr. Suzuki's system is the almost complete absence of etudes and scales. Very little time is spent on etudes, such as Kayser, Mazas . . .

It will be noted in the manuals that the child moves very quickly to music literature which is challenging, particularly to music by the Baroque masters Bach, Handel, and Vivaldi. This music is rhythmically and melodically interesting, and utilizes the solid bowing patterns begun with the very first piece.

While the child's progress for the first year may not be phenomenal, he picks up speed during the following years, and his good foundation, plus the repetition factor, cause very rapid growth.

The methods described here are not a panacea or a magic formula, but a live, experimental process, producing dramatic results. It should not be implied, however, that there are no problems or weaknesses. This would naturally be impossible. Problem areas include slow learners, sight-reading, musical materials for older students, the need for ensemble and orchestral experience, and ever-present financial problems for parents, teachers, and for the whole movement. But the spirit and determination are high among those who work in the Talent Education movement . . .

True, there is nothing new about starting youngsters

at an early age. We often quote, but seldom practice, the old adage: "Give me a child until he is six and you may have him after that."

Six weeks was not enough time to get a complete or final conception of this system, or movement. It did, however, convince the writer of several things: first, that this method, after twelve years of experiment in Japan, has achieved amazing results; second, that three-year-old children are not too young to learn to play the violin . . .

There are no contests, no vying for honors or "first class." Instead, there is a wonderful spirit of cooperation, of mutual respect, and of sympathetic enjoyment along with the serious study of the violin.

Can American teachers and mothers work together in teaching the child and will American mothers give their time, energy and patience on a regular and continuing basis to the lessons and practice of the children?

All of us who are interested in the future of string playing will now ask the question: "Can Mr. Suzuki's methods succeed in America?" It is this writer's opinion that they can succeed.

The next 50 years will be crucial ones in which the demands on human leadership will be found, and Mr. Suzuki's contention that developing the talents of small children is as important as atomic energy may not be as fantastic as it sounds. Certainly we must begin early to develop to the fullest, the human potential for thoughtful, sensitive, capable leadership.

Reading this report carefully, I admired Mr. Kendall's gift of observation and respected his wisdom in understanding the method and philosophy.

He had stated the importance of the mother's role, and this must be carefully explained. The secret of Suzuki's method lies in the participation of the mother. When the children go to the lesson, mothers must always accompany them. This is a strict rule. Of course in many other types of lessons, mothers usually accompany their small children, but their roles are different. While the children receive lessons from the instructor, the mother must always be near the teacher, listening intently, taking notes if necessary and often using the tape recorder. The reason is that they know that during six days of the week they must instruct the child at home. They realize that if their instruction is wrong, the child will be misled and it will be their fault. Since they know that they will have to make corrections, it is natural that they are very much in earnest. Few mothers have any knowledge of the violin. Most of them are wives of clerks, merchants, or farmers, belonging to the middle class rather than the rich or poor.

There is a story in Japan that a spy is trained to jump over hemp every day. As hemp grows very fast, within a short period he will be able to jump more than ten feet. This is just a story, and nobody believes it. But it contains a suggestion for learning. A child's ability to learn the violin develops very slowly, just like the growth of hemp. Still in a month or a year, the development is clearly noticeable. The mother's sensitivity will develop along with that of the child, and even when the child begins playing difficult pieces, the mother's ability will also develop so that she can easily check mistakes and instruct.

Often for some reason, mothers can not accompany the children, and a sister or father will go with the child. In this case, it is almost impossible for the mother to catch up and assist in the teaching process when the child is advanced. Sometimes this will be the cause of dropout.

One afternoon in May, Junko and I visited the Tamagawa Gakuen School which our two daughters were attending. It was in the outskirts of Tokyo, in Machida City. After walking five minutes from the station, we arrived at the entrance of the school. The road led up the hill, and on the left side there was a pond with big lotus leaves covering the water. As we climbed higher, a church steeple came into view. We stopped a little to catch our breath. Above the moaning of the wind through the pines, we heard a beautiful chorus floating from the chapel.

We climbed the steps and opened the door. A student ushered us to seats upstairs. It was a concert of the whole school. The conductor was one of their own classmates. I was astonished to hear everybody in the class join in the singing, and all sang their parts well and easily. I was very happy to hear and see them singing so joyfully. This is what music should be, not for a special person but for everybody, and everybody should enjoy and join in the singing. While one group was going off the stage, singing, another group caught the pitch while coming onto the stage. There was no hustle, and everything moved smoothly. The chapel was full of sweet music. The teachers' group sang last, and there was much applause.

After the concert we went to meet the president of the school, Mr. Kuniyoshi Obara. He said:

> Our school's guiding principle is total education. We are not trying to make a special elite, but rather to require every student to join in activities of his choice. Music is the best method to make students harmonize and happy, so every student joins in the singing. In fact, as you notice, singing is not only a lesson but part of their lives. They sing while they work. By the way, labor is important and we do not hire a special person to do labor in this school. Students clean their classroom, laboratory, and the objects they use. They must learn responsibility, which is important in a democracy. Culture is something which must not be enforced. They do this work joyfully. Our school motto is Do Things Willingly Which Others Dislike. One of the teachers will take you around and I hope you will enjoy your visit.

We thanked Mr. Obara and went out into the campus. It was large, about a hundred acres, utilizing the landscape to the fullest. There were hills, valleys, and woods and the school buildings were scattered over the campus. Mr. Koichi Maeda, principal of the elementary school, took us around.

There was a special room for drawing and a number of children were tacking up drawings on a big wall. The team was making wonderful combinations, and each child knew what he was doing, enjoying every moment. Some were drawing, creating their own pictures with freedom and beauty. The next room was for pottery-making or ceramics. Small boys and girls were molding clay and making vases and other small items.

In the next building was a music room. Children were being taught to develop absolute pitch. Mr. Shinichiro Sako was instructing the pupils in composition. Mayako was in this class and she was performing her own composition in an annex.

Mr. Yukinobu Chai was teaching a group how to make violins. There was also a half-finished piano. Yuko was working hard on finishing a violin. It was indeed wonderful for the children to make the instruments they were playing.

"Besides the regular classes," Mr. Maeda said quietly, "the children select some ancillary studies, such as drawing or ceramics, or making instruments, as you just observed. We do many other things, tending domestic animals, like sheep, hogs and cattle, or even bees. The students choose subjects according to their interests. Naturally, they enjoy this and as a result achieve mastery in this line. Once they master a subject, be it drawing or music, animal-raising or violin-making, they develop confidence in themselves and gradually conquer subjects which they dislike. Once they begin liking the subject, they will succeed."

On our way home, I discussed what we had seen with Junko. We thought our children were receiving a wonderful education. Besides, the walk to school every day, uphill part of the way, would make their feet strong, and the changing seasons would gladden their hearts.

WE PERFORM ON TV

One day in May, 1960, a man representing National Broadcasting Television (N. H. K.) came to our home. He told us that on the following Wednesday afternoon, N. H. K. wanted us to come to the studio to give a family concert on a program called "Ladies Hour." Mr. T. Isobe, a composer who lived near us, had recommended us. This was the first time our family was to be on television and naturally we were all very excited.

Mr. Ichiro Fujiyama, a well-known vocalist, was in charge of the program. We had several rehearsals with him before the program began. The title was, "Let's all sing 'When You and I Were Young, Maggie.'" Yuko began playing this melody and Mayako accompanied. Mr. Fujiyama sat on the sofa, listening to the music. As the music faded, Mr. Fujiyama approached and said into the microphone, "Good afternoon. The guests who will sing with you on the program are Dr. Honda and his family. Today's song is 'When You and I Were Young, Maggie,' and I hope you have memorized the verses. Please follow the notes while I explain."

He took time explaining the notes in detail. "Now let's all sing with Mrs. Honda and her family."

Mr. Fujiyama played the piano and my family joined in the singing. After the song ended, I came in. We exchanged greetings.

Mr. Fujiyama. What is the reason for your family learning music?

Dr. Honda. Because it develops wonderful feelings. I love this "Maggie" song very much. When I was a boy, we used to sing it in the public school.

Mr. F. May I ask you why?

Dr. H. I love the verses. Though the couple gets old, they love each other, cherishing their sweet memories.

Mr. F. Being a medical doctor must be very hard on your nerves. Maybe music does something to ease your mind.

Dr. H. Yes, very much. My happiest hour is to sing with my family after my work.

Mr. F. Will you please sing something for us?

Dr. H. All right, my family will sing "Midday Dream."

(Junko began singing; Yuko played obbligato, and Mayako also accompanied.) This music was written by Gekko Takayasu and composed by Tei Yanada. It is a beautiful song and Junko's favorite. I love it dearly.

Mr. F. It is just wonderful. Now will you all sing together? Of course Dr. Honda should join in.

Then, at Junko's suggestion, we sang Lullaby by Mozart, this time accompanied by Asami, our youngest daughter, who had been receiving piano instruction since she was four from Mrs. Keiko Endo.

Mr. F. Thank you very much. (Facing the camera.) Will you now all please sing "Maggie" again?
(The screen showed the verses and we all sang.)

It was a happy day. All our children were with us and were healthy, and our hearts were united with the television audience through music.

PREPARATION FOR THE TOUR TO THE U.S.

Mr. Kendall came to Japan again in March, 1962, to attend the national concert. The day after his arrival, Mr. Suzuki and I visited International House where he was staying. "Mr. Kendall," I began, "since your first visit to Japan, I understand you have given lectures and workshops about Talent Education in many cities. How are they received?"

"I am surprised to see how eager people are to know the idea and method of Talent Education in my country," he replied. "My opinion is that, in the near future, we should bring some children to the United States for a demonstration."

"Yes, I think that is a very good idea. It is very important for people to see and hear the children play. What do you think about this idea, Mr. Suzuki?" I asked.

"Hm, that's a good idea, but maybe in the future," he said, his face showing disapproval.

I thought it smart not to push him, and changed the subject. "Mr. Kendall, you need a textbook to spread the idea. As music is international and easily understood, perhaps you could sell our books in the United States?" I asked.

"Yes, for the time being, but if Mr. Suzuki allows, I would like to revise the books and publish them, probably through Summy-Birchard."

Mr. Kendall stayed in Matsumoto for several weeks, then returned home. I turned my attention to the Talent Education summer school, an event almost as important as the national concert.

We had our first school in 1951 in Kirigamine. The school was held in a big inn and all the children and instructors lived in the same building. But as the attendance grew from year to year, it was impossible to accommodate everyone in the same hotel, and the site was changed to Matsumoto. It was like a music festival and usually lasted for five days. Of course Mr. Suzuki was always at the center of the whole school—never tired, always vigorous, his face shining with happiness at being among the children.

The classes were divided into ten groups and the instructor in charge of Group 1 was to teach children studying Volume 1, and so on. Mr. Suzuki himself taught the college course. Children came from all over Japan with their parents. Instead of going to summer resorts, the parents came along, and all enjoyed it very much. There were many advantages. First, the children had the opportunity to study with different instructors. Second, the parents came to know each other and talked about various problems. Third, it was good recreation.

Every night there was a special concert in which those who were recommended by various instructors had the honor of playing solo in the big hall.

This was advantageous to the children who played as well as to those who listened. There was no competition, but the audience could distinguish between those who played with good bowing, posture, beautiful tone, and sensitivity and those who did not. In fact it gave encouragement to everyone, for no harsh criticism was given. Those who understood their own weaknesses were encouraged to correct themselves. Mr. Suzuki never ceased to move. He was tireless. Every morning at nine we all met at the big hall and he delivered a lecture. Then the small children played in ensemble before dividing into classes. Then he taught the advanced class. At noon, during lunch, he met with many people. I have never seen him let anyone down.

Everything was well planned and prepared. Still, as so many people with children were attending the school, many unforeseen obstacles developed. But we were always ready to solve the problems and never encountered real difficulties.

The word preparation is stressed in lessons. The motto is: "First, fingers; second, bow; third, start." Instructors always say this to the children. Needless to say, to play the violin, the left hand must be in the correct position and fingers must press the correct point on the string, and that point only. Fingers must always be trained to press this correct point and not shift up and down, seeking to find it. Unless fingers press the correct point, good tone will not be produced. This, how-ever, does not eliminate the need to adjust the fingers to the correct pitch. This technique is fundamental and should be mastered at an early stage. The tendency of human nature is to start before preparations are well made. Preparation must be made in attitude and mind before moving. For the begin-ners, the will to move the bow often comes before the fingers are ready. This produces very uncertain tone. The habit of preparation must be fixed in the early stages. As the music advances, it will be more complicated in tempo, rhythm, and melody. Fingers must move with skill, speed, and accuracy, always before the bow. This requires careful training and re-peated practice. Of course children must not be expected to master it quickly. They must practice slowly and accurately in the first period. Preparation will vary in quality and quan-tity, according to the difficulty of the piece. The motion of the right arm must never outrun the fingers. When the child is received into a violin class, the teacher usually will not allow him to play during the first period. He goes to the class with his mother and hears the other children receive their lessons. When his turn comes, he bows to the teacher, and the teacher tunes the violin and returns it to him. Repeating this for a month or so, the desire to play is aroused within the child. The preparation is being made, the motor is warming up. Then the lessons begin and the child starts with delight and eagerness. Often mothers are taught to hold the violin correctly and play "Twinkle, Twinkle" or small pieces. Naturally, in this case the desire within the children will be increased.

Not only in violin, but in our daily life this "get set, get ready, start" is very important.

Our daily life might be similar to playing violin. Sometimes the tempo is fast or slow or the rhythms change. We must always be prepared for what comes next. The difference is that we know what comes next in music but not in our daily life.

In the most recent summer school, Yuko was asked to play on the last night. We all decided to drive to Matsumoto. As the road was bad and dusty and the trip took more than eight hours, I was not keen on driving. But our friend, Father Taniguchi, who was in charge of Totsuka Catholic Church, proposed that he would drive half the way, so I consented. We left home at 3:30 in the morning and arrived thirty minutes later in Totsuka. The stars were shining, promising a good day, and the air was cool. But as the sun rose, the heat became intolerable. My car did not have air conditioning and it was like an oven; the only consolation was the wind that came in. But still we enjoyed the trip. We ate our breakfast by the lake near Mt. Fuji, looking at the towering mountain. For lunch we stopped at an inn in Suwa to eat a special dinner of lake fish.

We arrived in Matsumoto rather early in the afternoon and took a dip in the hot spring to refresh ourselves.

Yuko played the Mendelssohn Violin Concerto the next evening. She played with skill and good tempo, but, compared to Yukari Tate who played after her, she lacked volume and sensitivity. The difference came from the instruction she had received.

Mr. Suzuki has created a new word, "tonalization." The vocalist concerns himself with finding, through a series of exercises, the voice placement which will produce the most beautiful sound. This is called vocalization. So also the violinist should practice to develop tone similar to vocalization. Hence the new word tonalization. He also stressed that even in the early stage, children should put feeling into the music. Feeling can be developed by hearing records played by good artists. Feeling or sensitivity should develop along with technique.

The next day was hot, the sun scorching. We were to leave Matsumoto at 11:00 a.m. I drove my car from the hotel to the school to say farewell to Mr. Suzuki and the others. I left the car on the grounds and when I came back fifteen minutes later, I had a flat tire. This was indeed troublesome, but I had to fix it so I took out my equipment and, under the hot sun, I changed the tire.

Just as I finished the repair, I heard that dismal sound, which I had forgotten for some time, arise in my breast— hemorrhage, which I understood in a twinkling. I stood in dismay for a second, thinking fast as to what I should do. I knew if I visited a clinic, I must stay there at least two weeks and even then it would be doubtful if I could go home. I made up my mind to keep quiet and drive back. We picked Father up at the Catholic Church where he was staying, and off we went on the long drive back. I did not speak unless necessary, so naturally Father and Junko looked queer, thinking I was probably irritated by something. Every now and then I felt a surge coming up but by sheer endurance I held it back. Father took the wheel for more than two-thirds of the trip. I was glad that he enjoyed driving, and being a jolly person he chattered cheerfully, pretending not to notice my silence. Again a race between time and endurance began. The sun was scorching and the road rough and dusty. Finally at midnight, we arrived home and I lay down with relief on my bed. I knew the bleeding came from over-exhaustion and heat. Within a week, I recovered, and again followed my daily routine.

MR. COOK'S ARRIVAL

During the past four years, I had been a member of the Fujisawa City Council. I ran for the office because the medical association wanted one of its members to represent it in municipal politics. I had had no previous experience in politics nor any background, but in the balloting I ranked second among thirty-six. My four-year term expired in 1963 and I had to decide whether or not I would run again. I knew if I ran for city council I was sure to be elected again, but four years' experience was enough for me.

I ran instead for Prefecture Council, which I knew I would lose. The election was to be held in the middle of April. In the midst of my campaign, Mr. and Mrs. Clifford Cook came from the United States to study the Talent Education program. I went with Yuko to meet them at the airport. The plane was late, and when they finally arrived it was 4:00 a.m.

Mr. Cook had played a great role in introducing our movement in the U.S. Without him I wonder if the film would have been shown. Mr. Mochizuki wrote, telling me to give Mr. Cook every opportunity possible to investigate the program. In the midst of my busy schedule I took him to see many of the classes.

The cherry blossom buds were tight when the campaign began and the flowers gone when it ended. All those who helped me in the campaign were young students and, although I fought with all my might, I lost. I did not feel at all bad, because my campaign had been fair and straight. This was the end of my short political career.

Before returning to the U.S., Mr. and Mrs. Cook visited our home. The roses in our garden were beautiful. My friend Mr. Endo taught me how to raise them, and more than fifty different varieties were blooming. Roses are very difficult to raise; they require care and attention.

First the soil has to be selected and given plenty of fertilizer. When the bushes are planted, pruning is important; this must be done in February before the buds come out. Then, the roses must be disinfected and fertilized at least once a week. Raising roses is in some ways like raising children. The soil is equivalent to the mother. It is difficult for a mother who lacks physical and spiritual enrichment to have a healthy baby. Before the infant expresses his own desires, pruning is necessary to cut the strayed or withered branch and encourage the straight stem to grow. Then of course we always have to take care not to expose them to disease.

We visited Mr. Endo's house, where the flowers were abundant and in greater size and variety than ours. Then we drove to Kamakura. We stood by the big Buddha. He was clasping his hands and looking down serenely, eyes half-closed.

Mr. Cook said softly, "At last, here I am in Japan, looking at the great Buddha which I have seen so often in pictures. So it has finally come true, that we have visited Japan."

Mr. Sato, the priest of the temple, was a Rotarian and my good friend. We called on him at his new home. He took us to a big room, overlooking the garden. We sat on the floor talking about the garden. "We would like to serve you Japanese tea in full ceremony," Mr. Sato began.

"I imagine the ceremony is quite difficult," said Mr. Cook.

"Not at all. It is the spirit that is important, not the form. In ancient times, armored warriors sipped tea even in the battlefield. They sat on the soil and drank from crude vessels. Usually we do not speak while we drink, but observe the beauty of nature. That is why we always have simple flowers or a picture that we can enjoy and appreciate. The subjects should be of nature, avoiding stark realism as much as possible. Nowadays, the ceremony has become too formal. I say again it is the spirit that is more important. The host must do his utmost to welcome and serve the guests. The guests must express their thanks for the kindness of the host. This is in a way formal but it should come from the heart. Often we have tea outdoors. Every season has its beauty and even in the same place the scenery looks different at different times of the year."

We sipped our tea silently.

Mr. Cook left for the United States on May 1. The night before he left, we had a farewell dinner at the Hotel Okura in Tokyo. I talked to him about the possibility of visiting the United States with the children, and I asked whether Oberlin College would send us a formal invitation. He promised and we shook hands.

Two weeks after his departure, I received the following letter from Mr. Cook.

Dear Friends,

As we reluctantly leave Japan, our thoughts are of you. We have known for years that one of the principal aims of Talent Education is to make better people with warm and pure hearts.

Our six weeks in Japan have proven again and again how well this aim is being realized. Everywhere we have visited you have greatly impressed us not only as perfect hosts and hostesses but also as highly intelligent, warm-hearted people with lofty ideals for mankind.

I have asked our school to send you an invitation for the concert next year and they willingly cooperate. I am in close touch with John Kendall and he is writing many letters.

Mr. Robert Klotman, president of the American String Teachers Association (ASTA) is also very cooperative, and we four make a project team. ASTA will have its annual conference in Philadelphia and will extend an invitation.

The International Society for Music Education will hold a conference in Tokyo this summer. Alex Zimmerman, the president, and Vanette Lawler, the secretary of MENC, will attend the conference. I advise you to talk to Mr. Zimmerman and convince him of the importance of your tour. If you can give a small concert for him, this will be most effective.

Again I want to express our gratitude and appreciation for giving us such a marvelous experience to cherish as long as we live.

May God bless you and your family.

Clifford Cook

YUKO'S FIRST RECITAL IN MISONO

Yuko and Mayako were now going to Misono Girls' High School in Fujisawa City. This school was founded by Mother Theresia Misono, whose philosophy was based on the idea that the role of mothers is very important in education. She came from Germany in 1914 at the age of twenty-two to dedicate her life to work in this far country.

She came penniless, alone; all she possessed was Christian faith and love for humanity.

Thirty-six years ago she bought a whole mountain of ten acres and built a convent, orphanage, and schools. According to Sister Ignatio, her successor and principal of the school, Mother Theresia not only had profound knowledge of household management but also in surveying land and designing buildings.

I often wonder how and when this young lady acquired such extensive knowledge. Probably it was at her home. In the present school system, a girl of her age will talk logically of what she has read but will be very inferior in her practical knowledge.

When Mother Theresia bought the mountain, she stood on the top and pointed out sites for the chapel, orphanage, and schools. The experts were surprised that all these fitted just where she said they would.

During the Christmas season I have often brought candies and clothing to the orphanage.

One day I asked fifteen of my friends who owned cars to take some widows and their children for a drive and act as one-day fathers. The outing was somewhat of a failure, as the roads were bad and many got carsick. One of my friends reproached me for my headstrong action in not making thorough preparation for the day. But it was my temperament to do things impulsively once I thought they were right, not thinking through the details.

We planned a recital for our daughter Yuko at Misono Girls' High School on Sunday, May 17 at 1:30 p.m. We extended an invitation to our friends, telling them how we happened to meet Mr. Suzuki and also about Yuko's developing her character through violin.

The day was beautiful and the hall was full of sweet fragrances. On the program was Sonata No. 2 by Schubert, Concerto No. 3 by Mozart and, after intermission, "Rondo Capriccioso" by Saint-Saëns and some small pieces. It was a wonderful recital.

The school prepared a special room for the reception and the nuns and teachers helped to serve tea and sandwiches.

After the party Yuko came to my side with tears in her eyes: "Father, Sister Sapientia mopped and cleaned the corridor the night before. She said to me, 'Yuko, I am a Catholic sister and cannot give you anything. What I did is a very small thing but a present for your concert.'"

I swallowed the big lump that came to my throat and with difficulty held back my tears. It was the most wonderful present Yuko received.

THE TOUR MATERIALIZES

Alex Zimmerman, president of the Music Educators National Conference (MENC), and Vanette Lawler, the secretary, came to Japan that summer. I went to the hotel and talked to Mr. Zimmerman about our desire to introduce Talent Education in the U.S. He listened attentively and expressed an interest in inviting the children to the MENC convention in Philadelphia. Several days later, we gave a special program at a kindergarten in Shiba, Tokyo. We invited Mr. Zimmerman to the concert and he listened for an hour.

In the United States, Mr. Kendall, Mr. Cook, and Mr. Klotman made a project team to plan the tour. They worked vigorously, and Mr. Kendall wrote many letters to various schools. Our plans were materializing.

In September I received a letter from Mr. Cook stating that both MENC and Oberlin College were ready to print materials announcing the March appearances of the children, based on the assumption that all details were settled. Mr. Cook had serious doubts that the financial details were indeed settled. He pointed out that MENC could not provide funds or book any tours (including the Ed Sullivan show), and that if funds proved to be insufficient there was no way that he or John Kendall could guarantee funds for the trip. He asked that I let him know by October 1 if we were certain of having sufficient funds ourselves and that he would ask both MENC and Oberlin College to delay the printing of their program events until that time.

I read the letter with a sinking heart. This was indeed a blow which might shatter all our hopes. I meditated for a long time. After all, if we bought our own round-trip tickets here in Japan, at least we would not be stranded.

The October deadline was very near, but I would tell them that we would visit at our own expense. If they could give us hospitality in homes and provide land transportation, we could make the trip. I felt that we must make it, as there was no guarantee that it would be easier next year. Furthermore, there would be no music conference next year. But there were many difficulties in this venture, the most important at this point being to raise funds for the tour, not a small amount.

I wrote a letter to the project team telling them we would travel at our own expense. The letter was written on my responsibility.

As I had to commute to Tokyo every day to make arrangements, I moved my clinic to a center near the government railway.

I began contacting big firms and businessmen in Tokyo to find sponsors but after several visits I began to realize that it was more difficult than I had supposed.

"Taking small children to play the violin in America—what for? Music education in the United States is very advanced. If you are taking children who play the samisen (Japanese string instrument), maybe the American people might come to hear foreign music. But a Western instrument, I think not!" I told them that the method originated by Mr. Suzuki was unique and I was convinced it would create a sensation. They said no, and did not believe it. Besides, they added that they did not approve of taking small children abroad. The trip would be too strenuous and risky.

I was getting a little discouraged. What I needed was some success and encouragement but nobody seemed to understand my motivation. Then I received a letter from Mr. Kendall, giving a progress report on plans for the trip to America by Mr. Suzuki and the children.

He recommended that the trip as originally planned be cancelled. Though invitations had been accepted by Mr. Suzuki for appearances at MENC, Southern Illinois University, and Oberlin College and grants seemed possible from both the Presser Foundation and Summy-Birchard Company, no answers had been received from others who had been contacted; furthermore, needed financial support was not forthcoming.

He asked that we consider an alternate proposal: Bring four children, plus Mr. Suzuki and one Japanese mother to care for the children. (Others, including teachers, could come at their own expense, and hospitality would be provided for all who came.) The original planning committee would continue to make arrangements.

Mr. Kendall felt that this would satisfy the great interest in Mr. Suzuki and his work. Four children could demonstrate, perform, and work with Mr. Suzuki to show his methods; this would be a much better solution than abandonment of the project. He asked for our immediate reaction.

I was not keen on this compromise plan and knew that Mr. Suzuki would not go without me. Even if I did go I would have great difficulty in persuading him to go, as there were so many obstacles. I kept the bad news and the discouraging information to myself as long as possible, but copies of the letter went to him, and he seemed to understand the difficulties. He lost his desire to go. "Why do we have to go—with so much risk?" he asked me once. "I understand that this tour is a great risk. The first is the problem of funds. The second is that I don't know how the American people will receive us. Maybe they will merely think it child's play. In that case, our beliefs will be greatly shattered."

I replied, "Mr. Suzuki, I have been helping to spread your ideas for fifteen years and believe your method is valuable. But in Japan there are many people who are against it. Talent Education is not developing as it should and I know our financial situation is not favorable. Still I think it my mission to spread your idea to America. I am sure they will understand. There are difficulties in finding sponsors, but let us take children whose parents can afford to pay. I will pay my own way and the organization should pay yours and Mrs. Suzuki's."

I talked earnestly, but Mr. Suzuki did not reply and I knew from past experience that he did not approve of the tour. Indeed there were too many difficulties.

In early December I received an encouraging letter from Mr. Kendall. He reported that definite commitments had been received from:

Northwestern University	March 7
Southern Illinois University	March 9
ASTA-MENC	March 15
Oberlin College	March 16
Detroit	March 17

Confirmations for tentative dates had been received from Wichita University and schools in Trenton, Scarsdale, Tucson, and Los Angeles.

The Presser Foundation had promised financial assistance and had already been most helpful in making arrangements.

Mr. Kendall raised questions about programs, travel schedules, arrangements for the children's housing and rest before appearances, fund-raising, program format, accompanists, and television and radio appearances, and asked for our advice. The committee members were obviously hard at work behind the scenes. Things were moving very fast in the country beyond the ocean.

In the middle of the month, I met with the travel agent for the first time and asked him to set up our itinerary.

OUR UNITED STATES TOUR

As soon as the Near Year's holiday was over, we began the important procedure of selecting children and parents who would join the tour. On Mr. Suzuki's recommendation, ten children were chosen as candidates. I wrote letters to all the parents, asking about the possibility of their children joining the tour at their own expense. All answered yes. Mr. Hirose, a violin instructor, and Mrs. Shizuko Suzuki, an accompanist, also were recommended to join the group.

One day the travel agent called me to say the Department of Education had notified the agency that the tour would not be permitted. The idea of taking small children abroad during the school period was not to their liking. The Minister of the Foreign Office would not issue passports without permission from the Minister of Education.

This was a great blow that left me stunned. We had been working hard on this project for so long that this blow seemed fatal. Not only in Japan but in the U.S., people had almost completed the itinerary and if we failed to go, the people involved would be in serious trouble.

I sat for a moment and thought hard. Who had enough political power to persuade the Minister of Education to issue the permission?

The name of Mr. Aiichiro Fujiyama came into my head. He had been a foreign minister and still had strong influence. Besides, his home ground was Yokohama City in Kanagawa Prefecture and I, as a director of the Medical Association in Kanagawa, had helped him in his campaign. I phoned his secretary and fortunately received an appointment for that afternoon. Mr. Fujiyama was friendly and shook my hand warmly. We had met at Yokohama but I wasn't sure he remembered me. I told him about the situation and he listened attentively. He did not give approval but I felt I had made the right contact. Later, when Mr. Suzuki came to Tokyo, I asked him to accompany me and we met Mr. Fujiyama again.

Meanwhile I had to proceed with the arrangements. I asked all the parents and children to come to Tokyo and meet at our office. Most of those who came were the mothers. I interviewed each personally, asking about the child's health. This was most important, as it would not only be miserable to have a sick child on tour, but might develop into serious trouble.

The last thing I confirmed was their responsibility to pay their expenses for the trip. The children had already been recommended for their high ability to play the violin. The travel agent was present at the meeting and, after the personal interviews, everyone assembled in the hall and received information necessary for the trip.

During the following week, I again called the Education and Foreign Ministries but there had been no progress. Things seemed to be deadlocked. The Minister of the Foreign Office was more sympathetic but, without the consent of the Minister of Education, he was unable to issue passports.

In mid-February I received a letter from Mr. Kendall concerning further details of the trip. He discussed the nature of our programs. At each location, the children would be expected to give a full performance. If the sponsoring group requested it, he asked whether Mr. Suzuki would demonstrate his teaching techniques, such as having the children do some of the interesting games that are a part of the Suzuki method.

Mr. Kendall sent the final schedule of performances, substituting Seattle on March 5 for a previously scheduled Anchorage performance. At each location, we would be met, taken care of, and returned to the plane for the next flight. He would be with us at MENC in Philadelphia and at his school, Southern Illinois University, and Mr. Cook would go with us to Oberlin.

I already had information that Northwest Airlines would not land in Anchorage during March. Mr. Kendall was frantically making arrangements, but I was more frantic. At this time Anchorage or Seattle did not matter much to me. My deepest concern was, Could we go? And the answer was we must!

I suddenly recalled the name of Mr. Shunkyo Nakajima. He was the key man who had spread the idea of Talent Education in Central Japan when he was working in Aichi Prefecture in Nagoya. He had been transferred to the Department of Education and I was sure he was in charge of the work. I had already talked with the vice-minister, but perhaps it would work better if I approached someone at a lower level. I took the car immediately and went to Tokyo to meet him on the chance that he would be there, and he was. He had already heard about the tour and, of course, there was no necessity of explaining the purpose to him. His attitude gave me hope, which in the past I had not received from anyone.

This was February 15. Three days later I received the answer that the Education Minister had given his permission and the Foreign Minister would issue the visas. I do not know to this day whose influence made this possible. It might have been Mr. Fujiyama, or the vice-minister, or maybe Mr. Nakajima, or probably all combined. I was relieved but far from happy. We had overcome the first big obstacle, but I knew there were more to come!

On February 22 we all went to the Foreign Office to apply for visas. There were ten children and nine adults. Four of the mothers accompanied us. Each would not only look after her own child but would chaperone the other children. All the papers were to be finished in a week and every person would have to come again to receive his passport.

Now it was like a stone rolling downhill, gathering speed each moment. We had plane reservations for March 5, and before this date everything necessary must be done.

On February 27 when I came home after arranging things in Tokyo, I found that Mayako was not well. She often had stomachaches and, after examining her carefully, I found that she had appendicitis. The next day I asked the advice of Dr. Mori, a surgeon, who had performed appendectomies on Junko and her mother. His opinion was that the operation was necessary and that he would be ready to operate the next morning.

That was the day I had to visit the Foreign Office to get the passports and exchange money for the group—a very busy day. I knew Mayako's appendicitis was not acute, but still, leaving her without the operation and going on the tour would cause ceaseless worry throughout my trip. This indeed was a very trying situation, but I decided to let her have her operation. There is a proverb in Japan that mishap will call mishap. Junko had been sick in bed for the past several days.

The next morning I took Mayako to the hospital and Yuko went with me. Dr. Mori looked surprised when I told him that I could not stay for the operation. I told him my situation and left the hospital, leaving my heart with Mayako. Yuko sat in the chair outside the operating room praying, just as she did several years before when Mayako had the traffic accident.

I arrived late at the Foreign Office and found the group waiting anxiously for my arrival. One of the girls, Asako Hata, seven years old, had flushed cheeks and was coughing. She was a pupil of Mr. Hirose and one of the soloists. If she did not recover it would be difficult to take her, and besides there was no time to find somebody to replace her. As soon as she received her passport, I told Mrs. Hata to take her home and keep her in bed.

The American Embassy gave us visas within one day. I returned to Fujisawa in the evening and visited the hospital. I was surprised to find Junko there tending our daughter. She could not stay home and went to the hospital shortly after I left. Thank God, Mayako's operation was finished and she was feeling fine.

The days flew by and the day of departure, March 5, 1964, arrived. That evening we were asked to appear on a television program by 4:00 p.m. We took all our luggage to the TV station and after the appearance had supper and drove to the airport. The plane was to leave at 9:50 p.m. There was a big crowd in the lobby and lots of excitement. I noticed that the mothers who were not going were hugging their children and speaking softly in their ears, smiling bravely. I felt calm but inside I was excited.

When it was time to leave, I promised the parents that I would bring the children back happy and healthy. I took Chiaki Tamura and Keiko Fukuda, both six years old, and entered the immigration office. And so we marched single file out of their sight. Junko told me later that I had a grim countenance like a pioneer leading the group to the Wild West.

After passing through the immigration and customs office, we entered a lobby where passengers were waiting to embark. The parents were already assembling in the corridor. There was thick glass separating the corridor from the lobby, and in the middle of the glass were round plastic windows containing small holes so that people could talk through them. I held the small Chiaki close to the window. *"Sayonara,"* (good-bye) was all she said and her mother, smiling bravely, returned the same words. Nobody was weeping.

Before entering the plane we stopped on the gangway and waved our last farewell. Once inside the cabin, we were in a foreign country. I fastened the seat belts for all the children and observed that they were very tired. No wonder. Many of them had traveled several hours to reach the airport. The Northwest Airlines stewardesses were kind; they smiled and spoke to the children, who heard their first English.

The jet engines began to roar and slowly the plane started to move. Standing still in the runway it shuddered and then began to move, gathering speed each second. The lights of Tokyo flew backward and we were in the air, leaving Japanese soil. In another second we were climbing upwards and I noticed Keiko, age six, getting pale and leaning back helplessly.

I unhooked my belt and held the bag for her just in time. It was her first sickness.

Within an hour all the children were asleep; they didn't eat any of the food that was served.

I sat sleeplessly, thinking of the past and the future. So we were flying to the United States. I could not anticipate what would be waiting for us in that far country. Why worry? Tomorrow would come with all its new hope. I closed my eyes and tried to sleep. I slept until I was awakened by bright sun shining in my eyes. Somebody had opened the shade and the strong rays were coming in. I looked at my watch; the hands indicated that it was 3:00 a.m. Within an hour, breakfast was served and the children had their first meal on the plane.

The plane began descending before six and I again noticed that two of the children became sick. Yasuko Ohtani was with her mother, so I left her in her mother's care. I knelt beside Keiko and held the bag to her mouth. She was pale and her face looked like an old woman's. I wondered that even a child's countenance could change in a difficult situation.

The sun was bright and high when we disembarked and we were a little dizzy. The big sign reading Tacoma-Seattle Air Terminal jumped at my eyes and I realized that we were now in the United States of America.

Though my watch showed six-thirty, it was 1:30 p.m. local time and we had gained a day. We passed immigration and customs and went outside, still bewildered. Then a group of American people swarmed around us. One big man approached us with a warm smile and introduced himself as Vilem Sokol. He was a professor in the School of Music at the University of Washington and a good friend of Mr. Kendall's. After shaking hands we were all ushered into a car; I did not know where we were going, what we were doing, or even what time it was.

Though this was the first time I had visited Seattle, it was like returning to my old native city. The big billboards advertising cigarettes and movies were the same. Everything was neat and clean, and for the first time I felt a surge of joy.

After a thirty-minute drive we arrived at a big campus. It was the University of Washington. So we were to play at this beautiful big university, as we had long desired. Everything seemed like a dream. We were ushered into a big building with School of Music over the entrance. Refreshments were served in the lounge. I couldn't remember if we had had lunch. While we were having tea, milk, and cake, Mr. Sokol came in and told Mr. Suzuki and myself that the performance was to begin within fifteen minutes. I gulped my tea and coughed. I didn't expect to have the concert immediately upon our arrival, but the program was so arranged and the hall was almost full.

We all marched into a small but beautiful hall. Mr. Sokol gave a short address introducing Mr. and Mrs. Suzuki and myself. I introduced Mr. Hirose, Mrs. Shizuko Suzuki, the children, and their mothers.

Then the concert began. The first number was Sonata by Eccles. Since then this became a kind of rule and every year the children played this piece first. It was followed by Menuetto No. 3 by Bach. Then Mr. Suzuki went up onto the stage to speak; he asked me to interpret:

> Ladies and Gentlemen. It is a great pleasure to be here with you. For more than twenty years I have been convinced that every child can develop his abilities. Every child in the world can speak and understand his complicated native language, which is difficult for us adults to master. Children have a wonderful potential for adapting themselves to circumstance. These children are not special or selected children. They are from ordinary homes where there is no musical background. We are visiting your country to demonstrate that all these children have developed their abilities through the violin.

Again, though this was my first experience in translating Mr. Suzuki's words, I was calm and not excited. It was so easy and people listened so attentively that it gave us great encouragement.

Now we will have a little demonstration with the Bach Double Concerto. Of course you know well that this music is played by two persons, each playing a different melody, but today we will have six children play this music. Three will play the first violin part and the other three, the second. While they are playing, I will give them a sign, and they will begin marching while playing. This is not a stunt, but a demonstration to show how children's abilities have developed.

The children began the Double Concerto and when Mr. Suzuki gave the signal, one group marched to the right while the other marched to the left. They even went down the stairs and walked through the aisle. Then they came back, lined up facing the audience, and ended perfectly. "Wonderful!" "Unbelievable." "Amazing!" were the words I heard from the audience. The children then played several ensembles and solos, ending with Yukari Tate playing *Poème* by Chausson. When we all went out on stage, everyone in the audience was on his feet, clapping. It was our first standing ovation, and I was happy because I knew the audience understood and appreciated the performance.

We ate our supper at the school cafeteria that evening. It was our first experience with self-service, and the various foods, all different in color and quality, looked very inviting. Each child took a plate and helped himself to more than he could eat. We were told that we were going to have another concert at eight in the same hall. Mr. Sokol took us to a big lobby where we rested until the concert. I was not at all tired, but excited and happy, when I noticed Hitomi sobbing in her mother's lap. I asked what was the matter. Mrs. Kasuya replied that she had a stomachache. I felt her forehead, confirming she had no fever. It was a plain stomachache, resulting from fatigue and eating too much on an empty stomach. I recalled that we had not eaten since early that morning. Hitomi looked so fragile and small in her mother's lap that my heart ached, thinking of the heavy schedule which had just begun. I gave her a pill and she slept for some time; then she felt better.

The house was full that evening; there was standing room only. The concert was successful and there was even more applause than at the afternoon performance. But after the concert the children were exhausted, and they all hurried to the homes of their hosts.

I was invited to stay in Mr. Shober's house with Mr. Hirose and Ryugo Hayano, a ten-year-old boy. Mr. Shober, who worked for the Great Northern Railroad, lived with his wife and two daughters in a beautiful house. This was my first experience in staying in an American home, and everything was interesting. We forgot the time and spoke of politics, the economy, and other topics, but of course the main subject was education. I learned from Mr. Shober that the hosts who were accommodating the group were parents of students attending Ingraham High School. The reason was that the music teacher was interested in Talent Education and, besides, the school chorus was to visit Japan in the autumn.

Next morning we had to be at Ingraham High School by eight to appear on local television. I never had such a trying time getting up in the morning, and I presumed the children would have even more difficulty, but I found them waiting at the school, smiling and refreshed.

They performed a little concert and then Professor Sokol asked Mr. Suzuki and me to visit Holy Name Academy on Capitol Hill. We went up the hill and got out of the car near the school. It was very quiet and peaceful, and I fell in love with the place. The attractive building was constructed of large stones in an ancient style. It was dark inside and the ceiling was high. We were ushered into the corridor and told to wait a few minutes. Then one of the sisters beckoned us in. It was a small hall and I was surprised to see about twenty children, boys and girls of different nationalities, standing in a row holding violins. With a sign from the sister, they began to play "Twinkle, Twinkle, Little Star," "Lightly Row," "Song of the Wind," "Go Tell Aunt Rhody," and ended with the Brahms Waltz. Mr. Suzuki just stared, amazed to think that the seed of Talent Education had already taken root, even before our first visit.

Sister Mary Anella introduced herself and told us that she began the program after attending John Kendall's workshop. This indeed was a pleasant surprise.

We ate our lunch on our way to the airport to take the same Northwest flight #8 to Chicago. The plane was to leave at 2:55 p.m. I did not know or care how much time was left before the flight. So many things had happened in these two days that I lost track of time. When the Northwest Airlines agent saw us arrive, he called to us to hurry. The plane was leaving in a few moments. We all walked calmly, and I stopped on the way to buy some slides. Before we knew it, we were on the plane en route to Chicago. Keiko was sick again.

Mr. Shober wrote the following in my notebook before we departed: "We are honored to be your host. We wish you every happiness as you cross our country. May this be the start of an everlasting friendship."

We thought Chicago was a most beautiful city from the air. It was all light and bright. Nobody ever suspects, seeing it from the sky, that there is a dark side to this city.

Now on a domestic airline, we had no trouble with customs and went right through. Mr. Angel Reyes and his colleague from Northwestern University were waiting at the gate.

After greeting each other, we sped on the dark highway to Evanston without going through the city. All the cars pulled up before the North Shore Hotel where Mr. Reyes told me our lodgings would be. The children were happy to know that we all were to stay here together. Yasuko Ohtani's father, who was studying at the University of Wisconsin, was waiting for his wife and daughter. We gave them one room, Mr. and Mrs. Suzuki another, and I lodged with Mr. Hirose. Fumiyo Kaneko and Yukari Tate, both 14, shared a room, and each mother took one child besides her own.

Dividing and delivering the luggage was another job but by 11 p.m. everything was settled. Yukari and Fumiyo talked far into the night. I knocked on the wall and told them to go to sleep as tomorrow would be a busy day.

Next morning Mr. Reyes took us sightseeing around Lake Michigan. The snow was flickering down from the gray sky onto the black water. The horizon was misty, cloudy, and dark. Wood pilings, half rotten, were protruding from the water. Waves were splashing on the pilings and onto the shore. It was a dismal sight.

The concert began at 1 p.m. in University Hall. The building was old, but the atmosphere was serene and suitable for a concert. Besides the ensemble, Mr. Suzuki had each child play a solo. I felt that they did not play as well as they should, but the audience was enthusiastic.

Next morning, as Mr. Suzuki and I are Rotarians, Mr. Reyes took us to the headquarters of Rotary International. We trudged through knee-deep snow to the entrance. Though it was Sunday, a person in charge was waiting for us and took us around the building.

The objective of Rotary International is to serve others, which, in philosophy, is similar to that of Talent Education. The main difference is that Rotary is for adults and Talent Education is for children. While looking at the many flags of different countries, I thought that perhaps in the future our movement could be international like Rotary.

It was snowing when we arrived at St. Louis. Mr. John Kendall with his staff from Southern Illinois University was waiting for us at the airport. He had been recruited from Muskingum College to Southern Illinois University. This school, I was told, was newly established in Edwardsville and wanted to develop a good string program in the music department. When we met at the gate, we just embraced each other and no words were necessary. We understood what the other felt perfectly, and the silence was more eloquent than any words.

Late in the afternoon we sat in the lobby and talked about

the situation in the United States. Mr. Kendall told us that after returning from Japan, he visited various schools throughout the country and gave lectures and workshops. He had done a wonderful job of spreading the ideals of Talent Education. He acted as John the Apostle for Talent Education in America and indeed was worthy of his name. I am amazed to observe what wonderful potentialities humans possess. Of course, a man's power is limited in many ways. But when he acts as a match to light the paper, the fire will spread to wood and then to coal and great energy can be produced.

Early the next morning I was awakened by a call from Yasuko's host. She told me that Yasuko had caught cold and had a fever. Her mother wanted me to make a call and my host drove me to the home where the patient was. The snow was still falling and it was very cold. I shivered and felt a chill going up and down my spine.

I sneezed and I knew I had caught a cold, also. During the morning, the children presented a concert twice at the branch of Southern Illinois University in St. Louis. This was mainly for students and I did not know how it appealed to them.

Mr. Kendall and his colleagues took us to the Botanical Garden in St. Louis. It was warm inside and we appreciated the warmth more than the flowers. On our way back to Alton, the car Keiko was in stopped by the roadside. I got out of Mr. Kendall's car to see what had happened. Keiko was sick, and I took her out of the car and nursed her.

Snow was now falling heavily and I felt a bad chill go down my spine again. That night the concert was held in a church. The chapel was full of people who had traveled in the heavy snow, which nearly covered the windows. I had a headache and felt feverish. The scene of the audience giving a standing ovation blurred before my eyes.

When we arrived in New York the next day en route to Boston, Mr. Kenji Mochizuki was waiting for us at the airport. I met him for the first time and we talked about things that had happened and future plans. The plane to Boston was to leave at 2 p.m. By two o'clock the snowfall had turned into a blizzard and the announcement was made that the flight would be delayed. I went to the National Airlines counter to inquire about the time of delay. They told us they did not know and hinted of the possibility that the plane might not fly at all in such heavy snow. We had not, of course, reserved any hotel rooms, and besides, many people were waiting for us in Boston. But all we could do was sit on the bench and wait. Time passed slowly.

We sat waiting for an hour when suddenly an announcement informed us that the plane would depart and all passengers were to go on board. It was like a voice from heaven.

In Boston, members of the faculty of the New England Conservatory of Music were waiting for us. We were rushed onto the bus and driven to the school. Mr. Chester Williams, president of the school, was standing at the entrance and told us that the audience was waiting in the hall. I thought the concert was to be held at night and told Mr. J. C. Kennedy, who had escorted us from the airport, that we had not had lunch.

On hearing this, they took us to the president's office and served us some delicious apples. While munching apples, we tuned the instruments and then went out into the hall. The hall was big and the acoustics were good. That night at eight o'clock, the children performed for the second time.

The next morning, we flew back to New York and in the afternoon presented a concert in the Dag Hammarskjöld Auditorium of the United Nations building. Before the concert, Mr. Suzuki gave a short address:

> Dear friends, today we have come here from Japan to give you a concert. The children from six to fourteen will play various pieces of classical music. The main purpose for our tour in the United States is to demonstrate that every child in the world can develop his abilities. I do not know how many languages are spoken in this United Nations but all children in all countries will speak their mother tongue. This is eloquent testi-

mony that they can develop other abilities. We have brought children from Japan to play the violin. This is to demonstrate that even in a country where Western musical influence is not so popular, the children can play violin with wonderful skill and sensitivity.

We have been developing the hearts of children through violin. I hope you will do it with the children in your countries. The world's future lies on the shoulders of the children.

There were tears in many eyes, listening to the words and hearing the children's performance.

Next day we played at the Juilliard School of Music, the ivory tower of the musical world. There were many Japanese students studying in this school, and I heard the rumor that they were afraid of getting a bad reputation if the children did not play well.

I replied to these charges: "We are here to demonstrate what we are doing in Japan. If we are criticized, that is all right. It will be a good lesson to us. Our method is, of course, not perfect or ideal. We are here to demonstrate the Talent Education method and hear what people say about it. We will proceed with our program."

The hall was filled, mostly with students. Dorothy De Lay gave a word of introduction and then the concert began.

We received a warm reception but did not know how our ideal or method appealed to these people. A column in *Newsweek* gave us some idea of our reception:

Fiddling Legions
Seven-year-old Asako Hata playfully dropped a chunk of ice down her neighbor's back, and the long table of children at lunch one day last week burst into delighted giggles. Forty minutes later, Asako was standing on the stage of New York's august Juilliard School of Music, bobbing her head shyly to acknowledge the thunderous clapping that greeted her performance of a complicated Veracini violin sonata.

The solo climaxed a concert that was at once impressive and absurd, in which ten tiny Japanese children, ranging in age from 5 to 14, played Bach and Vivaldi with a skillful authority that drew bravos from a highly critical audience of Juilliard students and faculty. If their applause was tinged with sentimentality (when the children's teacher, Prof. Shinichi Suzuki, stepped on stage to tune a 5-year-old's quarter-size violin, the audience sighed), it was nonetheless wholly deserved. "This is amazing," said Juilliard violin Prof. Ivan Galamian. "They showed remarkable training, a wonderful feeling for the rhythm and flow of the music."

Playing without a conductor and using no scores, the youngsters were a living testimonial to the validity of Suzuki's unorthodox teaching method. He starts his children at about 3, but the first lessons are for the child's mother. She comes once a week with her youngster, and after three months has normally progressed to "Twinkle, Twinkle, Little Star." "By that time," Suzuki explains in a mixture of German and English as expressive as his thin face, "the child has watched the mother play and wants to imitate her." Only then is the pupil given a pint-size violin. Through exposure to classical recordings and constant repetition, the child is ready to tackle simple Bach gavottes within a year. The 150,000 children Suzuki's system has trained in 30 years are far from robots. They combine virtuosity with feeling so successfully that when Pablo Casals heard a Suzuki recital in Tokyo, he rushed to the stage, shouting "Bravo" and hugging the children.

Sensitivity Although about 5 percent of Suzuki's students make careers in music, the 65-year-old professor insists: "I just want to make good citizens. If a child hears good music from the day of his birth, and learns to play it himself, he develops sensitivity, discipline, and endurance. He gets a beautiful heart."

Suzuki thoughtfully crinkled a few of the paper-wrapped candies he carries for his musicians. "If nations cooperate in raising good children, there won't be any war."

Suzuki has done more than revolutionize violin teaching in Japan. Oberlin music Prof. Clifford Cook says: "What Suzuki has done for young children earns him a place among the benefactors of mankind, along with Schweitzer, Casals, and Tom Dooley."

It was cold in New York. Though the sun smiled shyly it did not have the energy to melt the snow. People were thronging to the West Chestnut Country Hall for the performance. The house was sold out. When we were in the hall preparing for the concert, a loud voice was heard near the entrance. Mr. Suzuki went to see the reason and found that a Japanese family—Mr. and Mrs. Okaya who could not obtain tickets was asking if there was any possibility of getting in. Of course they could. Later they arranged for their daughter to begin violin study and helped open a non-profit Talent Education organization in Hastings-on-Hudson, New York.

Next morning we traveled to Trenton by bus. The children were happy and began singing a song. This was our first opportunity to relax, and we were in good spirits in the bus all by ourselves. The name Trenton was familiar to me in connection with the Revolutionary War. The Delaware River was a rapidly flowing, large body of water. The city was old and quiet.

On our arrival in Philadelphia, we went to the Sheraton Hotel. Already the big lobby was crowded. Before the performance television cameras were shooting the children from all angles; then at 10:00 a.m., the concert began. The hall was packed and people were even sitting on the stairs. Mr. Kendall gave the following opening address:

There are moments in history when a place, a time,
a man, and an idea converge to produce results of great
significance . . .

Such an historical moment occurred when Shinichi
Suzuki began his experiments in violin teaching in Japan.
The results have attracted widespread attention and
have generated much speculation about the nature of
musical learning and the way in which every human
being develops in the early formative years. It is not
that any particular segment of Suzuki's ideas is new,
but rather that the totality of his concepts, together
with the results he has shown, throw a clear light on
a question we all wish to explore—how do human beings
become musical?

Suzuki's ideas have struck fire in America because
they go directly to the heart of a process universally
intriguing: how infant human beings emerge from early
shapelessness to the phenomenal powers of the formative years. In the understanding of this process, as
Suzuki points out, lies the future of the human race.

It would seem that we have only begun to recognize
the learning capacities of very young children. It is
likely that teachers and parents who seek an easy way
will be disappointed. However, those who have the
energy, the imagination, and the courage to experiment,
to change, and to grow with the teaching process will
certainly find stimulation in the ideas of Suzuki. In a
decade, the stimulation of his experiments has moved
violin teaching and performing to the forefront of
educational experiment and study—a move which can
only result in profound and positive influence on both.
Countless teachers, parents, and students in all parts
of America are already successfully illustrating that
Suzuki's ideas bear fruit in our own country as well
as in Japan.

The relevancy of Suzuki's ideas may be demonstrated
best through the constant work and expert teaching of

dedicated people, and it is appropriate that his faith lies ultimately in the great abilities of human beings to improve themselves and their way of life. In addition to the success of his teaching methods—a success so dramatically demonstrated by his own pupils—we owe a debt to Shinichi Suzuki for his wide and significant contribution to the human condition.

The concert began and the audience listened very attentively. The children played as usual without any rigidness or tension. People often ask why the children don't get stagefright. Maybe one of the reasons is that they have been playing since they were so young that it becomes part of their nature and they do not think they are doing something special. In a way, instead of speaking through their mouths they are speaking through violins. Second, in Talent Education, we often have concerts at classes and we also encourage the parents to have concerts at home as much as possible. So when they have guests visiting their home, the children are asked to play before them. Third, and perhaps most important, is that when you are doing something in which you have perfect confidence, you will not become overly excited. Mr. Suzuki stresses that real ability has developed when you can play even while doing something else. So we often have a game which will show these abilities. Children will play while marching or answering questions. To achieve this goal, practice is necessary, until the brain will work subconsciously. A concert cannot always be performed under perfect conditions and you are apt to get excited if the situation is not as good as you expected. If one has developed real ability, one can play without failure, overcoming all obstacles.

After each performance a murmur of astonishment ran through the audience who then burst into loud applause. When Yukari played the Chausson *Poème* at the end of the concert everyone was on his feet clapping.

Later Dr. Robert Klotman, president of the American

154

String Teachers Association, wrote the following article:

Suzuki: "Pied Piper of Fiddledom"

In 1964, as president of the American String Teachers Association, it was my privilege to serve on the committee, with John Kendall and Clifford Cook, that made it possible for the MENC convention in Philadelphia to see and hear the remarkable students of Shinichi Suzuki. For four years we had heard about Mr. Suzuki's wonderful achievements in Japan and here was our opportunity to observe the results for ourselves.

I shall never forget the impact of the convention performance. Teachers and musicians were so overcome with emotion by the artistry of these small children that there were tears in many eyes.

It is now eleven years since the name Shinichi Suzuki was introduced to this country. His concepts, his innovations in string instruction, and his imaginative approach have aroused an interest in strings that is unprecedented in the annals of string teaching.

Today pre-school centers and early elementary instrumental classes offer string instruction as an accepted fact. It could not have been accomplished without the inspiration and vision of Mr. Suzuki. He opened the doors and made us aware of the great potential inherent in small children. This man is truly a man of vision.

In addition Mr. Suzuki has added a dimension of parental involvement that has assumed a positive connotation which is contributing greatly to improved instruction. As the "Pied Piper of Fiddledom," he has forced all string teachers to reassess their value regarding the approach to string instruction.

After the performance, we went back to the hotel to have lunch and bring in our luggage. When we entered the lobby, Mr. Suzuki turned around and embraced me. We uttered no words, but understood each other's feelings perfectly.

In the afternoon we were to have two more concerts, one in Convention Hall, the other in some hotel the name of which I did not know, and then we were to fly to Cleveland. There was now a difficult problem of how to carry our luggage. It was impossible to bring it to the hall, then reload, find a sufficient number of taxis and move on. Fortunately, Mr. Stanley Ralph, a son of my friend Mrs. Dorothy Ralph, who was a student at the University of Pennsylvania, understood our problem and volunteered to ask his friends to bring the luggage to the airport. This was indeed a great help and without their assistance we would have been in great trouble.

We hired five taxis for the day and kept them waiting at each place during the performance. After each concert we rushed to the next place. Of course it was expensive, but I thought it was worth the cost.

When we arrived at the airport, Stanley was waiting for me at the counter. He had checked all the luggage and the tickets were booked. Everything was completed and we even had time for tea in the lobby. I tried to repay the expense which I knew Stanley had incurred, but he declined, saying that it was his pleasure to help the cause. I appreciated his kind intention and withdrew my hand from trying to put cash in his pocket.

We arrived at the Oberlin Inn about nine o'clock that evening. All the hosts were waiting and we divided the group. I was to stay with Mr. Peacock, a faculty member at Oberlin College who lived next door to Mr. Cook. We talked until late that night. I was feeling much better and, after the success we had, was in high spirits. Mr. Peacock even offered me a glass of beer, saying that the sale of alcoholic beverages in the town of Oberlin was prohibited and they had to go to Cleveland to buy spirits.

The name Oberlin has always been dear to me. It was Oberlin that first introduced our film. It was Oberlin that first extended an invitation for this tour. It was Oberlin that even made a showcase to display materials concerning Talent Education. Tomorrow I would make a speech before the concert to thank the dean, the faculty, the students, and the citizens of the town.

I had not taken a bath since I caught cold in Alton. As tomorrow was an important day, at least I should be decent and clean, so I took a bath and washed my hair.

The next morning was a beautiful day. It might have been the first bright sunshine we saw in the United States. I dressed and walked to Mr. Cook's house; Mr. and Mrs. Suzuki were staying with them. I rang the bell and Mr. Cook came out. I said "Good morning," or tried to do so. To my amazement I had lost my voice. Try as I might, I could barely whisper. The cold had gone to my throat. Probably it was the beer or maybe the bath. I reproached myself for this rash act. On this most important day, of all things to happen, I had lost my voice.

Oberlin was a beautiful town with many trees. It was like a town in a park. Traffic was light and people walked easily on the street. The school was a combination of old and new. The old buildings were like picturesque castles, surrounded by green lawns and many trees. It was dark and cool inside these buildings. To sit on a bench and hear the pipe organ was as peaceful as hearing music in a chapel. In contrast, the new buildings were modern, with many windows. They were designed by Mr. Yamazaki, the famous Japanese architect. There were many rooms inside the Conservatory of Music building, and each room was equipped with a Steinway grand piano. The rooms had long windows allowing plenty of light from outside. I thought it was good for the students to have a view outside. Music is not composed of notes only. It is important in music not only to read notes faithfully or touch keys skillfully but also to have a serene feeling which can be developed by appreciating the beauty of nature. Through windows the students were able to see the change of seasons and the white fleecy clouds floating in the blue sky.

Everything was so perfect, we caught our breath. Compared to this school our furnishings at Talent Education were meager and miserable. Still, I thought, in spite of our poor condition, we have developed something which will enrich the world of the future.

The concert began at three o'clock. I tried to speak, but my voice failed. I tried harder, but it became worse. I felt as if somebody had cut my vocal cords. Tears came into my eyes and the only words I said were, "Thank you, dear friends."

We next went to Detroit, where it was very cold. The wind that blew from the border of Canada pierced my light overcoat and I was cold to the marrow. The performance was held at Wayne State University. Dr. Robert Klotman was chairman of the concert. He is a modest man, but I am sure he did a great deal to help the tour materialize.

Next day the host drove us to Greenfield Village. There were many buildings inside the village, showing collections of various vehicles old and new. The ladies taking us around the village wore heavy coats and high woolen socks. They began to explain the history of the village. "We have many old things in this village. Some are as old as our nation, but compared to your history these are not old at all."

Indeed there was a chair in which Abraham Lincoln was sitting when he was shot in the theater. But as the children did not have much knowledge of United States history, all these things which to me were very interesting did not mean much to them.

Mrs. Norman Lyle, an elderly lady, was waiting for us at the gift shop. I had received her letter in Japan which told me that her son was a friend of John Kendall and was a music teacher. He was killed in World War II in the South Pacific. He loved music and believed that music could be the medium of international understanding. Mrs. Lyle had heard about our movement from Mr. Kendall and understood the aims of Talent Education. She had overcome her grief and bitterness when she heard about the children and offered to buy presents for all the children. I called the children, introduced Mrs. Lyle and told them about her story. "Now you can buy anything you want and Mrs. Lyle will pay." Needless to say the children had great fun.

The school provided a bus and a driver. A student from Wayne sat beside him. We took the highway to the airport to catch our flight to Wichita, Kansas.

I was sitting in the front seat. I always like to arrive at least an hour before the flight. It takes some time to book in and check the luggage, and besides the small children will always want to go to the toilet at the last minute. Time was going fast and the airport was still not in sight.

"Do you know how long it takes to get to the airport?" I asked.

"I don't know. Do you?" the driver asked the student.

"I am not sure," the boy answered in an uncertain voice.

Suddenly I realized that these boys were not sure of their way to the airport and for the first time I was upset.

"We are leaving Detroit at 3:50 p.m. Do you think you can make it?"

"I am not so sure," came back the reply. "I don't know the road that takes us off this highway."

While he was speaking we passed a sign reading, "To Airport."

"Oh, I missed it, we have to go three miles up and turn back. Now I know the road."

We arrived only ten minutes before flight time. I jumped off the bus and ran to the counter. We barely made it.

After playing at Wichita State University, we flew to Tucson, Arizona. It was the first really sunny day since we arrived in this country, and I felt my cold melting like ice in warm sunshine. The reception was held in a restaurant on the second floor of the airport. Beyond the big airfield continued a prairie or desert straight to the horizon. The sun had set and the whole sky was glowing pink and red. Slowly, very slowly, the color turned dark, vermilion and purplish. I sat looking, enchanted. Then the sky changed into deep indigo blue, and only the hue of the past glory was left in the western horizon. Twilight set in and stars began flickering. The dark veil covered the earth and night came.

The performance was held at the University of Arizona. The hall was so full chairs had to be installed on the stage. The children played with part of the audience at their backs. Sunny Southern California was indeed worthy of its name. We saw many oranges strewn on the ground on the way to San Fernando Valley State College. It was warm and we relished the sunshine.

Next day we took the children to Disneyland. This was their first recreation and they enjoyed it very much. Mr. Ross Beckstead negotiated with the office and they gave us free tickets to enter. But later we found that there was a request for the children to play at a restaurant. We did not like this idea, so I went to the office and explained that our concerts were for educational purposes, and I was sorry to say that it was impossible for the children to play for the sake of entertainment. Since this was the children's first recreation and as they were enjoying it so much, if necessary we would prefer to pay our admission. The man at the office understood us and said that it wasn't necessary to pay or play.

On Sunday March 22, late in the evening we arrived in San Francisco. We divided the group and each host took some of the children to his home. I was to stay with Mr. Jackson Trippy.

The California String Teachers Association was having a conference in San Mateo and we were invited to play at the convention. The room was flat and in the middle of the hall was a square platform about three feet high. As the children were so small, Mr. Suzuki sometimes had to put them on chairs so they could be seen at the rear. This was the last concert held on the mainland.

After the concert Mr. Trippy took us to San Francisco. We drove past my old home at 2039 Pine Street. Time had not changed it a bit. I walked up and down the stairs, then asked Mr. Trippy to drive down to Buchanan Street to the old Japanese school, Kinmon Gakuen. The distance from my house to the school was much shorter than I supposed, and the school and its playground was also smaller than I remembered.

Our next stop, Honolulu, was like a paradise. It was warm, even hot, in our coats, and I smothered in the sweet fragrance of the lei that was put around my neck. Half of our hosts were Japanese and the children enjoyed speaking Japanese and eating Japanese foods.

I stayed at the home of my old friends, Barney and Eiko Sato. It was the first time I had seen them since they were married. The flowers by the windowsill were bright and the hummingbirds flew with a buzzing noise. This was Hawaii.

The concert was held in a high school auditorium. The Honolulu Youth Symphony conducted by Peter Mesrobian played the first part of the program. Then our last concert began. During the intermission I went out on the porch to breathe the fresh air. It was warm, dreamy. The stars were twinkling. Tomorrow we would be back in Tokyo.

The Pan Am flight was to leave Honolulu at 1:15 p.m. All our hosts and friends saw us off, shaking hands, hanging leis and even kissing us on the cheek. We embarked on the plane and as soon as we sat down, we heard an announcement: "Ladies and gentlemen, due to engine trouble, the flight will be delayed. Please go back to the lobby and wait for further information." We all went back to the lobby and entered the cafeteria, where we ordered cool drinks. The breeze was blowing and we were glad to be delayed and stay longer on this beautiful island.

Yukari and Fumiyo were sitting by my side. They were old enough to understand what I said. "By mere fortune we are here, instead of flying with high speed in the air. The delay, as I know, will be four hours. I am sure you feel happy to be here another four hours, don't you?" They nodded. "Did you ever think of time? Time is moving every minute, every second. Here we are in this cool breeze enjoying our drink. But within a few hours, we will be on the plane and in another eight hours we will be back in Tokyo. Sometimes I feel life is like a dream. When we wake up tomorrow, we will find ourselves in our own beds. And all of the past will be like a dream.

"The difference between life and the dream is, in life we have lived every moment and left a spark which will kindle fire within many people's hearts. Some people will live for a hundred years and some only twenty. Of course those who lived one hundred years have been in this world longer, but that does not necessarily mean they have spiritually lived long. Compared to the busy schedule since yesterday, we are at this moment doing nothing. But this is a very precious moment, a moment you will cherish a long, long time."

In the plane I was busy again. I had to make a financial record of the trip and, every time I calculated, I had a wrong answer. I was tired and gave up figuring.

Returning home, I weighed myself and found I had lost twenty pounds in three weeks.

YUKO GOES TO
THE UNIVERSITY OF WASHINGTON

After returning, I often woke up in the night dreaming that one of the children was missing. My wife told me that I even screamed in my dreams, "Look out!" or "Take care!" My body was slow to adapt to the time difference, and every morning I woke up at four o'clock. I utilized this time in writing reports and finishing accounts.

I received a letter from Mrs. Lyle in Birmingham, Michigan.

April 9, 1964

Dear Dr. Honda:

I was very glad to have your good letter, and have gone over, in retrospect, many times, the very happy hour I had with all of you in Dearborn. My nephew, Douglas Lyle, heard you in Philadelphia. He phoned me and asked me to be sure to hear the children play, and also to meet you in Dearborn and give the children an opportunity to make their own choices of little souvenirs of their trip over here. I was very grateful for this opportunity, and to get to meet Professor Suzuki and his wife, your good self, and the precious children. Carol had taught some of Mr. John Kendall's students when he left Muskingum to teach at another college. She had not only her own little girls but others who had been taught the Suzuki method for over a year, and she was enthusiastic over the results she achieved with them. I wonder if you know that the audience that heard the performance in Detroit numbered almost a thousand, many of whom had traveled a hundred miles or more to hear the demonstration. All of our Detroit Symphony men were there and, of course, hundreds of teachers, all of whom spoke glowingly of Dr. Suzuki and his method.

Too many of our American children of this generation are glued to their television sets and waste their time during these fruitful years listening to good music which they cannot identify and which is background music for cartoons! Their lives would be so much richer if they learned to produce good music themselves. The music is a universal language that everyone understands and I am fully convinced that the "peace on earth" which we all desire can come about only through the riches of the mind which we can share as nations.

Surely the instruments of war have done nothing but engender bitterness and heartache. The beauty and dignity of life must be preserved at all costs and unless prejudice is taught these dear children, they readily love and enjoy one another.

I am interested to learn about your family and their musical interests. My dear little Japanese friend, who visited in Birmingham a few years ago and who is a fine little pianist, has married and gone to Kenya with her husband. She had about 30 piano pupils and I know she was not happy about this move away from Tokyo. She, too, had invited me to visit your beautiful country, and many friends here have visited you and I hope some day I can visit you, too.

My older son, of whom I spoke (an Oberlin student),

had many friends of other races and cultural backgrounds and one of them was a young Japanese gentleman who was working for his doctorate at Oberlin in 1943, when my son was killed in action. It was a senseless sacrifice of many young lives of promise who could have done so much to make a better world in a better way. He loved fine music and would have so enjoyed your children and their music. Give my regards to Professor and Mrs. Suzuki and tell them there will be a big welcome for them, and for all of you, when you come to us again. I am sending your letter on to Douglas Lyle—for his whole family will enjoy reading it.

Cordially yours,
Amy Lyle

I was very moved by her letter, so I translated it into Japanese and had it printed in our magazine.

Yuko had graduated from Misono Girls' High School while I was abroad.

I had already written to her about studying at the University of Washington and she and her mother had made up their minds to follow this advice.

It was of course very difficult for Junko to have her daughter leave home and live in a foreign country where the language and customs were different from ours. The most important thing was for Yuko to master English conversation, so she began attending Language School in Tokyo.

Meanwhile, in April, I received a formal letter inviting Yuko to come to the University of Washington. The condition was that if she would teach violin by the Suzuki method, she would be offered a full scholarship.

In June Miss Jeannette Scott wrote me a letter expressing her desire to visit Japan. I remembered her because during our stay in Seattle, she gave the children many postcards of Oregon. She was living in Salem, Oregon, and taught strings in a teachers college.

Professor Sokol and I exchanged letters paving the way for

Yuko. One day I went to the Foreign Office to inquire about the procedure for getting her a passport. To my surprise, I found that there was a government examination in English for those who wanted to study abroad. I knew Yuko's English was not sufficient, and usually those who enter a university in the United States finish their college course before going abroad. I told the man in charge that her case was different, that the University of Washington had already given her a scholarship and that all papers for her admission were completed. But the examination was required.

So one day she went to the Foreign Office to take this exam. She was the only high-school graduate, while all others were from universities. She failed. Now we were in trouble. We never thought of encountering such an obstacle, and everything had been prepared for her departure. I wrote letters to Mr. Sokol telling him of the result, explaining that the examination was purely the Japanese method of selection and if some person guaranteed an affidavit of support, she could go. His answer was not encouraging. Maybe my explanation of this examination system was insufficient and he could not grasp the idea. (This system was abolished the next year.)

Miss Scott arrived in Tokyo on June 12. I had promised to meet her at the airport. Junko and I arrived thirty minutes before her scheduled time, so, calculating the time she needed for immigration and customs, we thought there was a good full hour before she would come out.

When we went down to the gate, I found to my dismay that her plane had arrived early and all the passengers had already disembarked. As I did not remember her face, I was very troubled and slowly went upstairs to the lobby. At the top of the stairs a foreign lady with a smile approached and said, "You are Dr. Honda."

"Of course, of course, and you are Miss Scott."

We shook hands in greeting. Because of my stupidity we could have missed each other, making it difficult for both of us. I took her to International House in Tokyo, and we talked until late that night.

While she was in Tokyo, I took Miss Scott to many classes and later Yuko accompanied her to Matsumoto. Before she left for home after her three weeks' visit, we talked about Yuko's problem. "Why don't you have her come and visit me in Salem? She can stay at my home and attend the college lectures. Also I will be delighted to have her help me in teaching." Her proposal was like finding an oasis in the desert; we all were satisfied and grateful.

Yuko gave a farewell recital at Kugenuma Auditorium on July 18. The program consisted of the Brahms Sonata No. 1 in G Major and the Mendelssohn Concerto in E Minor.

During the intermission Mr. Suzuki gave a short talk on "How to Develop Sensitivity."

Then she finished her program by playing short pieces like "La Gitana" by Kreisler and Sicilienne and Rigaudon by Francoeur-Kreisler. Many people crowded the small hall, including Sister Ignatia from Misono Girls' High School, Mr. Egil Nygaard, the Norwegian Ambassador, and his wife came from Tokyo. We had a reception in the hall; it was a wonderful farewell party.

September 11 was my fiftieth birthday. We invited many friends and relatives to a Chinese restaurant in Kamakura to have a combined celebration and farewell party. Yuko was to leave the next day.

If I said we were not sorry to see our daughter off, it would not be true. But Junko and I agreed that there should be no tears. Next evening we saw her off at Haneda Airport. Many of her friends and mine came to say good-bye. Yuko kept smiling and so did we. A friend took a picture of her clasping her hands as if praying. "This," she said, "I will do to the immigration officers. I will not understand what they say, and they will not understand me. I will only say please, please." I looked away, hiding my tears.

She left, the first teacher from Japan to spread the ideals and methods of Talent Education in the United States.

Yuko's absence left an emptiness in our hearts and home. The sound of her violin was gone. I forgot she had left and called, "Yuko, Yuko" in a loud voice. It came back hollow and empty. I pretended I didn't miss her. And I think Junko, Mayako, and even little Asami were pretending as well.

Junko noticed the lonesome face of Mayako, catching her unguarded. But maybe Junko suffered more than the rest of the family. One day she went out and bought a puppy, a Maltese, three months old, small, fluffy, and white. I asked the price and gasped—200,000 yen. But I kept quiet. She was of good breed and her family name was Jupy Lord, an arrogant name. We named her Marshmallow but called her Marshy for short. The dog was not as clever as we thought she should be. I tried to teach her tricks but she just cocked her head and did nothing. I gave up.

The first letter from Yuko arrived within ten days. We all crowded around while Junko eagerly opened the envelope.

Dear Father, Mother, and Sisters:

You might be surprised but I am living in Seattle instead of Salem. When I arrived at the Seattle Airport, Miss Scott was waiting for me at the gate. Of course I recognized her immediately and she greeted me warmly. I was very relieved because if there had been no one waiting for me I would have been lost. Then she introduced me to a tall gentleman, telling me his name was Mr. Sokol. Of course I knew his name. It was ringing in my ears all through these past months. I thought he was just there to greet me, but to my surprise he told me that instead of going to Portland I was to stay in Seattle.

Miss Scott and Professor Sokol had been talking about me and they concluded that I should stay in Seattle and go to the University of Washington as was first decided.

Mr. Sokol said that during the summer vacation he had been away from home, had not seen my letters, and was not aware of our plans. Miss Scott called him when she returned and told him that I was coming to Salem. He was very surprised to hear this and argued with Miss Scott that I should stay here. Miss Scott consented and so I am now living in Mr. John Hilton's home. Mr. Hilton works at the Boeing Company as an engineer. There are six children; the eldest, Kathy, is about my age and attends Seattle University. Bob is 16, Judy 14, Butch 12, and the two small girls are Laurie, 7, and Rita, 5.

I think when Mr. Sokol asked for a family who would take a Japanese girl, the Hiltons volunteered because they have so many children that adding one more would not mean so much. The first night I sat at the table, everybody was very quiet. They knew I did not understand English, so in order not to embarrass me, they refrained from speaking with each other. The next day Mrs. Hilton took me out for a drive. The city was beautiful and the University so big and clean. I never dreamed that I would attend such a school.

We went across the lake by a floating bridge. Can you imagine a bridge, spanning a big lake? They say the road leads all the way to Chicago.

I feel a little lonesome but I will try to overcome it. I must get used to the customs and food here and, most important, learn English.

Goodbye,
Yuko

Listening to the letter, I was surprised to learn how the situation had changed in ten days, but was glad that it had turned out well.

I wrote immediately to Mr. Sokol, Miss Scott, and Mr. Hilton, thanking them for their kindness and for their trouble. Within ten days Yuko had jumped into a completely different situation and, though there was a little anxiety in the bottom of my heart, I was confident that she would adapt to her environment in a very short period.

We received a letter from Yuko every week, telling in detail of her life in Seattle in the home of the Hiltons, her relationship with the children, the ways of her American home and her schooling. So we knew well what kind of life she was leading and in a way we felt closer to her.

In early December, we received a very interesting letter:

Dear Father and Mother,
Last week Professor Sokol took me to the
Immigration Office to change my visa. In a very serious
atmosphere Mr. Sokol took an oath that he would
accept responsibility for me and also produced papers
that I was important in the school to help teach Suzuki's
method. It was called an affidavit of support. In this
paper, Mr. Sokol had to write the amount of his wealth
and guarantee that if something happened, he would
pay for my trip back home. I was filled with awe to
witness the solemnity of the procedure. I was told that
many people come from Japan and try to change their
visas, so naturally the procedure has to be strict. Will
you please write a letter and thank Mr. Sokol?
Every morning Mrs. Hilton drives me to the University
and I study music. During the first and second months
after my arrival I could understand almost nothing of
the lectures. But as music is international, I have no
trouble in performance and the students are very friendly. In the afternoon I change into a teacher.
Can you imagine a little Japanese girl teaching big
American university students? I use little phrases like
"right arm up," "not parallel," or "bend your fingers,"
and they seem to understand. Of course I demonstrate
and have them do games, which we usually did in Talent
Education. [I chuckled imagining big husky boys
following the instruction of small Yuko turning around
and bending down with her violin.] Most of my students
are in Music Education and they will be music teachers
in the future. Twice a week I teach children at Holy
Name Academy with Sister Anella. They of course come
with their mothers and I teach just as we did in Japan.
They study hard and I like them very much. American
mothers are very cooperative.
These days, I have almost no trouble with daily

conversation. It was a good idea to live with an American family.

If I did not speak English, I should starve to death or die of thirst. They say necessity is the mother of invention, but I think necessity is the mother of developing abilities.

Yours,
Yuko

It was indeed a surprise to learn that Yuko had developed her English in such a short period. Some months ago, she had failed an English examination in Japan and now she was not only studying at the university but teaching. It was the same Yuko and surely she had not changed physically. So it was, of course, the environment which developed her abilities. Her ears had been trained through music, but in the study of English she had no advantage.

We can consider that she had the potentiality to develop within herself. Not only she but all persons her age would do the same if they were given a similar chance. This is testimony that "man is the son of his environment."

Ability or talent will be developed by a good environment. It is difficult, however, to define what a good or a bad environment is.

WHAT IS ENVIRONMENT?

Environment is something organic or inorganic which surrounds every person in this world. No living thing can survive without air. Yet the amount differs at different atmospheric levels. For instance, if we suppose that the amount of oxygen at sea level is 100 percent, it will be half that at 580 meters above sea level. The people in Tibet live at the highest atmospheric level on earth, and as a result they have broad chests and many red blood cells. The body has to adapt to its environment. If we are to climb Mt. Everest, we must rest for some time on our way to adapt ourselves to atmospheric pressure.

We can say the same about sun, light, soil, climate, and temperature. Some living things will adapt themselves to an environment in which others cannot exist.

It is the life within that works in various ways to preserve itself. It can change physical conditions and also abilities or knowledge without which man cannot survive. It is this life that enables the body to adapt and to develop various abilities. To develop these abilities, be it in jungle or civilized society, it is important to have good human relationships; or, in other words, to receive good instruction.

Mr. Suzuki likes to say, "Man is born with the laws of heredity and develops with the laws of ability."

We receive from our parents various physical hereditary factors. Every Japanese has black eyes and black hair, while other nationalities have their own distinctive coloring. This is due to heredity. But if an American boy with golden hair were brought to a Japanese home at the day of his birth and brought up by Japanese foster parents, he would speak only Japanese, eat Japanese food, and live according to Japanese custom. It is the same with a Japanese child in an American family. Needless to say, these abilities are developed by environment. But millions of children, born in their own home, and of course speaking their native language, fail to develop good abilities. It is evident that they possess great potential, but something is lacking in their environment that prevents them from developing their abilities.

Everybody in the world makes his living with his various abilities. These abilities, good or bad, are the result of past environment. The circumstances in which we live from the day of our birth, the human relationships between our parents, family, teachers, and friends all combine to make up our present character and abilities.

It seems as though there is some limit to the age at which the brain can absorb things. The deadline might be at the age of puberty. But those who have training in the fundamentals can develop equally even at later ages.

There are so many factors in the development of human

abilities that it is difficult to define what is a good environment. One thing that is positive is the need for good instructors as early as possible. Without good instructors it is difficult to develop good abilities. Even in nature the importance of beginning at an early age is apparent.

The nature of the honeybee is well studied. The queen lays eggs in different rooms; some will be queens, others workers and drones. Any female egg is potentially able to produce either a queen or a worker. The difference depends upon the food given the larvae. Larvae in queen cells are fed only royal jelly; larvae in worker cells are fed beebread. It can be shown experimentally that if a queen larva is destroyed and is replaced by a worker larva within a certain number of days, the latter will grow up to be a queen. This is because it is fed with royal jelly.

We do not always remember what happened when we were very young, but the environment up to age three has a great effect in molding our adult character.

The relationship between the father and mother has much to do with making a happy home. Children brought up in good homes of course have a better environment than those who are not. Grandparents, brothers, and sisters living at home also provide stimulation for a child.

But it is very difficult to judge an environment as good or bad. People are apt to think that a good environment consists of having plenty of money, food, and merriment, with no work. But considering that without stimulation, no ability, mental or physical, can be developed, of course this is out of the question.

One way of judging a good environment is by the fruit it produces. If the fruit is good, the circumstances for the tree were good.

NEW YEAR 1965

We missed Yuko. It was the first New Year since she was born that she was not with us, but I was not lonesome. In a way I was happy and contented to know I had accomplished something which I had so long desired to do. Now I could devote more time to my practice, which I had neglected. I had used much of my time and money for Talent Education, and I thought the most important part of my work was over.

On New Year's morning, it is a custom for all the family to wear their best clothes and sit at the table and congratulate each other. The women cook all the previous day to make enough food to last at least three days, so they need not tend to housework during the holiday. This is the day of peace, rest, and merrymaking.

There is a sweet rice wine called *Otoso,* which has a special flavor. The wine is poured into a small wooden cup and each member of the family takes a sip. This is thought to bring good luck and health.

Anyway we are all happy, or try to feel happy, and even if children misbehave, parents refrain from scolding them. Of course the children are happy. They have received presents at Christmas and now they receive spending money from parents or elderly relatives.

Every family follows this same pattern, and they all anticipate good fortune and health in the coming year. Nobody expects to lose. Everyone is confident that luck will be with him and he will be sure to win the game. He waits with high spirits for the game to begin. But as the days go by, he will be disillusioned by reality. Only a few win, and those who do win have the ability to utilize what few chances come.

One day we received a phone call from the United States. It was a surprise call from Yuko, and Junko jumped to the phone. About two weeks earlier, Mr. Sokol had told Yuko that there would be a contest held at the school. All students could participate and he suggested that she enter. Yuko hesitated as she was still unfamiliar with the customs and did not have confidence. Mr. Sokol encouraged her to try, telling her there would be no harm even if she did not win a prize.

So she entered. All those who participated were seniors, and they played very well. Yuko did her best but never thought she would win. But today when she went to class, one of her classmates shouted to her, "Yuko, you won eight hundred dollars!" She was so astonished that she stood still for a minute and then, realizing what it meant, rushed to Mr. Sokol's office. He was teaching a class, but Yuko knocked at the door and asked him to come out. Mr. Sokol left the class to see what had happened.

"Mr. Sokol, Mr. Sokol, I have won eight hundred dollars." Mr. Sokol smiled and looked down at the excited face of the small girl. Then he said slowly, "You have not won eight hundred dollars." Yuko's face fell. The words weighed heavily on her heart.

"You have won eighteen hundred dollars, not eight hundred." Yuko could not grasp his words for a second, but when she looked up at the smiling face, she understood that he was not kidding and that she had won first prize.

She ran out of the school, took the bus and went right to Mrs. Hilton's room. "Mother, I have won first prize," she cried with joy.

Mrs. Hilton put aside her work and hugged her. "You have given me the best birthday present." It was Mrs. Hilton's birthday. "Why don't you call home and tell your parents about winning the prize? You can afford it now."

Hearing the good news, we were all very happy.

SUZUKI'S FIRST WORKSHOP

One day I received a letter from Mr. Cook that his school and some others would like to have a workshop with Mr. Suzuki. It was the first time I had heard the word workshop, and it sounded strange. What I concluded was that Mr. Suzuki would demonstrate and lecture about his method and ideas to string teachers who enrolled for a period of six days in June.

I consulted with Mr. Suzuki, and he willingly agreed to visit the United States and give the workshop, but he requested that Yuko help in translating.

Mr. Suzuki was scheduled to leave Japan on June 12 and to stay in the United States for six weeks. He gave workshops at the University of Washington, Southern Illinois University, Peabody Conservatory of Music, Oberlin College, and San Francisco State College.

The workshop in Oberlin was held for three weeks and Yuko traveled with Mr. Suzuki from Seattle to help interpret. Besides Yuko, Hiroko Yamada and Hiroko Toba, both of whom were teaching in the United States, also helped translate.

Mr. Cook wrote his impressions of the workshop:

> Instead of the usual 3-ring circus type of workshop, the Suzuki workshop for the teaching of violin, held July 17, was geared to a single purpose. It provided, in depth, an opportunity for teachers to become acquainted with the thinking and the violin teaching of Shinichi Suzuki and thereby to eradicate, as much as possible, the common misconceptions on this subject. Miss Yuko Honda, who was acting as an interpreter, finds Mr. Suzuki difficult to work with because he likes to coin phrases with his own special meaning: "Soft iron" . . . "Frog tone" . . . "Strike!" (when a boy plays a passage exactly right) . . . "Important *nothing*" (the gap between staccato tones). The audience laughed when Mr. Suzuki used this expression, but within a second they all became very quiet, reflecting the deep meaning of this word . . . "Up bow natural for babies" (they work everything up to their mouths) . . . "Please open door before entering" . . . "Nice face important in playing" . . . "We don't play piano sideways, and the piano doesn't move around while being played" . . . "Your tone is glass" (after a lecture on the difference between diamond and glass) . . . "Don't make accessories bigger than people" . . . "Kreisler highway" (the part of the string between the bridge and the circle of the F hole).

> The result of the workshop could be understood from

the comments of many teachers attending: "These were the best two weeks of my life." "In this relationship of teacher with pupil lies not only the secret of a great teacher of the violin, but also of a great-hearted man. We are all a little better, both as teachers and as human beings, for having had this privilege."

Yuko later described to me the following interesting episode:

Mr. Suzuki was demonstrating his method of how to produce good tone. He asked someone to come onto the stage and follow his suggestions. A gentleman came up and a screen was placed between him and Mr. Suzuki so that both could be seen by the audience but not by each other. Mr. Suzuki asked the gentleman to play something. When he began to play, Mr. Suzuki suggested that he lower the right elbow a little. He did this and the tone became better. Then he made several other suggestions, and every time the gentleman followed his instructions, his tone improved. Observing this, the audience was simply amazed.

The gentleman happened to be a player in the Cleveland Orchestra. For Mr. Suzuki this was a simple matter. For thirty years he had been teaching himself in the same way.

One day Yuko was assisting Mr. Suzuki. All of a sudden he called her to the stage and she went up, thinking she was to interpret for him. He said to the audience, "Now we are going to have a memorization test. Miss Honda left Japan in April and is now studying at the University of Washington. I will test her to see if she still remembers all the pieces she learned in the past." As Yuko told me later, her heart began to thump because, leaving Japan and living with an American family, it was all she could do to dedicate her time to understanding the new language and adapting to life in a foreign country. She had not kept up her practice. And now she was going to be tested before all the American string teachers. If she failed, not only would she disgrace herself but also Talent Education. Fortunately she played all the pieces Mr. Suzuki requested. This kind of test is often done in Talent Education. At the beginning it seems a little difficult for children to memorize the piece, but as their studies continue they have no difficulty.

One hot day in August, I walked to the mailbox and found a letter from Yuko addressed to me. That seemed queer as she usually addressed her letters to Junko and me.

> Dear Father:
>
> When I was in Oberlin with Mr. Suzuki, Dr. Donald Shetler of Western Reserve University in Cleveland asked me if I could do a workshop at his school. I was reluctant to accept because the responsibility was very heavy. I consulted with Mr. Suzuki and he told me to try it, so I began taking notes every day from Mr. Suzuki's lectures. It is surprising how you absorb things when you are in earnest.
>
> The workshop was last week. Every afternoon I took a bus from Oberlin to Cleveland and someone was waiting for me at the bus stop. As a result, I think I did a nice job. Can you imagine a little girl teaching real string teachers? I was surprised to receive five hundred dollars for this work, and since then have been thinking about how I should use it. Then suddenly a wonderful idea struck me. Mr. Sokol proposed that I give a recital in November in University Hall. Now I will mail the five hundred to you. Can you bring Mother and come to the concert?

This indeed was a wonderful surprise, but I had to plan carefully before telling Junko. First I would need to add a considerable sum for the two of us to visit the United States. Second, we had to find a person who could take care of our home.

That night I let it slip softly. But of course Junko was sharp enough to grasp the whole plan in a minute. Her face glowed. "Of course, we must go! Why don't we ask your parents to come and live in our house? I am sure they would enjoy living by the seaside for a change." I was surprised to realize how quickly Junko could arrange all these details.

Since I was going, I wanted to make the most of my visit, so I wrote letters to Dr. Walter Haderer at San Francisco State College and to Dr. Phyllis Glass at the University of Southern California asking if they could arrange a time for me to give a lecture at their schools.

I received a letter from Mrs. Hilton inviting us to stay at their home. I also received a letter from Mr. and Mrs. Trippy inviting us to stay with them in San Francisco. Dr. Haderer arranged for me to speak at a string teachers meeting in his school and Dr. Glass also invited me to speak at her school.

I VISIT THE U.S. WITH JUNKO

On October 30, 1965, we flew straight to Seattle. All the Hiltons welcomed us to their home and to their hearts.

Next day we visited the University of Washington for Yuko's rehearsal. The school had rented a beautiful instrument for her, a Guarnerius made in 1775. I was surprised to learn this and admired the generosity of the American people. Renting a precious instrument is never done in Japan. During the year Yuko's playing had progressed a great deal and her tone was lovely. The boy accompanying her, a senior at the music school of the university, was excellent.

We thought Seattle a beautiful city and we loved the quiet peaceful atmosphere. We often took walks in the park on Capitol Hill. Very few people walked there, and on the green lawn we saw squirrels feeding and scampering up the trees. There was a high tower in the center of the park and from its top Lake Washington and other lakes all connected by canal could be seen. The museum was famous for its collection of jade. It was a quiet vacation for us and we enjoyed every minute in the city.

Yuko's recital was held at the same hall where we had played the year before. The main number on the program was the César Franck Sonata, and she played it beautifully.

Listening to the music, I recalled the days when she was a baby, and the hard time we had with her at her first lesson with Mr. Yamamura. How fast time flew. Now, at this moment, she was playing in a university hall in the United States, something which we never even dreamed would happen. I felt my eyes getting warm and a tear streaked down my cheek. Junko was touching her eyes, and I knew she experienced the same kind of emotion.

Dr. Haderer had made arrangements for me to speak at his college. I had brought along a 35 mm film of the First National Concert, which I considered very important for the audience to see. I called Dr. Haderer and asked him to have the projector ready. He answered that everything was ready except for a take-up reel, which they did not have.

The day before leaving for San Francisco, I went to the largest camera store downtown and asked for a 35 mm reel. When the clerk replied, "I am sorry but we don't have any," I thought I didn't hear him correctly and repeated, "I want a 35 mm reel."

"Sorry, we have none."

I was at a loss and could not believe that the biggest shop in Seattle did not have an extra reel. Now I explained in more detail.

"I must have a 35 mm reel. Not a 16 or 8 mm. If I don't have it, people in San Francisco will be disappointed and I will be in trouble. I have brought a film from Japan to show to a string teachers meeting. It shows more than a thousand children playing the violin. It is very, very important for the instructors to see it. Maybe you can find one in your warehouse."

"I'm sorry, we have none."

"Can you order it? I really need it."

The man just shrugged his shoulders and spread his hands. I stood for a moment pondering when I heard another voice behind me.

"Pardon me," he said. "I did not mean to eavesdrop, but I overheard your conversation. Did you say you need a 35 mm reel?"

Turning around, I saw a young marine sergeant in uniform. "Yes. Tomorrow I have to speak at San Francisco State College and it's very important for the audience to see the film I brought from Japan. The school does not have a reel and asked me to bring one."

"If you can wait a little, maybe I can get one for you."

"Yes, of course," and I waited around the store for half an hour before the sergeant came back panting. He handed me the reel and said:

"I thought we had an extra one, but I couldn't find it. I unwound one and brought it to you."

My initial feeling of surprise quickly turned to a feeling of gratitude. I shook his hand and, thanking him from the bottom of my heart, said, "I know I cannot repay you for the trouble you took and for your kindness. But may I ask how much I owe you?"

He replied quietly, "It's all right, I just brought it from the barracks so you need not worry."

I was again surprised to hear this answer in the country where money shines and tipping is so common.

I insisted again, "I am sure I owe you more than money, but if I can just pay you something, I will be happy. Surely you used a taxi to go back to your quarters." Thus saying I took out a bill and tried to put it in his hand. But he gently shoved it back and said, "I have done nothing important. Besides, I am happy to know I helped you."

So saying, he left the store. To this day I can still remember the young man's face.

The fog was heavy the morning of our departure for San Francisco. Mrs. Hilton drove us to the Seattle-Tacoma airport, but we found out that due to fog the plane would leave from the Boeing private airfield where the fog was not so heavy. I was worried because I knew that the lecture was to begin at one o'clock and we could barely make it in time. Fortunately the plane did take off and within an hour we arrived in San Francisco where the sun was shining brightly.

Mr. and Mrs. Trippy were waiting for us at the airport and

we went downstairs to get our luggage. Within a few minutes, the luggage came jumping out onto the carousel. We found our bags and I carried them outside. We waited on the sidewalk while Mr. Trippy went to fetch the car from the parking lot. We stood in the sun enjoying the sight of the city until Mr. Trippy drove up. As I put the luggage into the trunk, I suddenly noticed that one shoulder bag was missing. In it were our passports, tickets, and cameras. I stood still and looked around. Yes, it was missing. I asked Junko excitedly, "Don't you have my shoulder bag? All our valuables are in it."

"I noticed that you left it on the floor when you were claiming the luggage. I thought you brought it." Hearing this I immediately began to run down the long corridor.

"Ah, foolish me, to forget the most important bag. The worst has happened." The distance to the baggage claim area seemed endless. I ran into the room. Nobody was there and the carousel had stopped. There was no sight of my bag. A sickening feeling came over me.

"You were standing on the other side," Junko, who had followed me, shouted.

I moved around, and there I found the bag sitting on the floor. I am sure it had been there for fifteen minutes. There are times when we feel like thanking God and this was my time.

The color of Seattle was green, and of San Francisco, white. There were very few trees and the houses nestled together without much space between them. When we arrived at the college, we were invited to have dinner with the teachers. The lecture began at one. Dr. Haderer gave me an hour and a half and I spoke on the subject, "How to Develop Children's Abilities." As a demonstration I had Yuko play, then for the last part of the program showed the film of the National Concert.

After two or three days in San Francisco, we flew back to Seattle. Mr. Sokol had invited us to attend a concert of the Seattle Youth Symphony Orchestra, which he conducted. It was held in the beautiful Opera House and they gave us the best seats in the balcony.

The concert was very good. I envied a country that could have orchestras in every big city, ranging from junior and youth groups to a full symphony. The last night in Seattle, the Hiltons invited us to an ocean-front restaurant named the Windjammer. Mr. and Mrs. Sokol were also invited and we all sat at a candlelit table. It was dark outside and we could hear the roar of the sea above the wind.

I described the events in San Francisco and added that if I had forgotten the bag in Haneda Airport in Tokyo, it would have disappeared in a minute. I also told about the kindness of the marine sergeant and concluded that since I had come to the United States I had been met only with honesty, kindness, and friendship.

Mr. Sokol smiled and said, "If I were to visit your country, I think I would feel the same way about your people."

"Yes, I hope so," I replied. "All human beings have faults. If we find fault with the people we associate with, we will never make friends. I think it is the same with nations. We all have faults but we also have good points and we should always think of the good points first. When I was in San Francisco, I met a man named Mr. Hacket. He was the first American to write about *haiku,* the Japanese seventeen-syllable verse form. In appreciation of his work, Japan Airlines invited Mr. and Mrs. Hacket for a month's tour of Japan. He enjoyed everything he saw and appreciated everything he experienced. He talked about the generosity and kindness of the Japanese people. Knowing my people I tried to disagree but he stopped me and kept praising them. Well, at least I was glad to know that he was happy in Japan and had the wisdom to see the good side."

Though the windows were shut tight and no wind came in, the candles flickered and we sat in silence listening to the sound of the waves.

"I should tell you about my own experience," Mr. Sokol began. Maybe the warm mood made him speak.

"In the second world war I was in Vienna. The Nazis were coming and we had to evacuate the city. I was on the last train departing from Vienna. There was a big sigh of relief among the passengers as our train pulled out. A few minutes later I noticed a conductor coming from the other end of the coach, checking tickets. I had my ticket and was ready for the inspection, when suddenly a man about forty came to my side. He spoke in a quiet voice. 'Sir, I am from a Jewish family and I have to leave this city at any cost. If not, I am doomed, since they will send me to a concentration camp. I do not have a ticket or cash, but only a check. Will you please sell me your ticket? I can pay any amount you ask.'

"I knew that a check would be a useless piece of paper and had no desire to part with my ticket. The man saw me pondering, fell on his knees and said, 'Please, please.' I thought again. When I got to Paris, I could go to the American Embassy and get money, if necessary, but if I did not help this man, he might be doomed as he said. So I gave him my ticket and all the dollars I had in my pocket.

"He was, of course, overjoyed and put in my hand a gold watch which he had in his pocket. I have this watch to this day."

I was moved. We all were.

Mrs. Sokol said quietly, "You have never told me that story."

He replied, "I meant to keep it to myself, but I felt like speaking in this atmosphere of true friendship."

In Los Angeles, Dr. Glass arranged a night for me to speak at the University of Southern California. Most of the faculty of the music school were there.

It began raining in the early afternoon and by night it was pouring. Los Angeles had not seen such rain for some time. The water overflowed the sewers and flooded the streets. But inside the building it was very quiet. I talked about Talent Education, and Mrs. Harlow Mills and Mr. Joachim Chasman added their experience with the children. Then Mrs. Trippy spoke:

"Dr. Honda, you should bring the children and spread this method and idea in this country. It's most important."

Her suggestion triggered a reaction from Dr. Raymond Kendall, the head of the music department, who sprang to his feet and shouted, "What kind of meeting is this, a conference of the Salvation Army, all blowing their horns in unison? I don't think Talent Education is an ideal method. We should study its curriculum before we bang the drum."

Silence fell over the audience. I stood up.

"I think what Dr. Kendall has said is true. We have never thought our method was perfect. The name of our movement is Talent Education Institute, which means that we must always study and investigate to find a better way. I am here simply to explain our ideals. Your system in this country is much farther advanced than ours and we would be glad to receive any advice."

I thought he was a frank man who spoke his mind. The program did not begin at U.S.C. until 1973.

LIFE OF THE SPIRIT

During our stay in San Francisco, we talked about having Mayako study piano at San Francisco State College. They had a very good piano instructor there, Mr. Istvan Nadas. A tape of Mayako's playing was sent to the school and she was allowed to enter the next semester. On June 19 she left to study in the United States.

Now, with Mayako gone, we had only small Asami at home. Also, the sound of her piano was gone and the house was very quiet. Even Marshmallow the dog did not move or make any noise and slept most of the day on the sofa.

My friends, who often visited our home, said, "We thought your home was the merriest in town. There was always laughter, good cheer, and music—violin, piano, song. Aren't you lonesome?"

Again, if we said we did not miss the girls or pretended not to be lonesome, it would not be true. Of course we missed them, and we missed the music, but we were not as lonely as people thought we were. People are apt to project their own feelings into the situation of others.

Yuko had been writing us in detail every week about her life with an American family, her life in school, and her thoughts. In fact, we understood her much better than when she was at home. In our daily life we do not always communicate with the family about subjects which affect our life spiritually. We're often occupied with trivia. We even argue, scold, or quarrel about small things, leading to nothing but unpleasant feelings. We had parted with our two daughters but, in a way, they were much closer to us. In fact, they lived with us in spirit even though they were not present.

Ever since Yuko began her violin lessons at four, music had been the bond between us. As she learned the technique and the music, we learned along with her; as she developed her ability, we developed our knowledge. It was something spiritual, not learned by experience or maturity. We climbed this lofty mountain together. We talked about music and every time a famous artist came to Japan, I took Yuko and we listened together.

When we reflect on our past life, we think of many people who have departed but who still live in our souls. Maybe a grandfather who told us fairy tales which we still cherish in our hearts, or a Sunday School teacher who taught us Bible stories and hymns. Perhaps a grammar school teacher who read us poems and taught us to appreciate the beauty of nature. These people are no longer around, but in some way or other, they are still a part of our lives.

We have heard many famous artists on records. Their tone lives in our hearts, stimulates us, and gives us peace. Mr. Suzuki has been listening to the records of Fritz Kreisler for the past thirty years. Kreisler came into his home day and night and taught him beautiful music. He never complained no matter how often Mr. Suzuki asked him to play. Of course, he did not come in person but in tone. His life was on records and Mr. Suzuki studied those records to copy and produce his beautiful tone. Several years ago, Jacques Thibaud, the famous violinist, had a fatal plane accident. Next morning, a reporter interviewed Mr. Suzuki on the phone, asking what he thought of this accident and of Thibaud. Mr. Suzuki, knowing for the first time about the death of Mr. Thibaud, felt tears gushing from his eyes and had no words to answer. He had lost a good friend. What can you say when you encounter the death of a dear friend? Later he told me, "It was indeed queer. I had never met Mr. Thibaud and only heard his records. But his tone has been living within me without my ever having seen him. There is indeed a life in tone."

Most of our attention in this world is concentrated on accumulating money or having high position or fame which, in several decades, crumbles to nothing. If our efforts were devoted to leaving good deeds and words, our daily life would be less tense. Our good deeds and words not only influence our children or our descendants but all those with whom we come in contact during our lifetime. People may forget who originated these words or deeds and may even think they had originated them themselves but these words and deeds live on through future generations.

THE SECOND TOUR MATERIALIZES

Mr. Suzuki received an honorary Doctor of Music degree from the New England Conservatory on June 12, 1966. When he returned to Japan he said, "An honorary doctorate is given to those who do not do anything for the degree." Nevertheless, people called him Dr. Suzuki after this.

The next tour was undertaken in 1966. John Kendall suggested that the tour should hereafter be managed by a professional manager. Many efficient managers were approached but they all were reluctant to undertake the managing of the Suzuki children. It was too risky. Norman Lloyd, past dean of Oberlin College, recommended Sheldon Soffer. He was not a large-scale manager, but even he did not want to undertake the tour. Later Mr. Mochizuki told me that one evening a party was held in Heinrich Roth's home. Many people were there, among them Mr. Soffer. Mrs. Roth talked to him about the importance of the tour and convinced him that he should manage the tour. That was how the 1966 tour materialized.

Mr. Soffer and I exchanged information about the tour. We decided that the best season for travel would be in October and, as the children would have to leave school, the tour should not last more than a month.

Yuko came back after her two years of study and teaching in Seattle. She had experienced and learned in these two years much more than we ever expected. In September we held a special recital for her in Kugenuma Civic Auditorium. The hall was small but had a home-like atmosphere. The night before her concert, a typhoon struck Japan, and all through the night we could not sleep, listening to the terrible howling of the wind, and the groan of the trees as big branches were torn off and hurled onto the roof. We all got up at midnight and sat in the living room. When morning dawned, we were utterly exhausted with strain and anxiety.

The concert could not be postponed, so it began at seven that evening. Yuko played the Franck Sonata, the same piece she had performed in Seattle. As soon as the first movement began, all the lights went out. She kept on playing and within a few minutes candles were brought for the accompanist. Yuko played the entire concert in the dark. At the reception held in the anteroom, the manager of the hall came up to me and shook my hand, saying, "I have never heard such a wonderful performance in my life."

The team for the 1966 tour consisted of two boys and eight girls. One of the girls was a cellist. The accompanist was Mrs. Katsuyo Suemitsu, Mr. Mochizuki's sister. She taught piano at Toho Music Academy and had no direct connection with Talent Education. Three mothers went along, but no instructor; it was a mistake. The first concert was held at the University of Oregon at Eugene on October 1.

Yukari Tate, the oldest of the group, played the first movement of the Concerto in D Major by Tchaikovsky. The hall was full and the audience, having already heard the first part of the program, was quietly waiting for Yukari to begin. The piano began the prelude and within a moment the violin solo came in sweet and low, like the beginning of a story. Yukari began with beautiful long bowing, confident and showing no sign of fatigue after the long voyage. But as she proceeded, I began to feel uneasy. There was something wrong, very slight, but something, and Yukari seemed to lose the elegant poise she always maintained. Then, in the midst of the music, she suddenly stopped. It was like a cord snapping and I almost jumped out of my seat. Silence, dead silence, fell over the audience. Nobody moved, and even Dr. Suzuki just stared blankly, glued to the chair. After several moments of embarrassing silence, Yukari gracefully tuned her instrument and began playing again. The reason was that this was the first time Yukari had performed with Mrs. Suemitsu and there was a lack of rapport between soloist and accompanist.

I arranged that the eight-year-old boy, Ken Kurokochi, would lodge with me throughout the tour. The first night we all stayed in a hotel in Eugene. Ken was sleeping in another bed beside me and on the night table between the two beds was a lamp with a big shade. At midnight, I jumped up in surprise, dreaming that a building was crashing over me. Instead of that, it was the lamp that came tumbling over my head. Fortunately, I was not hurt because the shade protected me, but I couldn't understand why such a heavy thing would fall on me. Then I saw Ken's feet reaching way out from his bed. He had turned a somersault and even though the lamp was out of reach, by unbelievable energy, he had kicked it down.

During the trip we stayed mostly in a host's home and several times a night I was awakened by the heavy thud of Ken falling out of bed. I put him back each time, which disturbed my sleep and drained my energy. Later I became wise and put some mattresses on the floor so he could sleep peacefully where he had fallen.

We arrived in Los Angeles more than an hour late. The concert was to be held in a high school auditorium in Pasadena at three o'clock. Mrs. Harlow Mills, our sponsor, was not at the airport to meet us. We crowded into cars that were available and sped down the highway to the hall.

We were thirty minutes late to Pasadena High School and, as the audience had already filled the hall, we began the concert immediately.

Asako Hata, a ten-year-old girl, played the Mendelssohn Concerto just before the intermission.

During the intermission, an elderly gentleman came backstage. He was Jack Benny, the famous comedian. We had not met, but I walked over to him, shook his hand and said, "Mr. Benny, how did you like the performance?"

"Wonderful. I play violin myself and have practiced the Mendelssohn. But when I heard that girl play, I felt like throwing my violin away."

Mr. Mochizuki whispered in my ear, "I wish he would throw his violin away. His fiddle is a Stradivarius."

"How old are you, Mr. Benny? Maybe you can still develop your ability," said Dr. Suzuki.

"I am thirty-nine years old and never get older," came the reply.

"Is that so? As I am five years your junior, then I am now thirty-four," said Dr. Suzuki. Since then Dr. Suzuki has always been thirty-four.

That night my hosts were Mr. and Mrs. Girvetz. Mayako, who came from San Francisco, stayed at the same home. The night before in Eugene I had not been able to sleep. The harder I tried, the more alert my brain became. I gave up, telling myself that since I was in the United States, I might as well enjoy every moment I was there. After talking with Girvetz, I went to bed. I was not sleepy at all. I told myself, "You must sleep tonight, tomorrow will be a heavy day in Phoenix." But somehow my brain revolted and I was neither sleepy nor tired. I did various tricks, such as counting from one to one hundred. It did not work. I got up and ate an apple, thinking it would lower my blood pressure. Another sleepless hour and the hands of my watch were pointing to one a.m. I got up and opened the door leading to the garden. The moon was floating high in the sky. The night was beautiful but chilly. I noticed a pool in the garden. The water was clear and inviting.

I took off my gown and slipped in. Oh! The water was cold, much too cold, and it chilled me to the bone. I jumped out, wiped my body and, shivering, jumped into my bed. The water cooled my body and I went to sleep.

On October 16 we went to New York to be on the Ed Sullivan Show. A week before the children had played in the beautiful Philharmonic Hall at Lincoln Center. The house was filled with an enthusiastic crowd who gave them a standing ovation. I was pleased that Ed Sullivan wanted us on his TV program. The day before the shooting I met the agent of the show. He explained to me that the length of the presentation would be about four or five minutes. I agreed to the proposal, provided that the title, "Suzuki Children—Talent Education" would be shown and that there would be some time for explanation. They were willing to cooperate, so Dr. Suzuki signed the contract.

Next morning, bright and fresh, we all went to the studio. The guard ushered us into a dark, dingy room where we waited for hours without any refreshment. The children were getting restless, and we all felt very uneasy. During this time, two boys disappeared and when I caught them later in the corridor, they were carrying a bundle of toilet paper in their hands. I scolded them for being away from the room and for their behavior, but could not understand why they had collected all the toilet paper in the studio. At last the time came for us to be on the air. The hall was dark and smoky and the atmosphere was not at all healthy or pleasant. The children played "Country Dance" by Weber. Later I understood that no title or explanation appeared on camera, and I was very displeased.

Next day we flew across the border to Montreal. It was very cold and Dr. Suzuki looked tired. The strain was showing. He had to tune all the instruments, give lectures, and conduct. I was busy interpreting and taking care of things backstage. All the mothers wanted to be in the audience and only the children were left.

Alfred Garson was waiting for us in the airport. In the lobby we had an orientation.

"Dr. Suzuki and Dr. Honda," he said, "here in Montreal there are citizens of both English and French descent. Though most of them understand English and French, English descendants will speak no French and the French, no English. Even in newspaper interviews, which we will have later, we must explain first in English and then in French. Before the concerts there will be an address in English and another in French. You might think it ridiculous, but the rule is very strict."

I was a little skeptical of what he said but later discovered it was the truth. Even in elevators of department stores floors were announced first in English, then in French.

The performance was held in Salle Claude Champagne, a beautiful Catholic Girls High School built on a hill overlooking the city. The introduction began, first in English, then in French. The explanation was translated into both languages. But the performances of the children were in an international language.

When the concert was over a dignified gentleman came on stage. He was a high official representing the Quebec government and was of French descent. At first he spoke in French but in a moment, to the amazement of all, he began to speak in fluent English.

"Dr. Suzuki, Dr. Honda, I know that you do not understand French. What we heard and witnessed is something very important for all human beings in the world. The aim, as I understand it, is to develop love among small children through music. In this era of misunderstanding and disbelief among many peoples on earth, this movement should be carried throughout the world. You have heard of the feelings between the two ethnic groups in this country. After I heard the children play, these feelings seem so trivial."

As we did not have this kind of divisiveness among people in Japan, it was a little difficult to understand such harsh feelings, but considering what I had heard from many people, I was convinced it must really be a very difficult problem.

That evening the mayor invited us to dinner. The restaurant

was an old fortress by the St. Lawrence River. An old cannon pointed toward the river guarding the city. Everything was preserved as it was in the eighteenth century. We ate by candlelight and the waiter wore eighteenth-century costume. By the time we arrived in Rochester, New York, Dr. Suzuki was limping. He had developed rheumatism and I knew he was in pain. He never complained but was silent during the rest of the tour.

Eastman School of Music had received funds from the Federal Government and from the State of New York to study our method to see if it could work effectively with American children. Dr. Donald Shetler had been recruited from Western Reserve University to Eastman and he worked energetically to promote this project. It was called "Project Super," an acronym from SUzuki approach in Penfield, Eastman, and Rochester. Several string teachers were employed to carry out this project and each taught a number of children from various ethnic and socio-economic backgrounds. So far, the project was successful and we heard numbers of these children play in the hall. Project Super would be carried out for one year but had the possibility of being extended.

After leaving New York in October, our schedule was very heavy: Montreal, Rochester, DeKalb, Ogden, Dallas, and Seattle, traveling every day, giving workshops in the afternoon and concerts at night. It was a great relief when we arrived in Honolulu and stayed there for two nights.

Dr. Suzuki had returned East from Seattle to give some workshops so there was no instructor at the concert held at McKinley High School Auditorium. Receiving help from Mr. Peter Mesrobian, conductor of the Honolulu Youth Symphony, Yukari and I tuned the instruments. When the group lined up on the stage, I went out and gave the sign to begin. I was pleased when the girls came back giggling, telling me how well I conducted.

On our way back home, I reflected about the past tour and concluded it had not been so successful. I could not anticipate another trip but, if one ever materialized, we should bring at least two instructors. The disadvantages of bringing mothers outweighed the advantages. First, the children behaved much better with instructors. Second, those children whose own mothers did not accompany them felt very lonesome. Traveling and playing every day was too strenuous. We needed a day's rest after each two or three days of travel.

THE NEW CENTER BUILDING
OF TALENT EDUCATION

The year 1967 will always be remembered by people connected with Talent Education. The building in Matsumoto, which we had so long desired, was completed and the dedication ceremony was to be held in August.

I received a letter from Mr. Howard Van Sickle, president of the American String Teachers Association, informing me that quite a number of American string teachers would be visiting Japan that summer to attend what we call summer school.

This was indeed a great event, as never before had so many foreign specialists visited Japan to study something which originated in this country. I told Mr. Akeo Mizuno, a man in charge of the Tokyo office, to make preparations to welcome them. We would have a big party in Tokyo after the concert and invite all the American teachers and also the officers of the Japan String Association and professors of the Music Conservatory in Tokyo.

It was my idea that by inviting these people and letting them make friends with American string teachers, they might be led to understand the truth. So the American teachers, fifty-eight in all, came in the intense heat and humidity of the Japanese summer.

When we toured abroad, people in America thought we brought only the best students. In order to have them see that this was not so, we divided these teachers into several groups and had them visit classes in all parts of Japan. Later they met in Matsumoto for summer school.

Our movement had a history of more than twenty years and had done much to enhance the status of music in our country. Still, music critics and professors of music were against the idea and the movement. The reasons varied. First, jealousy, because the Suzuki method was gaining popularity throughout the world. Second, Dr. Suzuki was not a graduate of any music conservatory. Third, there was general misunderstanding of both the idea and method. If one hound barked against the movement, the whole pack joined in without knowing why the first one was howling. The undercurrent was cold and strong.

Before the opening of summer school, we had a general meeting of the Talent Education organization in the hall of the new building. Delegates from all over Japan sat in their seats and the officers sat on the stage flanking Dr. Suzuki who sat in the center. Instead of a pleasant atmosphere which should have enveloped the meeting, the mood of the hall was solemn, even grim.

Dr. Suzuki began the session, thanking the whole delegation for their cooperation in building this new center. Then Mr. Takasugi began to explain the total cost of construction. The sum was staggering and people held their breath. After paying some expenses, the remaining debt was very high. This amount must be paid within ten years, and heated discussion began on how and to what extent each school should take responsibility. Discussion changed into argument and dispute and the hall filled with loud voices. Dr. Suzuki stood up and tried to explain the nature of the contract between Talent Education and the contractor.

His voice was drowned out. Mr. Kamijo, the chairman, banged his hammer and shouted for order. The hall became quiet. I stood up. "I am very sorry to witness such feelings among the delegates, who should meet to rejoice in the construction of the new center. Education is not business and naturally we are always suffering from financial trouble. But please consider that from this center, the ideal of our movement will spread throughout the world. I have been visiting

America for the past two years and have witnessed what wonderful inspiration this ideal has brought to people there. Calculating these things, which are indeed priceless, I think the debt does not mean much. The important thing is to appreciate what we have done and discuss how we should pay the debt. I am convinced that we will, we can, and we must."

Again there arose a large outcry in the hall. It was already after 6:00 p.m. We had invited the American teachers to dinner but now it was impossible for either Dr. Suzuki or myself to join them.

I sat down distressed and broken-hearted. At last the meeting was over. That night I tossed in my bed, unable to sleep. During the past twenty years, I had done my best to spread the idea. I never received anything for what I had done, but was only happy to acknowledge the development of the movement. It had been a kind of mission to me and I had done my best. But today, like it or not, I had to face the limitations of my ability. I needed help. I needed advice from those who had influence, power, and money.

Suddenly, an inspiration struck me. I recalled the name of Mr. Masaru Ibuka, founder and president of the Sony Corporation. He was coming to the ceremony for the new building tomorrow. I would approach him and ask his help. I would talk to him in earnest and even if he did not understand, even if there was no improvement, things could be no worse.

Next day we had a ceremony for the dedication of the new center. We were glad to have all the American teachers attend the ceremony. Though we had suffered much, financially and spiritually, this would be almost nothing when people in the future reflected on the history of Talent Education. The ceremony was badly arranged and things did not go well.

After the ceremony, I caught sight of Mr. Ibuka and Mr. Masanori Hiratsuka, president of the National Institute for Education. I was busy talking with many people, but this was a chance I could not afford to miss. Mr. Yoshisuke Kurosaki, a famous children's portrait painter, had come with me and was standing beside me.

"Mr. Kurosaki," I said to him, "will you go to Mr. Ibuka and Mr. Hiratsuka and tell them that we need a kind of advisory board? If you will just engage them in conversation for several minutes, I will join you and take it from there." While finishing talking with my friends, I noticed from the corner of my eye that Mr. Kurosaki was doing a good job.

Things worked very well, and Mr. Ibuka proposed to meet me in Tokyo. In early September, Mr. Ibuka invited me to a dinner at a Chinese restaurant on the ground floor of his mansion. Dr. Seiji Kaya, former president of Tokyo University, and Mr. Hiratsuka were there. I stated everything to them and they seemed very surprised. I asked them if they could make an advisory board which could help this organization. Mr. Ibuka agreed to consider it.

TOUR WITHOUT SUZUKI

Dr. Suzuki announced that he would not join the tour for the next year. I wrote to Mr. Soffer, informing him of the fact, and asking that he inquire of each school whether they would like to sponsor the program even without Dr. Suzuki. Mr. Soffer answered that all were willing and not even one had cancelled. I myself was a little concerned about traveling without Dr. Suzuki. How would the audiences receive my talk?

The first city was Pendleton, Oregon. The scene of our arrival was described by Bernice Riley in the *East Oregonian:*

You never saw such excitement as there was at Pendleton Airport Thursday afternoon. The lobby of the building looked the way a Japanese railway station must appear with the crowd filling every bit of floor space.

Mayor Eddie Knopp was there and Chief Clarence Burke, of the Umatilla Indian Tribe, was present dressed in his ceremonial costume. So was beautiful Carla Walker, winner of the 1967 American Indian beauty contest. And overflowing the building and spilling out onto the grounds were hundreds of children and adults. Some of the adults were parents of the children, many more were teachers. Most of the children carried violins and they were similarly dressed in blue and white.

The plane came in and a hush fell over the crowd, now congregated outside. Shirlene McMichael, director of the string department in the Pendleton schools, approached the steps of the aircraft. Then there appeared the Suzuki Talent Education troupe, ten children and seven adults. This was the reason for all the people at the airport. They were there to give a rousing Round-up City welcome to these visitors from Japan.

Pendleton is the first stop in their 1967 tour of the United States which will take them to New York City and back across the continent to California.

The welcome was a surprise to Dr. Masaaki Honda, leader of the tour, and his party. They all looked a bit stunned as they stood uncertainly for a moment in the bright sunshine.

Then the children, led by Martha White, began to play "Twinkle, Twinkle, Little Star," and broad smiles appeared on the faces of the visitors.

For this simple tune (with variations) could well be called the theme song of the Suzuki Talent Education program. This is the melody a child learns to play first, before going on to Bach and Vivaldi.

Next evening, a welcome potluck dinner was held at West Hills School. It was a merry evening, with children of both countries playing games and exchanging songs. Just when we were to begin dinner, three men with masks came in with pistols in their hands.

"Where is he? Where is he?" The men began looking around. A hush came over the party. The men saw me and came to my side.

"Here he is—Honda. We're taking him along." He stuck his pistol in my side and ordered me to move out of the room. When we moved to the door, the men took their masks off and roared with laughter.

"Were you scared?" one of the men asked me. I knew from the beginning it was some kind of joke, but not wanting to make them unhappy I just smiled and said nothing.

"Dr. Honda, you have passed the test. Now you are a member of the Pendleton Cowboys. Here is your certificate." They gave me a blue card on which was printed: "This is to certify that Masaaki Honda is a member of the Pendleton Cowboy Association."

When I showed the card to the people in Oklahoma, they just sniffed and said, "Pooh, we have real cowboys here."

This year's troupe consisted of girls only. The youngest was six-year-old Yasuko Fukuda. I did not know why Dr. Suzuki had not selected any boys; probably it was that we had had a little too much trouble with the boys on our previous trip.

Mr. Hachiro Hirose, Mr. Mitsumasa Denda, Miss Yuko Mori, and Miss Yoshiko Nakajima came with the group as instructors. Yuko Hirose, a fine pianist and the wife of Hirose, was the accompanist this time.

Pendleton is famous for its cattle rodeo and pageant. Many thousands of people visit the city for the show, but as it was out of season, the city was very quiet. The city's main businesses are wheat and lumber. Pendleton is the junction of the famous Oregon Trail from Fort Walla Walla to Northern California. When we arrived, hunting season had just begun and people were talking about deer hunting in the mountains. The medical doctor with whom I stayed told me a sad story. Several years ago he had gone hunting with his only son and mistook his son for a deer, wounding him fatally. Since then, he never touched his gun again.

We took very small planes from Seattle to Bellingham, a Cessna and a Beechcraft. The group was divided in half, and I embarked on the smaller plane with five of the girls. The plane flew very low and we were able to see the bay, mountains covered with spruce and pine, lakes large and small—scenery typical of the Northwest.

The workshop and performance were held at Western Washington State College. I saw many familiar faces from Seattle in the audience. Charles North was the chairman and the young instructors handled the workshop very well. I divided each teacher's responsibilities so that everything worked smoothly.

Odessa, in the heart of Texas, is barren, like any place that produces oil. Many Russian laborers worked on the construction of the Texas and Pacific Railway in 1884. The place was named Odessa after the city in their native country. I was surprised to learn that even in this remote place, there was a great deal of interest in our movement. Mrs. L. Croft had been teaching the Suzuki Method for the past several years.

I was very much surprised to meet Kenji Kobayashi in Oklahoma. He was one of Dr. Suzuki's first students, and he went on to study at Curtis Institute in Philadelphia. He was now the concertmaster of the Oklahoma Symphony Orchestra. The sponsor for our concert in Oklahoma City was this symphony orchestra. This was the first time that a professional orchestra had sponsored our concert. Maybe they were interested in our playing, maybe they wanted some of the fiddlers from Japan, or maybe they had extra money. But we were glad to play in this city and to meet Kenji Kobayashi.

I once read that the American string teacher's dream was to have an established position and also to have some private students in Winnetka. When I told this to Milton Goldberg he just shrugged his shoulders and said nothing. A wealthy friend sitting beside him spoke in his stead. "Well, it's true there are many rich people living in this suburb of Chicago, but as we do not have any factories or business establishments, the taxes are very high and the public facilities are not as well equipped as they are in other cities. There are always two different points of view and there is never perfect contentment on this earth." But Mr. Goldberg had a nice school and wonderful violin classes. He had attended our first performance at Northwestern University in 1964. Since then he had followed the program of Talent Education, introducing the idea in the North Shore area school system.

The performance was held in the Skokie Junior High School auditorium. As it was small and not a first-rate hall, it corroborated the words of the rich man.

The next concert, which was held at Ithaca College, ended late at night. We enjoyed our stay in Ithaca, the beautiful city of the Finger Lakes. People were friendly and there was no hurry or rush. The next day, October 16, the children were to play at Philharmonic Hall at 3:00 p.m. It was to be the highlight of the tour. Because of the close schedule we decided to charter a plane and have the pilot fly us to New York immediately after the concert.

The concert was well received and several encores and curtain calls were requested. Backstage, many waited to talk about the success of the concert and get autographs from our children. Suddenly a man came in and shouted, "We should leave immediately. The airport in New York will be closed at midnight. We have only an hour." It was the pilot.

I rushed the children into the car and off we went with the pretty blue clothes they wore in the concert. Waving a hasty good-bye, we boarded the twenty-five seat plane and flew to New York.

We divided the group and took a taxi from the airport, arriving at the hotel at one o'clock. But something unpredicted happened. Mrs. Fukuda had taken one taxi with her two daughters, Keiko and Yasuko. Yasuko was six, the smallest of the group. In the hurry and excitement, they had forgotten Yasuko's violin in the taxi. Now this was indeed a very serious problem as Yasuko could not participate in the concert without her violin. Because we were in a rush from the airport, we did not think to write down the number of the taxi. The hotel manager called the police and announced on the radio that a reward would be given to anyone who brought the violin to the hotel.

Heavyhearted, we all went to bed but, as we were very tired, went to sleep immediately and woke up late in the morning refreshed. While I was dressing I received a call from the desk. I went down, anticipating that the violin had been found but, to my disappointment, it had not. The caller was Mrs. Okaya, a lady we had met in Scarsdale in 1964. I told her about our unfortunate situation. When she told me that her daughter was using the same 1/10 size violin and she would immediately go get the instrument and bring it to Philharmonic Hall before the concert, Mrs. Fukuda was extremely happy as she had reproached herself all night for her carelessness.

It was a beautiful day. We arrived at Lincoln Center a little past noon. People strolled easily, casually enjoying the pleasant weather. Many pictures were taken before we all went in. Philharmonic Hall is beautiful inside, with nearly three thousand seats sloping gently toward the stage. I usually test the hall from various places while the children rehearse to evaluate the acoustics. The sound seemed quite good even in the last row.

We did not know how the audience would turn out. If only a very meager number were to be seated in such a vast hall, it would not only discourage us but would also hinder any future big city performances. Like it or not, it is the big cities that attract the critics and journalists, and by their articles people learn about the movement. The house was full. Every seat was taken and probably one-third of the audience was made up of children. We were told that critics in New York are severe. But all the papers published favorable comments, and we were happy to know the concert was a success.

Our hotel in Brooklyn was neither pleasant nor well-heated, so we asked the agent to find a better one. The new hotel was in Manhattan near the Empire State Building. The rooms were clean and there was even a small hall available for rehearsal. The location was convenient for shopping and we liked it very much.

We had three free days in New York and we used them for

sightseeing and shopping. I discovered that to have the group stay in this city was very expensive and exhausting. First, to feed seventeen mouths three times a day was quite a job. At first we used the hotel restaurant but the bill ran very high and the service was not good. So later we bought bread, ham, and sausage from the grocery nearby. This was much better. For lunch we used a self-service restaurant nearby. Each one carried his plate and I had to keep a keen eye on them lest they only take jelly, cakes, and desserts which were attractive to their eyes.

One day I took them to the Metropolitan Museum in Central Park. The things that attracted them most were paintings by great artists. These children had never seen these pictures but something seemed to attract them and I learned that when children develop good abilities, they can understand other arts.

One morning I took some of the instructors and children shopping. It was rather early in the morning and streets and shops were not crowded. They were enjoying buying small gifts when I received a call from the hotel, telling me to return immediately as an accident had happened. I took a taxi and hurried back, fearing something bad had happened.

When I went up to my room Mr. Denda, an instructor, told me that a thief had entered Mr. Hirose's room. I ran to Mr. Hirose's room and knocked at the door. As it was not locked, I opened the door and looked inside. There stood Mr. and Mrs. Hirose, looking very miserable. He wore his raincoat and had no trousers on. What I found out in a short time was that while they were in the bathroom, somebody came into the room and took his clothes, cameras, and all the valuables. I picked up the phone immediately and asked the operator to call the police station. Then I called Mr. Mochizuki who had returned to his home in Manhattan and explained to him what had happened. As he was working for the Consulate General, he told me he would go immediately to the office and replace their passports. Clothes of any size could be bought in New York so there would be no trouble. This cheered me up and I went to Mr. Hirose's room. When I entered the room, a man came in and introduced himself as a detective. He searched the room and, finding nothing, went out in the corridor. I followed him. He opened the door of the next room and there on the floor were Mr. Hirose's clothes. We found the cameras and passports and the only thing missing was cash, three hundred and thirty dollars. We were glad to get back his property and did not ask for further investigation. Later I found that the detective was a private one employed by the hotel. Though I liked this hotel, we never used it again.

We left New York the next morning by train. We were hurrying along the dark platform of Grand Central Station when suddenly Mr. Mochizuki called me in a loud voice. "Dr. Honda, Dr. Honda." I turned back and found myself face to face with a dignified gentleman with white hair, smiling. It was Leopold Stokowski, the famous conductor. We shook hands and began talking about Talent Education. As all the children had boarded the train I shook his hand again and said goodbye. "Please remember me to Dr. Suzuki," he called. Mr. Stokowski was traveling as a visiting conductor with the Philadelphia Symphony Orchestra.

Yukari Tate had always wanted to play in a church to dedicate her music to God. The atmosphere of the art museum of Worcester, Massachusetts, was much like a chapel. A low platform was placed in the middle of the big hall and there were two winding, broad stairways facing the hall. The balcony looked down from three sides and a number of small room annexes to the hall were filled with antiques, pictures, and statues of saints, knights, and kings. The concert was held in this center and people crowded the hall, filling the chairs, sitting on stairs and looking from balconies. Yukari played Concerto in D Major by Brahms with all her devotion. People gave the girls a standing ovation and the reviews in the papers were superb.

Our next concert was at Oceanside, Long Island. It was sponsored by Rockaway Music and Art Council. I was told that this council had been founded by Jewish people in the vicinity and the chairman was Sam Levenson. His name was not familiar to me but I found that he was quite a well-known person.

We arrived late at night by bus and the driver had difficulty finding the hosts' homes. My host was Milton Zinar, whose home was located at the extreme end of a street only a block from the Atlantic Ocean. Mrs. Zinar is a piano teacher so we had many topics in common and we chatted until midnight. I was surprised when Mr. Zinar told me that I was the first Japanese person he had met. I thanked him for receiving me into his home and also expressed the hope that the first Japanese had given him a good impression. While teaching piano, Mrs. Zinar was working for her doctor's degree at New York University. I found out that her dissertation topic was Suzuki Talent Education.

Next morning Mr. Zinar took me for a walk by the ocean. I was surprised to see the clean blue water of the Atlantic compared to the dirty sea in New York harbor. The waves were high, running to and fro along the white sandy beach. There was a wooden sidewalk parallel to the shore as far as the eye could see. I sat on the sand and scooped some in my hands. It was white, clean and fine.

After breakfast Mr. Zinar took me to Coney Island. I had always heard and seen pictures of this colorful center. Now, under the bright morning sunshine, it seemed to have lost its past glamor.

"Young people are not attracted to these kinds of amusements anymore," Mrs. Zinar explained. Indeed the world is changing and so is the taste of youngsters.

On our way back we were invited to visit a Jewish synagogue. It was during a religious festival and there were many decorations and offerings placed on the table in one corner of the chapel. There were pumpkins, carrots, corn—the harvest of the field—offered as thanks just like Thanksgiving day. In Japan there was a custom of offering the first crop of rice to god and it was interesting to know all countries have some way of extending their gratitude for blessings they receive. The rabbi gave us the special privilege of looking at the Holy Script written in Hebrew. Though I could not read or understand the writing, I felt reverent beholding the scripture.

In the afternoon our group joined us and there was a goodwill meeting between the two nations. The children played games together and sang folk songs. Sam Levenson acted as chairman and he made people laugh by his wit and humor.

"Did you read my book?" Mr. Levenson asked.

"I am sorry," I replied.

"I just published a book titled *Everything But Money.* You see I was born in a large family and my parents were poor. But they gave us a good education and we were all happy."

"Yes, I can understand. There are so many people who have 'Nothing But Money,'" I answered. "I think we understand each other quite well."

Later he sent the book to Japan and I found it very interesting. That night after the concert while we were having a party in Dr. Mauss' home, I received a phone call from Miss Mori.

"Dr. Honda, I am scared. There are two big husky men in this house. They are always following me, telling me they want to make my bed or serve tea and other things. Of course they mean to be kind, but I am afraid."

I told Dr. Mauss about the call, and he burst into laughter. "I vouch for them. I have known them since they were infants. Though they look big and husky, they are still teenagers. Their parents are visiting friends in New York but will return late this evening. Tell her to forget her fears. There is nothing to be afraid of." I called again and consoled her as best I could, but I really understood how she felt.

When we arrived in Owensboro, Kentucky, the sun was strong and bright. Sister Mary Cecilia and other friends welcomed us with beaming smiles at the airport. We all scrambled into the bus and off we went to the school. I was surprised to hear a police siren, and was even more surprised to learn we had a police escort. The traffic of this small city was not at all heavy and we were in no hurry to reach the school. The police of that city were either very kind or had plenty of free time.

My hosts were Mr. and Mrs. Walt Davis. Their home was white with many columns and a wide veranda in the front, surrounded by a big green lawn. The Stars and Stripes fluttered on the flagpole. It looked very much like the home of Ashley Wilkes of Twelve Oaks in *Gone with the Wind.* The bed was high, old, magnificent, a four-poster with a white lace canopy. It was much nicer to look at than to sleep in. That evening a reception was held at Mr. Payne's home, a grand mansion. Mr. Payne offered me a drink with leaves of peppermint floating in it. I asked what kind of drink it was. He answered casually: "It's only a Kentucky Derby."

I took a long draught, thinking it was a soft drink. I almost choked. The hot liquid ran down my throat into my stomach. It was bourbon whiskey specially produced in Kentucky. I make it a rule never to drink liquor before a concert. Looking at my face, Mr. Payne roared with laughter and said, "You need spirits to pep you up." Yes, it did put me in good spirits.

The concert being held that night was not in an auditorium or hall but in a gymnasium as big as a baseball field. Sister Cecelia came to my side and whispered in my ear. "We want to accommodate as many people as possible. Nearly five thousand people can be seated in this hall. We have to sacrifice acoustics. You cannot have everything, you know." I wish she had sacrificed the seats and saved the acoustics but it was too late. People were pouring in by the hundreds. Buses arrived and unloaded boys and girls from grammar and junior high schools. When the concert began, the ensemble could be heard, but the solos of the small girls were hardly audible. I took my seat way in the back and indeed the girls looked very tiny. It was quiet at the beginning but, as time went on, the surroundings became noisy. After the intermission it really became more like a gymnasium. Children raced and jumped. I felt a little miserable, but could not blame anyone. After all, everybody had worked for the best. And the audience had endured to their limit, listening to hardly audible, difficult classics played by tiny, tiny children.

I cannot withhold my admiration for American people who love their land, wherever they live. In Albuquerque, New Mexico, by the Rio Grande, people say this is the best place in the United States. So do people living in the desert of Tucson, Arizona, and in the heart of Kansas, where the smell of the cattle stings one's nose. In the extreme cold of Anchorage or Fairbanks, they love the climate. They love Iowa with its corn and New Orleans with its high humidity. Maybe the spirit of the pioneer makes them adapt to any situation or circumstance and even the fierce cold of Minnesota stimulates and develops whatever abilities they need. In Japan, there is a proverb, if you love your land, your work, your wife, you are sure to succeed.

I think every city has its color and in my opinion Albuquerque is light brown. There are very few trees in the city and most of the houses are built of brick, clay, or stone. My host, John Gaston, took me sightseeing in the city. The Rio Grande, contrary to its name, is small, narrow, and ungrand. Probably, it gathers more water as it flows through Mexico and becomes the true Rio Grande. We saw an Indian village where Indian crafts were on sale in shops and by the roadside.

The children played a concert in the beautiful big hall of the University of New Mexico.

The next concert took place in Pasadena, California, at the Civic Auditorium with a seating capacity of three thousand. Since Mikie Naito had lost her concert costume in New York, I had told all the girls to wear ordinary clothes even on the stage. On our arrival in Pasadena, Mrs. Elizabeth Mills took me to many department stores to find a similar dress, but it was hopeless. Finally we found cloth very much like the color of the costumes, light blue. We bought the fabric and Mrs. Shulster made Mikie a dress ready to wear that night. She was very happy and so were all the girls.

They played three concerts, two in the daytime and one in the evening. Each time the house was full and I was told that many people had to return home as all tickets were sold. The stage manager was kind and very helpful. In a tour with children, especially girls, this makes a great difference and I appreciated his cooperation very much. The three days in Pasadena were very pleasant for all of us. We had time to visit Disneyland and enjoyed it much more than I can express. In the evening Dr. and Mrs. Goulard invited the whole group and all the host families to their home in Orange Grove, Arcadia. We enjoyed the barbeque in the garden sitting comfortably under the starlit sky. It was good to rest for a while after the journey.

The sunshine in San Diego was strong and we felt that we were indeed in sunny Southern California. Dr. Ted Brunson and Dr. Robert Forman, both professors of music at San Diego State College, took me to the point overlooking the bay. Many battleships were sleeping peacefully in their berths and a small destroyer was coming into the bay, making white streaks on the blue water.

The last concert on the mainland was held in the hall of San Diego State College. Compared with the previous tours, I felt this whole trip had been easier. We had enough instructors who did their part efficiently and all the girls behaved very well. Besides, my ability to handle the tours had developed considerably. On the first two trips, I was concerned with the children being too tired after the flight, so I usually divided the group in two and ordered half to rest in the host's home, while the other half attended the workshop. Examining the condition of the children carefully, I noticed that those who participated in the workshop were much better than those who rested. The playing seemed to stimulate them and lift their spirits. I ordered all children to join the workshop and this worked out very well. None was sick and everybody enjoyed the trip very much.

The last three days in Honolulu were like paradise to the children. Besides the performance, we were on TV and radio but it did not place us under any stress. Mr. and Mrs. Carl Panfiglio gave us a reception at their beautiful home by the ocean. The next day Mrs. Barney Sato took the children to

Ala Moana Shopping Center. This was the first time they had plenty of time to shop.

It was indeed "aloha" all over.

FOUNDING OF E.D.A. AND THE 1968 TOUR

Yuko returned from Seattle and again the sound of the violin filled our home. She was practicing the Concerto in D Major by Tchaikovsky, and every time she started to open her violin case, Marshy, our dog, came running to her side, sat on her haunches, and listened as Yuko practiced. When Yuko practiced in her room, annoyed by Marshy's presence, Marshy sat by the door, cocking her ears, listening. Sometimes she just listened, but one day she suddenly raised her voice and sang with the violin. This was the beginning. At first it was just howling, but as time went on she learned to put more feeling into it and even changed pitch following the melody. Asami was then studying Volume 2, but when she began to open her violin case, Marshy would run precipitously out of the room. Needless to say, Asami's pride was terribly hurt.

I received an invitation from Mr. Ibuka to meet on January 11, 1968, at Zakuro Restaurant in Tokyo. There were two other men with Mr. Ibuka whom he introduced to me: Mr. Toshiyuki Miyamoto, an ex-editor of Asahi Newspaper, and Mr. Hirano, President of the Mathematics Association of Japan. The main subject was to establish a new organization adopting the idea of Talent Education. The idea and method of Talent Education had proved successful over the past twenty-five years. But considering the vast number of children who have no chance of studying violin or piano, we should apply this idea in other fields like foreign language, drawing, reading, calligraphy, gymnastics, mathematics and so on. We discussed the matter thoroughly and concluded that a nonprofit organization should be established. The name in Japanese would be *Yoji Kaihatsu Kyokai* (Infant Development Association). I suggested that the English name be Early Development Association. The potentiality of humans is at its highest on the day of birth and decreases gradually. But though people get old there is always a possibility for them to develop themselves. I once wrote about Mr. Kurosaki teaching brush painting to people over sixty. They had never drawn before, but after taking lessons for a year, all of them were able to do a beautiful brush painting. This made them and their families very happy. It is also eloquent testimony to the fact that abilities can be developed in old people. Indeed, I believe ability can be developed at any age, if one tries hard and repeats often. But there are some limits for an adult to acquire facility, for instance, in language or music. It is almost impossible for an adult to acquire perfect pitch or speak a foreign language perfectly. The boundary line seems to be puberty. The decision was that the organization would be named Early Development Association, E.D.A.

The fourteenth National Concert was held at Nippon Budokan in Tokyo. This was the third concert held in this circular hall, which was not originally made for music but for sports. Thus the acoustics were poor. As there was no other place besides Tokyo Gymnastics Hall, like it or not, we had to use it.

One of the highlights of the event was that a five-year-old girl, Terri Goulard, from California was to appear; she would be the first American child to participate in the big concert.

We had often been invited to Dr. Goulard's home in Orange Grove, Arcadia, and I knew that Terri played quite well. I asked Mrs. Goulard how it happened that the child began playing violin. I received the following letter from her:

You asked about Terri so I will give you a bit of the background on her and how she got started in music. When Terri was born, we had four older children ages 10, 12, 14, and 16. When she came home from the hospital, we put her in the room with her oldest sister who at that time was 14 almost 15. Helen was very interested in music and had studied violin with Elizabeth Mills for 5 years in the traditional method. Helen did, however, greatly enjoy playing the pieces she was learning as well as other classical compositions and the record player in her room was in use most of the time. She found that one of the pieces that her little sister seemed to enjoy the most was Haydn's Toy Symphony. Helen used to play this piece over and over for Terri—even before Terri could talk. And Terri could *whistle* this music when she was less than a year old. In fact, Terri never sang nursery rhymes as such, but would hum concert or symphonic music. (Of course this was along the lines of the Suzuki training, but we had no idea that we were subconsciously developing the right habits for listening.)

When Terri was two, the Suzuki group made its first appearance in the Los Angeles area—in San Fernando, I believe. Helen attended the afternoon workshop with Mrs. Mills and other pupils. When she got home, she was just brimming over with enthusiasm. This was for her little sister. She was going to start her right away, etc., etc. Both Dr. Goulard and I were a bit less than enthusiastic, I'm sorry to admit now. (Of course, we hadn't seen the children perform and were getting all of this through the eyes of a teenager.) Helen wouldn't be stopped, however, and kept at us to get Terri a violin. We did—a toy violin—which Terri promptly threw across the room and we were sure that we had proved our point. But Helen wouldn't give up. Also Terri kept asking for a *real* violin. For Christmas that year she purchased a 1/16 size violin for Terri. Then she announced that she had talked to Mrs. Mills and that Mrs. Mills had agreed to start several young children on the violin in the spring. Mrs. Mills had been using the Suzuki method with her beginners at that time, but her beginners were older than pre-kindergarten. Helen also extracted a promise from me to continue Terri's lessons when Helen would be leaving for college in the Fall. I agreed, for I thought that surely by then the violin would be forgotten and covered with dust in the corner somewhere and that I

would not have any concern with it. *How wrong I was!!!*
Before long I found myself attending lessons with Terri.
I found that I was developing patience that I didn't
know was possible to possess. Some lessons we made
it just as far as the studio door only to have Terri
announce, "I don't want a lesson today." And smiling
(though surely not feeling like it) I would drive her
home. The progress didn't make itself known at first.
Sometimes it seemed like a real losing game. But I had
made a promise to Helen, and by now she had left for
college and I carried on as she had requested.

Then came Dr. Suzuki's workshop in San Francisco
in 1966. Terri was three and a half at the time and we
went to the workshop at the request of Mrs. Mills. Dr.
Suzuki worked with Terri every day for two weeks and
at the end of this time she was putting down the correct
fingers to "Twinkle, Twinkle." She knew all of her
rhythms and had been listening to the records for over
a year. Her progress seemed to go in high gear for a
great period of time. The biggest drawback I can see
in Terri's development is that the older children who
started at the same time she did, more or less fell by the
wayside. This means that the competition up to now in
her peer group has been nil. Somehow she needs a bit of
stimulation to keep at it. However, we are well pleased
with what she has accomplished in her short life thus far
and we are most happy with the time and effort that has
been given to Terri by Mrs. Mills. Terri has just finished
the Seitz Rondo and is starting on the Vivaldi A Minor.
(This is probably a misstatement, for Terri has in essence
been practicing the Vivaldi for the past year by listening
to the record of it.) She is also learning to read music
and seems to take to it very rapidly. Her progress here
is very fast.

Terri's life is not only filled with music, but she has
many other interests as well. She is a good swimmer and
is most fond of animals. She enjoys the friendship of

other children and loves to play with her Barbie doll whenever she has the time. She is outgoing and affectionate and tends to give a great deal of herself in every occasion. We do feel that her musical training has given her a great deal of confidence and security. When a child is the "tail end" as this one is, sometimes he seems to lack this security.

I failed to mention that Terri was very ill at 7 months of age and was given no hope for survival. As a baby, she was quite fidgety and nervous and music did seem a great calming factor. We do feel that music did give her that *something* that she needed.

I do hope that this is the information that you desire and that it will help you.

We are surely looking forward to seeing you very very soon.

With our very best,

Terri looked tiny and lost among two thousand Japanese children; of course there were smaller children, but they were among their own people speaking their language. Terri understood no Japanese, so when she lined up among the big group, she must have felt very isolated. Observing her lonesome figure, Yuko went and knelt beside her and talked to her. "Don't be afraid, Terri. Play just as you have been taught in your country. Pluck up your courage, there's nothing to fear." Terri smiled and played beautifully, forgetting she was an American girl. Later when Yuko went to visit Dr. Goulard's home, Terri invited her to swim in their pool. Yuko stood at the edge hesitating, when Terri came up to her and said:

"Don't be afraid, Yuko. Do just what you have done in your home. Pluck up your courage and jump in. There's nothing to fear." When I heard this story I laughed until my sides ached.

After organizing E.D.A., I was often in touch with Mr. Ibuka. After graduating from Waseda University, Mr. Ibuka applied for a position with Toshiba Electric Company but failed the examination. In 1946, he established a company named Totsuko and asked Mr. Akio Morita to cooperate with him. Later they changed the name to SONY, a name now well known throughout the world. SONY and Talent Education began at about the same time. SONY has developed financially and internationally while Talent Education, although well known internationally, is always poor financially. Of course SONY is a business company and our business is education. SONY's purpose is to make money and ours to make individuals, but the philosophy is quite similar. So naturally Mr. Ibuka easily understood our idea, and I could also understand SONY's management. For members of the Board of Directors of E.D.A. Mr. Ibuka recommended important persons in the country. Dr. Seiji Kaya, former president of Tokyo University, was the first to be on the board. The other directors are Mr. Shigeo Nagano, chairman of Shinnihon Seitetsu; Mr. Kazutaka Kikawada, chairman of Tokyo Electric Inc.; Mr. Hideo Edo, President of Mitsui Estate Inc.; Mr. Hideto Furuoka, President of Gakken Publishing Co.; Mrs. Chieko Akiyama, a famous journalist; Mr. Seiji Tsutsumi, President of Seibu Department Store; Mr. Tomiji Yamazaki, President of Yamatane Security Co.; Mr. Bunbei Hara, Representative, Upper House; Mr. Minoru Mori, Executive Director, Mori Building Inc.; Mr. W. Buckner, President of Ken Foundation; Dr. Glenn Doman, Director of the Institutes for the Achievement of Human Potential; and of course Dr. Suzuki, Mr. Miyamoto acts as managing director, Mr. Ibuka as chairman, and Professor Akira Taga of Chiba University and I as executive directors.

Thus a new page in the history of children opened.

Another tour for 1968 was materializing. It was to start from Honolulu on October 4 and end at Anchorage, November 2. In Honolulu we gave three presentations in the big beautiful International Center. Thousands of children from kindergarten to grammar school filled the house. I always give a message at the beginning. "Good afternoon, children." They echo, "Good afternoon." "Now we will have a concert, maybe slightly different from what you hear daily, but I am sure your teachers have had you listen to the record. It is classical music composed by Beethoven and Mozart and Bach, whose names you probably have heard. The music is played by small children about your age. They are speaking to you through the violin. We are here to let you know that all children can develop their abilities. Our children can, and of course you can. How many of you in this auditorium cannot speak English? If there are any, please raise your hands. I see no hands raised. Naturally you all speak and understand English. But you must remember that it is very difficult for an adult to learn a foreign language, so you all have wonderful abilities. The music will not be so long, so please have patience and listen quietly."

They all had patience and were very quiet during the concert. The children also gave a formal concert at the same hall and it seemed that people enjoyed it very much judging from the following:

Suzuki Strings Amaze Audience
By Robert C. Loveless
Star-Bulletin Music Critic

The Honolulu Youth Symphony opened its fall season last evening in a joint concert with the Suzuki Strings of Japan.   .

It is with no intent to belittle the fine performance of the youth symphony in its opening group of three numbers, that we say that it was the unbelievable Japanese children that utterly flabbergasted the modest crowd gathered in the Honolulu International Center Concert Hall.

The program of the Suzuki children progressed from the amazing to the incredible to the fantastic.

It was amazing to hear the ensemble of five then seven string musicians, aged 5 to 10, play Bach, Vivaldi, and Mozart with technical precision, feeling, and careful attention to the terraced dynamics, and timely rallentando.

The program reached the level of incredibility with the performance of 5-year-old Kimiko Kitazawa of Bach's "Loure" and 6-year-old Akihiro Miura's rendition of the Presto movement of Vivaldi's A Minor Violin Concerto.

These youngsters performed the technically difficult works with precision and flair. It was exceedingly difficult for one to believe what he was hearing.

But fantastic is the only word that is nearly adequate to describe the performance of 13-year-old cellist Koji Yanagida of the first movement of Boccherini's B-flat Concerto. The cadenza was magnificent. The total rendition was worthy of a mature musician.

The same could be said of 9-year-old Hitomi Kasuya's reading of Vitali's Chaconne. The intricate bowing techniques were taken in stride like a veteran. The interpretation was mature. The overall effect was—well, as I said, "fantastic."

Shinichi Suzuki's rote method of teaching has received world-wide attention and acclaim. His concept of enriching the lives of the youngsters, whether or not they go on to be career performers, is one from which we should learn.

For those who did not hear last night's concert, you have my sympathy.

Honolulu Star-Bulletin
Reprinted by permission

On the island of Maui, we had a nice rest. Dr. Izumi and others took us to their homes. We enjoyed sightseeing and picnics on the island.

The concert was held in the Baldwin High School auditorium. In the daytime the children gave two concerts especially for junior and senior high school students. In a way I was more concerned with their response than that of younger children. Most of the music they know is rock or jazz, and I felt they might be restless at a concert of classical music.

My worry was needless. They were quiet, attentive, and seemed to enjoy the music very much. Often we make prophecies from our own viewpoint, thinking others might not like this or that, especially if they are children. We must acknowledge that children possess much higher potentiality than we think; thus it is important to give them what is good. And it isn't necessary to consider if they like it or not from our standpoint. Dr. Blakely in Hilo, Hawaii, has been for the past several years promoting a movement to have people hear good music. I always admire the zeal and enthusiasm of people who dedicate their time and money working for the good of people, asking nothing in return.

In Hilo I had a little free time and Mrs. Blakely took me to the barber. The shop was managed by Japanese and girls who did hair-cutting were second or third generation, speaking almost no Japanese. We had a brief conversation of not much importance. But suddenly they became quiet. When the girls went to the corner to change towels, I overheard one speaking in a low voice, "I am ashamed, he speaks much better English than me." I had noticed her queer manner of speaking, pidgin English, they say. In Japan, different provinces have different dialects. Since TV and radio spread throughout the country, and teachers usually teach standard Japanese, dialects are disappearing rapidly. When young people come from the country to enter school in Tokyo, they are sometimes made fun of because of their dialects and this often leads to an inferiority complex. In E.D.A. we teach standard Japanese to children. It is important for them to master good language skills at an early age.

We left Hilo very early in the morning. It was dark and, even in the tropical climate, it was cool. As our plane gained altitude, the eastern horizon became pink and bright. The sun was rising and the weather fine. The sea was indigo blue, clear and beautiful. The islands strewn on the ocean were like emeralds. No wonder they call the islands of Hawaii the "Jewels of the Pacific."

We left Honolulu en route to San Francisco. I was surprised

to see Mrs. Carlos Panfiglio waiting to see us off at the Honolulu airport. She put a fragrant wreath around my neck and kissed me on the cheek. Every time we visit Honolulu, the Panfiglios open their home and entertain, not only us but those who have worked for the concert. Mr. Panfiglio came from Italy and worked his way through college with the help of a football scholarship. He built the American Electric Company which is the second largest industry in Hawaii.

The trip to Redding in Northern California was strenuous. We changed planes in San Francisco and arrived in Sacramento in the evening. Mr. and Mrs. Jacoby and their friends were waiting for us, and we divided the group and drove up the highway. I thought the drive would take about an hour or two, three at the most. We had a light supper on our way which refreshed us very much. Again we drove hours and hours on the dark highway and the strain was beginning to show on all of us. It was midnight when we finally arrived at Shasta College in Redding. It was very cold and the children were shivering. We had left Hawaii in the morning wearing summer clothing and now the climate was like winter. All the hosts had been waiting for us at the school, but it took another good hour before the children were tucked into bed.

Three days in Northern California were very strenuous. We would have enjoyed the beautiful scenery with its tall spruce and pines if the weather had been good. Unfortunately it was not and every child caught cold, some with high fever. I went to the homes in which they were staying and gave them shots and medicine. We conducted the workshop in the afternoon and gave the concert that same night. I learned two lessons from this experience: for the sake of the children's health we should travel from north to south—never the other way around; and in order to assure sufficient time for everyone to rest, we should avoid strenuous scheduling.

The children played at Paradise High School on October 11. The high school band, with Mr. Jacoby conducting, played some pieces. At the conclusion of their performance, they played "America the Beautiful." I was listening backstage and when I heard this music a wonderful inspiration came to me. During the past tours through the United States we had always played classical music and, though people call it Western music, it is essentially European. I have always wanted to play something that was original to the United States. "America the Beautiful" was just what I was looking for. Traveling all over the United States from east to west and south to north, I always loved its majestic beauty, loved the people living in this country. The verses and the music of this piece symbolize the country. It would be a perfect encore.

In the Los Angeles area there were two sponsors, one in the Pasadena area and another at El Camino College. They took turns inviting us every other year. Dr. Robert Haag was the director of the program in El Camino and the school budgeted funds to present good music to the district. Besides the Suzuki children they sponsored the Vienna Boys Choir, the Don Cossack Chorus and other performances. Mrs. Elizabeth Holborn, instructor of violin in this area, helped house the group and prepare for the workshop. Mrs. Holborn told me several years later that when I told the audience that the children on the tour were not the cream of the crop and that I could bring any number of others, she did not believe it. But when she visited Japan to attend the summer school, she witnessed the truth with her own eyes and ears.

After the performance at Northwest Nazarene College, we flew south to New Orleans. Mr. Mochizuki and I stayed in the home of Mr. Godchaux, who owns a women's department store. He is a dignified old man who lives alone with his servants in a big home in the best residential quarter. Next morning, I felt like taking a walk downtown, so I asked one of the servants how to take a streetcar to the downtown area. He told me he would go with me to the car stop. We left the house from the back door and strolled down the street. He put me on the car and after some time I got off at Canal Street.

Walking down the street, I suddenly felt a pain in my stomach. Maybe it was the water which was the cause, but the pain became worse and I could hardly endure it. Just then, fortunately, I spied Mr. Godchaux's department store. The atmosphere was elegant and, of course, the customers were all ladies. The lady in charge approached me and asked, "Can I help you?" Help, of course, was what I wanted. I asked where the restroom was. The lady answered calmly, "This is a women's store but you can use the employees', which is on the third floor." Thanking her, I ran up to the third floor. This was perhaps the most trying time for me of the whole trip. As my pain eased, I began strolling through the store. There were floors that sold only underwear, and floors that sold dresses, suits and coats. People looked at me queerly, and I became a little embarrassed, so I told one of the salesladies that I would like to see Mr. Godchaux. She took me to the president's office and when I entered, he looked very surprised. I told him I was interested in women's clothes, which made him very happy. He began telling me the history of his store which began in the early eighteen hundreds. From the shelf he took an old account book on which was written, in beautiful fancy penmanship, all the names of customers and the details of purchasing and selling. "My grandfather wrote all these," Mr. Godchaux said. "He seemed to have difficulties after the Civil War. The story, I understand, was that Confederate money became worthless and the store was in financial trouble." He then escorted me through his store and this time when I looked at the ladies' clothes I was more at ease.

After saying good-bye to Mr. Godchaux I got on the same streetcar. Then suddenly I realized that I had not asked the name of the stop at which I embarked. I had been talking with the servant and did not bother to notice the place or name. I racked my brain and then happened to remember passing a grammar school just after we got on the car. In Japan, though it be government or private railroad, the name of the stop is always written both in Japanese and English, but not here. I looked out of the window, saw a grammar school, and got off at the next stop. I began walking toward what I thought was the direction of Mr. Godchaux's home, but nothing looked familiar. I now recalled that I had come out of the back door, and didn't look back to confirm the landscape. I walked and walked but could not find the place. I again racked my brain and recalled that the name of the street was something like "Estate Place." I asked many passersby but no one recognized the name. At three o'clock in the afternoon we intended to have a workshop in McAlister Hall auditorium at Tulane University. It was already one o'clock and I started perspiring nervously. Just then I saw a Catholic Girls High School, so I went inside and asked the lady in charge to help me. She smiled at my story and began calling on the phone. At last she found the number and location of Mr. Godchaux's house. No wonder people did not know the name. It was a private estate.

That night, after the concert, Mr. and Mrs. Peter Hansen drove us through the French Quarter. New Orleans was very exotic and quite different from any other city in the United States.

On this tour we brought two boy cellists, Koji Yanagida, thirteen, and Tomoyuki Nomura, seven. Mr. Nomura, cello instructor and father of Tomoyuki, was in charge of the cello workshop. When we arrived at Indiana University at Fort Wayne to perform the workshop, Koji Yanagida came to my side with a distressed face. "Dr. Honda, I have lost the end-pin of my cello and it is impossible to play." Yes, it was impossible to play without the end-pin and it was only thirty minutes before the workshop was to begin. I asked one of the faculty members if he had an extra, but as Koji's instrument was not full-sized, there was none available to fit. People were expecting a cello workshop and we had to find something to substitute. I searched my bag and found a pair of chopsticks made of bamboo. One fit but when he tried to play, it was not strong enough to sustain the weight. I began to get worried and searched my bag again. In it I felt something long, thin, and hard. It was the steel stem of the Rotary banner of my club, Fujisawa North. The length was about eight inches. I gently pulled it out of the flag and installed it in the cello. It fit perfectly and I cried hurrah in my heart and shook hands with Koji. Even the short end was perfect to hold the cello on the floor. That afternoon, the children played with the Fort Wayne Symphony Orchestra.

We visited Oberlin again, and the events at the school were given in honor of the tenth anniversary of Talent Education in the United States. The program had been specially arranged by Mr. Cook and Mr. Mochizuki. The concert and workshop were held on October 20 at Warner Concert Hall.

Way up in the mountains of North Carolina in Chapel Hill is the University of North Carolina. I was surprised to see, even in this district where the population is not dense, there was a parking problem, and my host had to drive around and around in search of a parking place. The performance was arranged by Dr. Edgar Alden of the University of North Carolina. The concert at Hill Music Hall received a tremendous ovation. People stood on their feet, clapping their hands and calling "bravo." The warm reception of the people went straight to our hearts and we were happy.

In East Chicago, Indiana, the performance was held at Washington High School auditorium. The children trooped backstage after they played Allegro by Fiocco. Yukari Tate, who was marching at the end of the line, stumbled, fell, and hit her right elbow. She sat still on the floor for some time, holding her elbow. I ran to her aid. I was relieved to find there was no fracture or serious injury. At the end of the program, she played a Paganini concerto. She played the first part beautifully, but, when the music proceeded to the cadenza, she suddenly stopped playing. Her elbow hurt her and she could not continue playing. Backstage, she sat on the chair and burst into tears. I could do nothing. She had to pull herself together. This would be a good lesson for her though the medicine was bitter.

We are often asked the percentage of children who will follow professional careers in the future. One of the important points I stress in my lectures is that Talent Education is not a movement to make professional musicians. We expect children to develop various abilities through playing the violin. Parents will not pay tuition for teaching manners or concentration. By learning violin or piano children will not only learn music but also many other good qualities. In short, it is education *by* music, not education *for* music. As a result there are some who want to become instructors or performers, but the percentage is not high, probably about 10 percent.

Yukari is one who will make music her career. But there are many obstacles in her way before she becomes established. Thus far she has walked in sunshine, but in her future there will inevitably be days of rain and storm.

In New York City, the children performed in the Assembly Hall of Hunter College. I did not think that the hall would be equal to the Philharmonic or Carnegie Hall, but when I saw the pictures of famous artists who had performed in Assembly Hall, I acknowledged it to be so.

A school bus was waiting at the entrance of Manger Windsor Hotel the next morning, to take us to Oceanside, Long Island. The children were to give three short concerts for the public school. We all tumbled into the bus and I, as usual, sat in the very front. The driver inserted the ignition key and turned it but the engine just murmured and stopped. Again he tried but the bus failed to start. Before I knew what was happening, the driver jumped out of the bus and began pushing from the side. As it was parked on the hill, it began to move slowly. The driver came running and hopped into the bus, and the engine started. My skin crawled to think what would have happened if the door had closed and he was unable to jump in. It was far too risky a thing to try and I did not like it. But the driver was very happy and sang all the way to Oceanside.

Eastman School of Music had been continuing its "Project Super" and Yuko had been invited to teach for a year. The schedule in Rochester was rushed. On the afternoon of our arrival we had workshops, and a concert that night at the big Eastman Theatre. Local schoolchildren joined the workshop. They were making good progress under the direction of Dr.

Shetler and Miss Anastasia Jempelis. The next day we had to leave. It broke my heart to see Yuko weeping as we left the airport.

At O'Hare Airport in Chicago many passengers stood by waiting for us. Actually they were waiting for the American children to welcome us by playing violin pieces. Every year since we had visited Chicago, the children of Winnetka played the violin for us as we arrived in the lobby of the airport. Each year they played better. It gave a warm feeling not only to us but to all the people who heard the music. Even the passengers of this busiest airport in the world stopped to listen.

That day another incident took place which made my hair stand on end. We had finished the program in Winnetka and were going to O'Hare Airport on a school bus. The driver was driving casually when I happened to notice that he was doing something funny with his right foot. Then, gradually, the bus slowed down and suddenly made a right turn on the red signal. It glided into the gas station and stopped. The driver had pulled the emergency brake. I asked him, "What is the matter, are you out of gas?" No," he replied, wiping his forehead, "it was trouble with the brake, the foot brake wasn't working." While we waited for a substitute bus, I asked Mr. Mochizuki to take a taxi and hurry to the airport to inform the agent of United Airlines of our accident and request that the flight be held until we arrived. Consequently, we made the flight safely to Anchorage, Alaska, later that night.

Anchorage was enthusiastic from the first, in 1964. They had been preparing all things necessary for our appearance, but as Northwest Airlines had stopped their service in March of that year, we had to cancel the concert. After four years, our visit finally materialized and we owed much to the effort of Mr. Frank Pinkerton, Director of Music, Anchorage School District.

My hostess, Mrs. Loraine Harrison, President of the Anchorage Music Association, a widow in her late sixties, is a wonderful lady. She did not indulge herself in sorrow long when she lost her husband, but opened a ladies' hat store in the corner of the hotel. Hat-making was her hobby and then it became her chief means of livelihood. She later enlarged the shop, making dresses, especially wedding gowns. Being successful in her business, she spends her time and money for social activities and, as she majored in music, helped establish the Anchorage Music Association. Mrs. Harrison is always smiling. In spite of some troubles in her personal life, she never complains. She is a great lady and I admire her very much.

Alaska is indeed a wonderful state and it has a great future in economy, in nature, and in culture. For the brochure of the tour, John Kendall wrote the following, which expresses his thoughts as well as those of his colleagues:

> Just ten years ago, an historic showing of a film sparked the beginning of a movement in America which was to have far-reaching results. At that time, it was my good fortune to attend a meeting of string teachers who reacted incredulously to the film brought by Kenji Mochizuki at Clifford Cook's request, showing 700 very young Japanese children playing the Bach Double Concerto.
>
> The impact of this experience resulted in a visit to Japan in 1959, when Mr. Suzuki urged me to bring the Talent Education movement to the attention of American musicians. Since then, it has been my opportunity to travel twice more to Japan, and subsequently, to explain and demonstrate Mr. Suzuki's ideas to over 2000 interested teachers in forty states.
>
> Now, ten years later, every corner of the nation, including Alaska and Hawaii, has been touched by the excitement, enthusiasm, and curiosity surrounding these ideas. It truly has been a decade of dramatic development in American string teaching.
>
> Experiments with these teaching approaches have not been confined to one single area, or level, but significantly have been carried on in universities and colleges; community and settlement music schools; laboratory

schools; public schools; government projects; and, of course, by many private teachers.

The possibilities for very young violin students, as well as older ones, to play beautifully has been demonstrated for us by the appearance in this country of Mr. Suzuki and his talented students, beginning with the first trip in 1964. These performances are a source of inspiration and a challenge to all who experience them.

The need for dedicated, skilled, and enthusiastic teacher-performers to carry on the development of our own young talented students is a pressing need which we must face with imaginative efforts.

If the next ten years bring to fruition the seeds so far planted, we will have taken a great step in strengthening our musical life in America, and in cementing a fine relationship, through music, with our friends in Japan.

To the fine young violinists of the 1968 touring group, and to their teachers, we extend a warm and cordial welcome.

I have already written about the introduction of the Suzuki Method in the public school system in the United States. Compared to private lessons in Japan, the adapted method has some disadvantages, but by giving a chance to every child through teaching in the grammar school it is ideal for American children. There are several cities and districts in the United States where boards of education are really helping carry out this program. Miss Shirlene McMichael wrote an article about her work in Pendleton, Oregon. This article is an eloquent statement of the positive results and the ways in which they have been achieved:

> Here in Pendleton we are starting our fourth year of experimentation with Talent Education in the public school string program. The program itself, starting its seventh year, is complete with the first high school orchestra. The strength of the program in terms of student interest and quality of performance is greater

since the adaptation of Talent Education ideas.

The success of a program depends on many factors, but the key role is that of the teacher. More teachers need to look at their own beliefs about teaching and the goals they set for students. Very often instructors involved in performance music activities become so preoccupied with the end result they forget about the process and the individual students. How a student learns; how his interest in, and sensitivity to, music is aroused; how parents can be helped to create a musical environment for children . . . these are the key concerns.

Adaptation of Talent Education to the classroom makes use of individualized instruction within the class. Students progress at their own pace, receiving individualized attention in turn. As a group they play material all students know. This classroom situation offers the best solution for working with the main objective of Dr. Suzuki's philosophy—that of developing the potential of each individual student to the highest degree.

After an enlightening trip to Japan this past summer with ASTA to observe Talent Education, we are convinced that we should go ahead with the experiment in our school system. In doing so, we must consider:

1 *Teaching Environment:* Teachers must have love for children, interest in each individual child's development in music through fun, musicianship, listening skills, and motivation for individual achievement.

2 *Home Environment:* Parents should be interested in the program and understand its philosophy. They should offer support by coming to lessons and programs. Their role is to *encourage,* not *force.*

3 *Cultural Development:* Practicing the violin is a cultural accomplishment. Children should not receive *rewards* for practicing but always *praise.*

In Japan, parents play an important role in the education of their children. Mothers supervise music practice. They are the key factor in creating the musical home environment and in stimulating the children to practice.

In our program, time is spent at the beginning of instruction with coordination skills. Each step of playing is carefully introduced so that the student will not be rushed into all phases of playing at once. Much emphasis is placed on listening and memorizing so that class time can be spent on tone production and musicianship. Learning to read takes its proper place in the sequence of skills to be learned. Material once learned is constantly reviewed so that a student develops facility with and control of his instrument.

Note reading is introduced to a student when he is ready technically and handles his instrument proficiently. So far, most of the students have done above-average work in note reading, and the rhythmic reading has improved. Now, after learning how to listen, students play in tune first, and are used to concentrating on doing things carefully one step at a time. They do not get bored with practicing because repetition is an important part of the vocabulary. We believe that our Talent Education program will develop better all-around players for our school orchestras.

When we visited Pendleton last year I personally observed the results. I admire the good experiences which the public schools are trying to give children in the United States.

E.D.A. STARTS TO WORK

During my visit to the United States, E.D.A. had rented two floors of a building in Kitamagome, Ohta-ku, Tokyo. The building was still under construction. Within a month, it was beautifully furnished with a thick carpet and good furniture. The atmosphere was luxurious. As soon as I was settled, I began designing programs for the project. Besides violin and piano, we would experiment in various fields. The number of children accommodated would be limited, but in the future we ought to be able to send materials which had been tested and developed in the center to homes of the poor or where children are neglected.

Newspapers, radio and TV stations were interested in our project. It was news to them, a new idea in education. We explained carefully, trying to avoid misunderstanding as much as possible. They listened intently, asked questions and took notes. But quite a number of articles misinterpreted our motives, which did great harm.

The American lady who was to take charge of the English class suddenly returned to her country without notice. Now I was in trouble, as more than fifty children, ages ranging from three to six, had applied for the class. If we did not find an instructor, we would be in deep trouble. Then I happened to remember a young lady who was helping in the office of the Committee of Cooperation for English Study in Japan, Miss Kathy Irving. I called her on the phone and found her English accent was perfect. The pitch of her voice was pleasant, neither too high nor too low. I asked her to come to the office, told her about our situation and asked her to be the English teacher. She was reluctant. Her main reason was that she had never had any experience with small children. "This is a new experiment. Nobody has taught a foreign language to children of three. I know you do not have experience. Nobody has. But I am sure you can make it." I coaxed, pleaded, and explained that the class was to begin within a week and I desperately needed an English teacher. At last she consented and the class began.

Each class consisted of less than fifteen children. Kathy taught three classes a day, spending approximately forty-five minutes in each. It was the first time that many of the children had ever seen a foreign lady, much less heard English spoken. I told Kathy to quit the lesson as soon as the children showed any sign of weariness. In the beginning their concentration is not yet developed, so they tire easily. But to my surprise they all seemed to be very happy with the young

American teacher. She was indeed a very good teacher and with the assistance of Miss Emiko Koyama, who spoke excellent English, managed to keep the children interested. Children do not feel any obligation to the teacher, so, as soon as they get tired, the instructor loses control of them. The important thing is to have song and movement in the curriculum. The E.D.A. method is to have the teacher engage the children in some activity like singing or marching.

To teach a foreign language to children in whose homes their native language is spoken from morning to night, the cooperation of the mother is as important as it is in the teaching of violin. Attending a class for forty-five minutes once a week will not develop abilities, so we give every child a tape of the curriculum. This tape consists of ten volumes and, when the children master these ten, they should be able to carry on a simple conversation. Kathy spoke to the children in the way she would speak to American children and within a month these Japanese children understood what she was saying.

OUR SILVER WEDDING ANNIVERSARY

March 21, 1969, was our silver wedding anniversary. People often say that life is like a dream and when I reflect on the past, maybe it is like a dream, but every detail of our life comes clearly to my mind. I can still recall the day I first met Junko in her home. When we went on our honeymoon, a scroll was hanging on the wall and on it was written a script by Lord Tokugawa Ieyasu, the first Shogunate of Tokugawa era. It began like this: "Life is like walking a long road carrying a heavy load. Don't hurry!" Twenty-five years had indeed been a long road and we had carried heavy loads, but we never grumbled and I think no one knew how heavy they were.

Junko is still as young and beautiful to me as she was the day I first met her. Maybe one of the reasons we have both remained young is that we always face tomorrow. It gives us happiness to think there are so many things for us to do. Because our wedding was held during the war, we did not have a reception, so we planned to invite many friends to celebrate our twenty-fifth anniversary. Junko's old friends, Mrs. Mituishi, Mrs. Ito, and Mrs. Sugahara, gave us a big wedding cake. I took Junko's hand and we cut the cake together.

Our second daughter Mayako returned home from her studies at San Francisco State College. She was doing nothing, sleeping until late in the morning. One day I talked with her: "Mayako, I have been observing you and, in short, you are leading a lazy life, serving nobody but yourself. You must learn how to serve others. This is a very important thing in life." She nodded.

A month later, she came to me and said, "Father, you told me to serve other people. I have taken an examination for PAN AM and passed. Of course, you will allow me to enter the service." I gasped and was speechless for a time, but could only say "Yes." Within two weeks, she flew to Miami to receive training as a stewardess.

After finishing her two year contract at Eastman, Yuko returned home for her summer vacation. The school wanted to renew the contract but she seemed at a loss whether to continue her teaching at Eastman or not.

TOUR, 1969

It is indeed a surprise to see how time flies. There is an old saying in Japan, "Time flies like an arrow." There are very few things on this earth that are given equally to all people. But time is given equally to all. When we are unhappy, we pray that time will pass quickly and when we are happy, we hope that time will forget us. But time moves steadily, regardless of events on earth. It depends on the ability of the individual to make the most of it.

The 1969 tour began from Anchorage. Mr. Soffer had taken my advice and arranged the itinerary beginning from Alaska and ending in Hawaii. The morning after our arrival, one of the host families took me to see a glacier located in a suburb outside of Anchorage. We drove along the gray coastline that was cold, desolate and barren. A stream was flowing from a lake, so clear you could count the pebbles in the bed. Occasionally, a big salmon glided by, showing his red belly. The salmon had come to this spring after climbing many miles up the river from the ocean, to lay their eggs and then wait to die. The big lake was the tomb of the glacier. Moving inch by inch, taking thousands of years, these ice floes had moved down to this place to melt and end their long journey. The color of the ice was indigo blue, clear and sparkling. I stood for some time, breathless, just looking at nature's beauty. I have never seen such beautiful color in my life.

The performance was held at West High School auditorium in Anchorage at 7:30 p.m. on October 6. The full house gave us a standing ovation which we appreciated very much, a good omen from the start.

Like Eastman, Iowa received a government grant and began a project under the direction of Mrs. Mohatt. They named it "Project Star" and began the program in different schools in different cities.

When I first received the 1969 itinerary from Mr. Soffer, I found that Peoria, Illinois, had been included, and my heart leapt with joy. We were to fly from Burlington, Iowa, to Peoria and then drive to Bloomington where we were to give a performance. I wrote to Mrs. Charles Funk asking the distance between the two cities and understood it to be about a thirty-minute drive. I wrote another letter to Mrs. Funk asking her to reserve the two best seats on the night of the performance, telling her I would pay for the seats.

After having dinner in Bloomington with Mrs. Everett Walker, who had visited Japan in 1967 with her husband, we arrived at the Scottish Rite Temple where the concerts were to be held. During the intermission, many people came backstage, telling me of the wonderful performance. But I stretched my neck, waiting for a certain person I had never met. A few minutes later, I saw a lady of middle age in a pink coat, walking toward me. I needed no introduction. I knew instinctively that this was the lady I was waiting for.

"Mrs. Fran Block," I said.

"Yes, Dr. Honda."

We took each other's hand for some time, without a word. This was the moment I had been awaiting for a very long time.

In 1966 there was a big domestic air strike in the United States. A daughter of my friend Dr. Ono was visiting the U.S. on a summer vacation. Sometimes it is difficult to understand what is happening in a foreign country, and though I am sure the agent told her of the strike, apparently she didn't think she would be in trouble. As a matter of fact, she was stranded in Los Angeles en route to Chicago. She sat in the lobby waiting alone for the plane to take off. Even in this city of Southern California, it became quite cold as night came on, and she shivered with cold, fright, and loneliness.

Then an American lady approached her and asked what was the matter. She tried with all her might, with limited English, to explain that she must fly to Chicago on the next plane or she would be in serious trouble. There was one plane leaving for the East and hundreds of people were clamoring for the seats. Hearing her story and observing she was shivering, the lady took off her sweater and put it around the girl's shoulders. Then she walked to the counter and talked with the clerk in charge. The lady came back with the clerk and told her to have no fear as everything had been arranged. The agent ushered the girl to the plane and gave her a first-class seat. I do not know to this day how she managed to get the seat. Maybe she had given up her own seat.

When the girl returned to Japan, she told this story, with tears flowing, to her parents on their way home from the airport.

"Dr. Honda. This was the best lesson my daughter learned from her trip to the United States, to help others in time of need. I really admire the generosity and the warm heart American people have," Dr. Ono related. I was moved beyond words. I got her address and her name; she was Mrs. Fran

Block and she lived in Peoria, Illinois. That night I wrote her a letter thanking her for her kindness. I wrote that her noble deed was surely not only for one Japanese girl but for all humanity. I could not but have deepest admiration for what she had done.

After two weeks, I received an answer. It began like this:

> Dear Dr. Honda, I am surprised to receive your letter. Anybody in my place at that time would have done the same. The poor girl was so lonesome. We walk daily a path which we will never tread again. Why shouldn't we do for others what we think best?

I was deeply moved again by her letter and resolved that if ever I should be in Peoria, or in the vicinity, I would invite her to the concert. Finally my dream was realized, and I was glad beyond words that I could repay her for her benevolent deed.

In New York, we played again in Philharmonic Hall, this time with the Little Orchestra Society. When Hitomi Kasuya played the Mendelssohn Violin Concerto, Koji Yanagida, who played cello, was invited to play as a member of the orchestra. We could well understand his pride, being given a seat beside the principal cellist and playing with adults in full orchestra. It was indeed a big day for him.

Three days in Washington D.C. were very busy. Mrs. Mary Disler and Mrs. Joseph Greenwood and their friends were waiting for us at the airport with a school bus. We all got on the bus and of course thought that a husky driver would take the wheel. We were surprised to find that the lady with white hair was to drive. I was relieved to find she was a very good driver.

After appearing on TV, we were taken sightseeing in the city. Before the tomb of John Kennedy, we all made a deep bow. I remember the time I wrote a letter asking if there was a possibility of playing in the White House. His secretary gave me a polite answer hinting the possibility, but all this faded away with his sudden death. The next morning I got up at six and took two children to be on TV. It was a morning show and the President of Ghana and his cabinet were being interviewed before us. The performances were presented in the Jefferson High School auditorium at 1:30, 3:00, and 8:00 p.m.

One of the girls I took to the TV interview that morning was Mikie Naito. She played a piano solo and in the midst of her solo, she stopped abruptly and ran backstage. She was holding her face and I noticed blood oozing between her hands. Her nose was bleeding. After taking care of her, I went out on the stage and apologized to the audience. During the intermission a handsome looking gentleman and his wife came backstage. I could not identify him. He said with a smile, "I am Captain Porter."

Then I remembered. He was Commander of the Naval Air Base in Atsugi. My Rotary Club and the base were on good terms, and we often had joint activities.

"I saw you on TV this morning and asked various places to find where you were to perform. I am very glad to meet you."

So was I. It is indeed a small world.

That night a reception was held. I stood with Mr. Richardson, Undersecretary of State, greeted and shook hands with many people for a long, long time.

Next morning we all got up at six. I was so tired I dragged myself out of bed. We took a chartered bus from Falls Church to Washington, D.C. The first concert was held in the National Cathedral. The gigantic Gothic chapel towered above us and we were awed at the magnificent building.

The performance took place at the Great Crossing, the heart of the cathedral where two transepts intersect, forming the shape of the cross. Benches from three sides faced the space and though the concert began at 8:45 in the morning, every bench was occupied. As the hall was so big, I was afraid that the tone would not carry to the far distance but I found that acoustics were good.

It was the first time we had played inside a church and the children knew that this was the House of God. Forgetting all their weariness, they played beautifully. It was indeed a marvelous and solemn experience for us all.

The next performance was at 10:30 a.m. at Beauvoir Cathedral Elementary School, another at 2:15 p.m. at Sheridan School, and the last at 4:00 p.m. at George Marshall High School.

On arrival at Blue Grass Airport at Lexington, Kentucky, there was a red carpet placed from the aircraft to the lobby. I told the children that there must be some important person on the plane and they should not tread on the carpet. Later I was surprised to learn that the carpet was for us. The weather was beautiful but cold. I told my host that I had always thought the weather in Kentucky and Tennessee was mild, but he laughed and said they even have frost in winter. We had frost on the morning of October 14.

On arrival in Louisville, Miss Jane Burke, Mrs. Virginia Schneider, and our host took us to the famous zoo. The children had a wonderful time with the animals, and then we were all invited to a garden party given by the Mayor, Mr. Schmied. After lunch the mayor gave me the keys to the city and the following certificate:

The City of Louisville
In behalf of its illustrious citizens, confers on
Dr. Masaaki Honda
who, through distinguished deeds has exhibited the qualification necessary of a Louisville
Ambassador of Good Will
and the responsibility of furthering the fame of Louisville's business progress, civic accomplishment, cultural and intellectual achievement, and gracious living, wherever he may be,
As authority of this commission, we present the
Key to the City of Louisville
Presented at Louisville, in the Commonwealth of Kentucky, this 24th day of October, 1969
Kenneth A. Schmied
Mayor

The concert was held at the Atherton High School auditorium at 8:30 p.m., and the workshop in the same hall at 8:30 the next morning. Nearly one hundred and fifty children joined the Japanese children in the workshop. It was indeed a beautiful sight to see children of both nationalities play on the stage. As soon as the assembly was over, Mr. Robert Whitney, Dean of the School of Music, University of Louisville, came on the stage, took the microphone and began speaking. His words shook with emotion:

> What we have witnessed is a matter of great importance. Many American children have traveled far to join the concert. These children are descendants of different nationalities. They have played with the Japanese children side by side. It is not the matter of difference in skill but the important thing is to play together with no prejudice or discrimination. I hope that all children in the world will play like this in the future.

When we left Louisville at ten-thirty, there were buses everywhere loaded with children. We all waved good-bye. Though we were separated by a glass window, the warm feeling communicated straight to every small heart.

The three-and-a-half hour drive to Muncie was a good rest for all of us. Most of the children slept, and I enjoyed the scenery. On arriving at Ball State University, we were ushered to beautiful Emens Auditorium. The workshop was performed at four, and it was followed by rehearsal with the Muncie Symphony Orchestra conducted by Dr. Robert Hargreaves.

Our performance in Milwaukee was at Alverno College. This is a Catholic girls' school and Sister Laura Lampe was in charge. Our housing was on the first floor of the girls' dormitory. There were three male instructors on the tour, Mr. Chuichi Takasugi, the chief instructor, and two others. We were probably the only males in the history of the school who were allowed to sleep in this dorm.

Our 1969 tour ended after performances in Boise, Idaho, Los Angeles, and Hawaii.

The following article written by Miss Anastasia Jempelis explains the recent development of the Talent Education movement in New York State, which has ramifications for all of the United States.

When Shinichi Suzuki arrived in Rochester, New York for his first two-week Teacher Training Institute at the Eastman School of Music during the summer session of 1966, no one could have predicted the tremendous impact his unique approaches to the education of young children would have in the next few years. The Eastman Institute was the beginning of "Project Super"—the Suzuki program in Penfield, Eastman, and Rochester.

The Project was designed to evaluate the Talent Education approach to violin teaching, using American teachers and students. It was partially supported by grants from the New York State Arts Council and the National Endowment for the Arts. Students came from the Preparatory Department of the Eastman School; the Rochester Public Schools; and the Penfield Central Schools. Teachers were trained by Dr. Suzuki, who guided the early development of the Project and spent almost twelve weeks during six visits to the Rochester area in 1966, 1967, and 1968.

In 1966, less than 100 children between the ages of four and seven began study with members of the Project staff. At present over 600 children are playing the violin, viola, or cello in the Greater Rochester area as part of this program. Talent Education programs have been started in six local school systems: at the Hochstein Music School; at the State University at Brockport; at several parochial schools; and in other cities in New York State.

When Dr. Donald Shetler, Director of Project Super (1966-68), asked me to become a Suzuki teacher in the

Project, I was delighted. I had read about Dr. Suzuki
and his methods and was eager to try them in my
teaching. The results have been astonishing: Parental
cooperation and depth of understanding has increased
over the years, with subsequent improvement in
children's progress.

I have also used the Suzuki approach in my teaching
of string methods for music education majors at the
Eastman School of Music, with excellent results. This
year an elective course on Suzuki Violin Pedagogy has
been added to our curriculum for the intensive study
of the *Suzuki Violin School* and its application to
specific teaching situations—both in music and in
general education.

At the present time, we estimate a total population
of over 1500 young students are studying stringed
instruments by the Suzuki approach in New York State
and in three Canadian centers. Because of the
unprecedented growth of Talent Education, we began
an annual tradition last year at Ithaca College. Each
year, at a different center, there would be a concert,
demonstrating the work accomplished by teachers,
parents, and students involved in projects based on this
approach. Mr. and Mrs. Sanford Reuning and staff
hosted the first concert at Ithaca College on June 16,
1968; 250 young performers participated.

This year, the author and several members of the
Talent Education staff at the Eastman School of Music
were hosts. This event took place on June 21, 1969, in
the Palestra at the University of Rochester's River
Campus. Guest of honor was Dr. Shinichi Suzuki, who
took part in the program throughout the day. Over 500
children, ranging in age from 4 to 13, performed. After
an early registration and "run-through" of the printed
program, luncheon was served at the Dining Center, then

everyone returned to the Palestra for the "real" concert at 2 p.m.

Dr. Suzuki began the concert by starting nine children, three boys and six girls, in the first movement of the Vivaldi A Minor Concerto. Gradually, piece by piece, the nine children were joined by the others, until all 500 children, with Dr. Suzuki at the piano, performed the "Twinkle" Variations to the delight of some 1500 people in the audience. For the first time in an annual concert, violists and cellists also performed. After tumultuous applause from the audience, the Variations were repeated, and the Festival Day was over.

The motivating factor for the success of our festival was cooperation, not competition. There was a wonderful attitude among us all, with great mutual respect in evidence. Therefore, many people contributed to our program. First, Dr. Suzuki, whose dynamic personality is a source of inspiration to all who meet him. Then, there are the New York State Arts Council and the National Endowment for the Arts, who, through their substantial support, have enabled us to bring Dr. Suzuki to Rochester and other New York State centers for his important assistance as teacher and adviser. The members of the Project Super staff at Eastman and all area teachers gave generously of their time and efforts, as did the teachers, parents, and friends of Talent Education who are so enthusiastic and dedicated. Above all, of course, there are the children themselves, who worked so hard and gave such a magnificent concert.

Now that we begin the second decade of Talent Education in America, we can point with pride to past achievements and work together to make this wonderful movement, that has already enriched so many lives, continue to grow and develop. We now have the "tools" to make our profession of teaching more fruitful, joyful, and meaningful than ever before.

DEVELOPING SENSITIVITY

I adjusted myself within three days after the tour. I was amazed at the development of my own ability not only mentally but also physically. After five trips abroad with the children, though the place, climate, and situation were different, I could adapt myself to any circumstance very quickly. Often on our tour we arrived at the hall at the last minute and, after speaking with the sponsors for a moment, I could understand what kind of workshop they wanted.

Dr. Suzuki writes in his book about the blind boy who began taking lessons with him. One day Mr. Tanaka brought his son Teiichi, about five, to receive lessons. The boy had glaucoma after his first birthday and the doctor told Mr. Tanaka that without an operation, which meant total blindness, the boy's life was doomed. Thus a life of darkness began and Mr. Tanaka thought if the boy would learn to play the violin, it would bring light to his life. Hearing the story, Dr. Suzuki was at a loss for a moment, as he had never taught violin to a blind person before. He told Mr. Tanaka to give him a week to think about the method. That night he sat in his room thinking how he would teach a boy who was sightless. He put the light out and began playing the violin. He discovered he needed no light to play the instrument. He could play in the dark as well as in the light. This gave him confidence.

The next week Mr. Tanaka came with the boy. Dr. Suzuki told the boy to hold the bow with his right hand and feel it with his left. This gave the boy the idea of how the bow was made. Then he told him to hit his left hand with the tip of the bow. This was difficult for the boy and Dr. Suzuki gave this as homework. Next week the boy was able to hit his left hand. Then the next week he was to hit his left thumb. After they left, Dr. Suzuki tried this himself and found it quite difficult. He regretted that he gave the boy such hard work. This was difficult even with sight and surely must be impossible for a blind boy. But within a week or two the boy managed to hit his thumb. The time had come for the boy to begin the violin. His sensitivity had developed, and it was not at all difficult for him to study. A year later Teiichi played the Seitz Concerto in D at the concert. Everybody knows the saying, "If there is a will, there is a way." But few find the way. If a boy who sees nothing can play the violin, why can't those who have two healthy eyes be able to do things they want?

In southern Japan there is an inland sea called Setouchi. It is strewn with thousands of islands and is most beautiful to see from the ship. When you go on deck, you will see many islands which seem to block the course of the ship. There seems to be no way to pass between the many islands. But as the ship proceeds, you will notice a gap between the islands and then a wide path coming in sight. Sometimes this is true of life. When we think of the future, it seems as if all roads are blocked by many obstacles. You think it is impossible to go on, but if you try to keep going, you are sure to find a path.

At the E.D.A. center we added a few more subjects. Drawing was one, and Mr. Kurosaki took charge of the younger group, ages up to three, while Mr. Susumu Nemoto took those from four to six. Drawing pictures is fundamentally different from playing the violin or learning how to speak English. Especially when children are very young, we must not restrict their imagination. Mr. Kurosaki lets the children draw as they like. They are simply trying to tell their stories in pictures.

Mr. Nemoto has to attend more to the older children. Sometimes he blindfolds the children and has them feel different articles. Then they must draw what they have touched. This method develops sensitivity of feeling and imagination. He sometimes takes the children to a grocery store and shows them pears and apples. Coming back to school, they draw what they have seen. Many adults, including myself, cannot draw things accurately. Sometimes I find it difficult even to draw a map showing the location of the E.D.A. center or my home. In scientific research one needs to draw with accuracy what is under the microscope. Both the development of imagination and accuracy of observation are important facets of the teaching process in the drawing classes at E.D.A.

Another experience offered at the E.D.A. center is what we call thinking class. This class is instructed by Mr. Fujinaga and Mr. Saiga. The purpose of this class is to have children think by themselves. For instance there are several ways to make the number seven: $6 + 1 = 7$, $5 + 2 = 7$, $4 + 3 = 7$. The children have to think of various ways of making these numbers using marbles, blocks, and other small materials. They are also taught how to read Japanese sentences.

Sesame Street began about the same time as E.D.A. Their programs are distributed to homes in TV, but the route is one way. Thinking class is just the opposite. Children have to make characters themselves and solve problems. Besides these subjects we teach calligraphy, reading (in Japanese), and gymnastics.

THE FIRST VISIT TO EUROPE

In early spring of 1970, I received a letter from Mr. Soffer telling me that England and Germany were interested in inviting the tour to stop en route to the United States. This was indeed big news and I was overjoyed.

The person in charge was Dr. Stephen Moore, Secretary of The Schools Music Association. I phoned Dr. Suzuki immediately informing him of this good news. I also added that he should accompany us, as this tour would be as important as the first one to the United States. Dr. Suzuki also expressed his delight in hearing the news, but he did not express his desire to go and I was much concerned.

In March, we had the 16th annual concert in Tokyo Metropolitan Gymnasium. The day before the concert, I had a private talk with Dr. Suzuki, expressing my feeling that this tour was of the utmost importance and he must go by all means. He said he was not feeling well and would not be able to go. He urged me to undertake the direction of the European tour.

His wife, Mrs. Waltraud Suzuki, would accompany the group to Europe and my wife Junko decided to join us for the first time.

Ten children were selected as usual by Dr. Suzuki; this time we brought a boy pianist, Seizo Asuma, 7 years old, and a boy cellist, Tomoyuki Nomura, 9 years old. Mr. Denda and Miss Nakajima were the only two instructors and Miss Misako Yanagida was the accompanist. The whole group left Japan on September 27 and after a fourteen-hour flight arrived in Hamburg.

While waiting in the lobby to change planes for West Berlin, I noticed that it was very quiet, not at all like an airport in the United States, where loud talk and laughter echo. Here the people were silent, even grim looking. Before embarking, the searching of hand luggage was done in a strict manner; the epidemic of hijacking was at its most virulent.

Mr. Koji Toyota, who was now concertmaster of the Berlin Radio Symphony Orchestra, and his wife were waiting with their two sons at Tempelhof Airport. Mr. Michel Schwalbe, concertmaster of the Berlin Philharmonic Orchestra, also welcomed us. The bus drove through the city to our place of lodging, which was called a guest house but was more like a youth hostel. The streets were wide and clean. There were many trees and unlike Tokyo the air was not polluted.

That afternoon we all slept like logs. I thought I heard a voice downstairs but was again dragged into deep slumber. In the evening Mr. Toyota came for us to take the adults to the Berlin Opera.

The ladies wore evening clothes and the men were in dark suits, but the glamorous atmosphere of the Metropolitan was missing. People were quiet and there were no smiles or laughter. The opera was "The Marriage of Figaro" and though the singing, acting, and everything were wonderful, I had to fight the drowsiness that occupied my brain and tried to make my eyelids close. I knew the audience was enjoying the opera very much. Der Senator für Wissenshaft und Kunst, our sponsor, had reserved special seats for us; otherwise it was very difficult to obtain tickets. If I were to fall asleep, I knew I would disgrace my country. I pinched my thighs and with strenuous effort kept my eyes open. After the first curtain, I asked the instructors if they wanted to stay and they all in one voice echoed, "Let's go home to sleep."

Breakfast was bread, butter, and milk, very simple. At 10:30 a.m. the first performance in Europe began in the hall of the Music School of Juli-Stern Institute. The program opened with the Concerto in A Minor by Bach. After this piece Mr. Denda began the workshop with Mrs. Suzuki acting as interpreter. The program ended with my address: "If all the children in the world have music in their hearts, people of tomorrow's world will understand each other much better." I thought the people understood and enjoyed our workshop.

The school art museum had many kinds of instruments from all over the world. We were especially interested in the old instruments. The lady in charge played several of these for us.

That night all our members were invited to a concert by Radio Symphony Orchestra. The Philharmonic Hall was very different from an ordinary hall. The stage was in the center surrounded by twenty-two hundred seats arranged unsymmetrically on six sides. No one was sleepy this night.

The city provided a sightseeing bus for us the next morning. When I climbed the wall that divides East and West Germany, I thought I understood why the people had such solemn faces. Near the market where many things were sold from stalls was a church. Mrs. Suzuki exclaimed, "In February, 1928, Dr. Suzuki and I were married in this church."

The concert was held that night at seven-thirty at Herman-Ehlers High School. The hall was not large enough to accommodate all the people who wished to attend. All the tickets were sold out. The program began with Sonata in G Minor by Eccles, followed by Allegro by Fiocco. We had a marching demonstration while the children played the Bach Double Concerto. The audience was thrilled.

We left West Berlin the morning of October 1 and landed in London at 6:00 p.m. Dr. Stephen Moore was waiting for us at the airport. He was lean and tall, a typical English gentleman.

At ten-thirty the next morning, we went to St. Mary Abbott's Hall for a TV session with the BBC. I was interviewed by Mr. Kenneth van Barthold, explained the Talent Education idea to him, and then the shooting began. Besides the Eccles Sonata, several ensembles were filmed. Then they began the setting up to shoot Hitomi's Mendelssohn solo. The man who was in charge of lighting never seemed to be satisfied. Hitomi played over and over in the glaring light, and even I admired her endurance. Finally everything was fine, the rehearsal over and the shooting began. When Hitomi was almost finished, there was a strange sound and the video tape snapped. Inserting a new tape, the producer asked Hitomi to play again, but she shook her head.

"I think the girl has had enough," I cut in and the day was over.

After two hours of sightseeing in London, we arrived at the Royal College of Music and at 3:00 p.m. the workshop began. The hall was full; all 650 seats were sold. As this was the first appearance, Dr. Moore did not want to risk a bigger hall. That night the concert was held in the same hall and we had equal success. I think the people in England understood the method and the philosophy very well. It was indeed worthwhile to undertake all the trouble to arrange this visit. The importance which must be stressed is that The School Music Association was the sponsor and if they thought Dr. Suzuki's method could be introduced, it would spread throughout England. The BBC filmed us at the airport and even wanted the children to march as they played, a performance which had attracted wide attention in the lobby.

When we landed at Lisbon, Portugal, the sun was shining bright and the sky was deep blue. The stewardesses wore lemon yellow suits which just matched the climate. An elegant oriental looking lady approached us and said, "Welcome

Dr. Honda, welcome children. Welcome to Lisbon." The lady
was Mrs. Vera Franco Nogueira, president of the Music Academy of Santa Cecilia. She had received a most enthusiastic
letter from Alvaro Cassuto, a young Portuguese conductor,
telling about our performance in New York. Last year Mr.
Cassuto served as assistant conductor of the Little Orchestra
Society in New York and he was present when the children
gave the concert in Philharmonic Hall. He also sent Mrs. Nogueira newspaper clippings which convinced her it was worthwhile inviting us.

I am often amazed what wonderful things a person can do
when he or she is willing. Mrs. Nogueira is the wife of the
former foreign minister. She could sit in her living room enjoying her social life and live in luxury. But her idea was to
spread music, good music to the people. Thus she began collecting funds, which of course is no easy task for any person
in any country, to build the Academy of Music. She had succeeded and now her project was to invite the children of Talent Education. This she had also realized. Our lodging was a
dormitory of the Catholic College Pio XII. The rooms were
simple but adequate.

After changing to summer clothes, we were invited to a
reception given by the Japanese ambassador. Mr. and Mrs.
Hattori welcomed us. The site of their home overlooking the
Tagus River was beautiful.

The old city was interesting, public squares and sidewalks
paved by alternate white and black mosaic tiles. Mrs. Nogueira
took us to a picnic at a fishing port and swimming resort,
Cascais. By the shade of an old citadel we ate our lunch.
There were two skinny dogs prowling for bones. Portugal was
like a nineteenth-century western country. Life seemed easygoing, unhurried, not like Japan or the United States. It
seemed very attractive. If I ever retire I would love to live in
Lisbon. Even in the dormitory, the food was good: meat,
and plenty of wine, white and red. The only trouble was that
we spoke no Portuguese and the sisters spoke no English.

The concert was held at Monumental Theatre, the largest in the city, at 9:30 p.m. The house was filled with an audience of three thousand. I stepped on the stage and Mr. Vasco Barbosa, professor in the Music Academy of Santa Cecilia, translated my English into Portuguese.

"Western civilization was introduced to Japan five hundred years ago by your people. I have brought ten children from Japan to repay your kindness . . ." The people enjoyed my short talk very much and flattered me by saying it was a brilliant speech. But the performance was more brilliant, and after the program we were called back to the stage many times and given a standing ovation.

Next morning at eleven we performed another concert. After the program was over, a gentleman introduced himself. The Assistant Director of Music for the Gulbenkian Foundation, he proposed that the Foundation, which was very interested in the Talent Education movement, cooperate with us in the future. This proposition materialized two years later in England. When we embarked on the bus, hundreds of small children waved their hands good-bye. They were students of the Music Academy of Santa Cecilia. That afternoon we left Lisbon for New York, and when the plane roared up into the air, my sincere hope was that the seeds we had sown in Portugal would grow and produce good fruit in the future.

When we arrived at Kennedy Airport, it was completely dark. Mrs. Mary Lou Tuffin was waiting for us. She is Sheldon Soffer's secretary, a very able lady; it was she who arranged the itinerary for our tour. Yuko once told me that her phone conversation was simply perfect—without useless chatter but still warm and polite.

We all got on a bus and drove three hours to Albany. I did not like the schedule at all. We should at least rest a night in New York and refresh ourselves after the trip across the Atlantic. Later I wrote my complaint to Mr. Soffer. Children recover very easily, but there is a limit, which I knew from my past experience, and this exceeded their limit. The next day two of the children got sick. I gave them shots and pills and they recovered in a day or two.

Our hosts were Mr. and Mrs. Patrick Hernandez and their home was far outside the city. Next morning I took two of the girls, Kaoru and Kumiko, out for a walk. It was a beautiful day and the trees were just turning colors. I picked a small wildflower and showed it to the girls.

"You see this is a very simple flower that grew by the road unnoticed and even trampled. But if you observe it carefully you will see the beauty of the shape and color. We are apt to be attracted to something more colorful and glamorous, but you should know that beauty exists even in these unknown flowers."

Oneida, New York, is famous for its silverware. It was originated by the Oneida Community, where selected people lived in one big house, ate the same food, and worked for the same project. The first business was making glass and now they make silverware. The concert was held in the Civic Center. Though there was no Talent Education program in the district, the Oneida Area Arts Council sponsored our tour. We gave three forty-five minute concerts for them.

There is nothing in the world that is supported 100 percent by everybody. There are criticisms of Talent Education in Japan, especially among professional musicians. But here in the United States I have always admired the broad-mindedness of the people. Still there were some criticisms among professional musicians. In this atmosphere, Mr. George Shick, president of the Manhattan School of Music, invited us to play at his school. We gave workshops for those people who were specially interested. I did not hear the report of how we were received, but I think the workshop went well.

The next day I took the children sightseeing by boat on the Circle Line. Seeing New York City from the sea and the Hudson River, you can get a commanding view of the skyscrapers in Manhattan. I remembered the day I first visited this big city more than thirty years ago by ship. It was before

World War II, and this country seemed to be in its prime. I stood in Times Square and looked up at the colorful illuminations all through the night. Time has changed the same Square so much I don't dare to visit it late at night anymore.

After Columbus, Ohio, and Winnetka, Illinois, we arrived at Lexington, Kentucky. It was through the efforts of Mrs. Kay Sloane that our visit was arranged. People often say that our tours must be very arduous, but compared to the work of the sponsors who must make all the arrangements, our part is quite easy. Mrs. Sloane was the key person who dedicated her time and energy to make our visit a success. Without her work and that of others like her, we could never make our tours. They have a wonderful program in Lexington; they even publish a newspaper for members of Talent Education.

William Starr, Professor at the University of Tennessee, his wife, and many instructors, including two girls from Japan, were waiting for us at the airport in Knoxville. Mr. Starr had visited Japan after the first tour and then during his sabbatical leave came with his whole family to Matsumoto to study with Dr. Suzuki. He was the first full-fledged American professor to study the Talent Education idea and method intensively.

After lunch, a workshop was held in Bearden High School. At the beginning of the program, pupils of Mr. Starr played the Bach Double Concerto and Allegro by Fiocco. They played beautifully, and I congratulated Mr. Starr for his wonderful work. At four the next afternoon the concert was held at the University of Tennessee. During the intermission a lady came to me and said: "Dr. Honda, I was wondering whether to speak to you or not, but I made up my mind to do so. I am from a Dutch family, and during World War II my parents and our people suffered very much at the hands of the Japanese Army. To this day I can't help but nurse a hatred for the Japanese for their deeds. But when I was listening to the music which your children performed, I felt my hatred melt away. The beautiful music they played with such delicacy brought tears to my eyes, and now I can forget and forgive the past." I just bowed my head and thanked her. Words were unnecessary.

After returning to the home of our host, Mr. Compella, I asked Kaoru and Kumiko to play a piece for Theresa, his daughter. Theresa had fallen down the steps and hurt her back badly; she was unable to move. Of course she could not attend the concert, so I asked the girls to play her favorite piece, Sonata by Eccles. Theresa closed her eyes and listened to the music and I felt tears surging up.

The performance in Lincoln, Nebraska, was held at Union College. Junko had left us in New York, joining Yuko in Des Moines. She called me in Tennessee saying that they would take a Greyhound bus from Des Moines and arrive in Lincoln by noon. I asked my hostess Mrs. Ravnau to drive to the bus stop to meet them. The bus arrived but I was disappointed to find they were not on it.

Later when we were having the workshop in Engel Hall of Union College, Junko and Yuko came and sat in the rear. The hall was overcrowded, so many extra chairs had to be brought in.

We arrived at Madison, Wisconsin, at 12:30 p.m. on October 10. Marvin Rabin and Richard Wolf from the University of Wisconsin were waiting for us at the airport. Our hosts were Mr. and Mrs. Michael George. Mrs. George was young and pretty, the mother of two boys and a girl, the eldest six, the youngest two. I marveled that she volunteered to host myself and two girls with all her small children to care for.

I had an appointment with Dr. Rick Heber, Professor of Psychology at the University of Wisconsin. He had written an article about his work in developing low I.Q. babies. In Milwaukee among low income groups, the I.Q. is very low. Even the mothers are below 70, so naturally the children will not go beyond this point. Dr. Heber, receiving a government grant, established an infant center and began the experiment. Every morning twenty-five babies, their ages ranging from eight months to three years, were brought to the center. There the instructor taught these babies to recognize figures and words as the first stage. They were given triangular and square blocks and taught to insert them into holes. They were also taught language. Their I.Q. was below 70 but within three years it reached 130, which is equal to that of middle-class children in Madison. The control group remained below 70. This was proof that intelligence or culture is developed by circumstance and not inherited. The results coincide with our theory perfectly. Mr. Rabin had been doing the same kind of experiment with violin teaching. He taught numbers of children in Milwaukee with very good results.

Though both Dr. Heber and Mr. Rabin were teaching in the same university, they did not know each other. They shook hands, laughing, saying it took Dr. Honda from Japan to introduce them.

At noon I lunched with Dr. Wolf, Mr. Rabin, and Dr. Sarig, all three from the University. Dr. Wolf questioned me: "Dr. Honda, what do you think of the connection between heredity and circumstance?"

"In physiology and in anatomy I believe there is a hereditary factor. But in culture, I think circumstance has more than 80 percent effect. I think we all receive different hereditary traits from our parents and ancestors, but to develop these traits depends on circumstances."

Dr. Wolf looked at Mr. Rabin and said: "This man does not believe in any hereditary factor. What do you think about what Dr. Honda said?"

"I believe culture and intelligence are developed 100 percent by circumstance, and hereditary factors have nothing to do with it," Mr. Rabin spoke strongly.

"These things are not yet clarified. But our visit to this country is to demonstrate how circumstance is important in developing abilities." The time came for us to leave and the discussion ended. At four o'clock we were to have a rehearsal with the Youth Symphony. I visited Mr. Rabin's office and at three-thirty we went to his car in the parking lot. He inserted his key and turned it. No reaction. He gasped and hit his head. "Ah, what a fool I am. I forgot to turn off my lights. You know it was foggy this morning."

I remembered the fog, but we were in a tight situation. All the children were waiting for our arrival. My orders were always to assemble thirty minutes before the concert. Fortunately a lady came to drive her car out of the lot. She kindly helped Mr. Rabin to charge his battery. The car began murmuring.

"Don't let it stop," she said as she waved good-bye. We moved on smoothly. At the crossing the light turned red. Mr. Rabin had entirely forgotten his previous trouble, and he took his foot off the gas. The engine coughed and stopped dead. It was worse this time in the midst of all the heavy traffic; people were honking their horns and yelling. But he was very calm, opened the door, looked at the engine, and then walked slowly to a gas station nearby, leaving me in the car. Several minutes later he brought a man who charged the battery and everything was fixed. We were only a few minutes late.

The concert was held in Stock Pavilion. We had never played in a hall where there was a dirt floor, but it was the biggest hall in Madison. Many people drove hundreds of miles to hear the children play; the house was full, nearly three thousand people.

We enjoyed three good days' rest in St. Paul, Minnesota. Our hosts were Dr. Marcel Richter, a professor of mathematics at the University of Minnesota, and Mrs. Richter, niece of Mrs. Harlow Mills in Los Angeles. They were very kind and the two girls and I felt very much at home.

We usually divide the group into five or six, and they are accepted in different homes. We enjoyed staying in people's homes so that we could make friends. The children make friends with each other easily and though there is a language barrier they seem to understand each other well. I don't know how the people volunteer to accept us, but usually the hosts are connected with Talent Education in their district. It

is indeed a great sacrifice on the part of the hosts, opening
their homes and undertaking all the trouble.
We played a concert accompanied by the St. Paul Symphony and Hitomi played the Mendelssohn concerto. The hall
was beautiful, all the members of the Symphony were friendly, and we enjoyed each other very much.
Later I received a copy of the following letter from Mrs.
Richter to Mr. and Mrs. Mills:

Dear Aunt Elizabeth and Uncle Harlow,
We can't express what a wonderful time we had this
past weekend with our Japanese guests—Dr. Honda,
Kaoru and Kumiko. The house seems empty and quiet
now and we all wish they lived near us always. Not only
did we have a most pleasurable time, but also a most
worthwhile, even inspiring one. Much of what Dr. Honda
patiently expressed to us we heard before, and he
expressed it many times (to us and to guests in the
house) and *finally* we began to feel it sinking in. There
is such a difference between knowing and really
knowing. This morning we both had the experience of
waking with the Vivaldi Concerto ringing in our heads
(as a result of hearing it almost constantly for two days
at two concerts, rehearsal and practice sessions), and we
said, "So that's what Dr. Suzuki is talking about!"—The
involuntary sense of being filled with a certain sound.
We had of course known one should listen and listen but
had never *experienced* a piece of music "entering our
blood." It is very exciting.
We talked to Leila's teacher, Mark Bjork, at the
airport this morning and we are planning to get together
with the other parents of his students next week so
those of us who were fortunate enough to host our
Japanese guests can share with the others and with each
other what we have learned.
Sheila

The schedule for the last week at Reno, Nevada, Pocatello and Caldwell, Idaho, was heavy. When we arrived at Los Angeles we were all quite tired.

After the performance at El Camino College, Mrs. Holborn drove me to Mr. Quon's house, which was way up in the hills of the peninsula. I was tired, but I knew she was exhausted. I kept talking about our trip to boost her spirits. The street led to a winding road up the hill, where she stopped the car. It was very dark and my watch indicated 11:00 p.m.

"I am out of gas," she sighed in distress. My heart almost stopped. But of course I could not reproach her.

"You can move on a little. I see a gas station over there."

She moved the car to the station. It was closed. We found another one a little further. It was also closed but a light was in the window. A man popped his head out of the window. She went to talk to him and came back with her shoulders drooping. "He says it's closed and he will not respond to my plea." I got out of the car and walked to the station. I spoke to the man, "My name is Dr. Honda and I am from Japan. I brought ten small children to play the violin at El Camino College tonight. We are now on our way to my host's home and Mrs. Holborn is out of gas. Tomorrow we fly back home and, if we cannot buy gas, not only I but all the group will be in trouble."

The man came out and filled the gas tank. I paid him, giving all the change for a tip. He put it back in my hand and simply said, "It's my pleasure."

On the morning of our flight back home Dr. Phyllis Glass came to see us off at the airport and gave me the following certificate:

> *American String Teachers Association*
> *California Unit*
> *Certificate of Award*
> *To Dr. Masaaki Honda*
> *For contributing to the happiness and welfare of children throughout the world through your service as Director of Talent Education.*
> *Date: Nov. 1, 1970*
> *Signed: Phyllis Glass President*

Each of the children received a Certificate of Award for outstanding performance.

E.D.A. ENGLISH CLASSES

The E.D.A. English classes were having good results. Miss Emiko Koyama, assistant to Miss Kathy Irving, wrote a report on two of the children, Mami and Chico.

Mami entered the class when she was twenty-two months old, Chico when he was fourteen months. The teachers were reluctant to have them in the class as they were so small and could not join in the activities. But their mother insisted she would take care of them. So they were more often in the hands of their mother than a part of the class. They still toddled in their diapers and, when necessary, they crawled with great speed.

Ten months passed since the English classes began. The children were instructed always to repeat after their teacher. Mami and Chico never spoke a word but always listened smiling. One day these children spoke their first English. They were sitting in the group and suddenly they were opening their mouths and speaking in a loud voice. When Miss Irving spoke to them individually, she found that they knew all the words which had been taught in the class. For ten months they had been silent, absorbing and accumulating English. This is the secret of learning to speak one's mother language.

Mami's mother told us that after Mami began learning English, her vocabulary, even in Japanese, increased. The first phrase she learned in the class was "up and down." At the sound of the piano all the children stood up and raised their hands; then at the word "down," they lowered their hands. This was great fun to Mami and Chico.

Babies, from the time of birth, absorb from their surroundings. But it is more than a year before they begin to speak. The period until this time might be interpreted as an incubation period. Later when the children begin to study violin, there is a difference in the length of this incubation period among them. Teachers and parents sometimes estimate their children's ability at this time by comparing them with others.

We have an interesting article written by Mrs. Kazuko Ichimura. The Ichimuras had two daughters; but their first son, Yoshiyuki, wasn't born until they had been married eighteen years. It was natural that he was overprotected. So when Mr. Ichimura heard Mr. Ibuka's lecture about E.D.A. at the Rotary Club, he and his wife decided to have Yoshiyuki join a violin class in the Center. Yoshiyuki was three and a half years old.

The lesson always begins with a bow to the teacher. Yoshiyuki always waited patiently in his chair until his turn came. "Yoshiyuki, you are next."

When his name was called, he would suddenly crawl under the chair or roll on the carpet. This continued for a month, two months. When he practiced at home, he could bow perfectly. Mrs. Ichimura expected each week that her boy would receive a lesson, but she was always disappointed. She was discouraged that her son could not do what others did so easily. Mothers of other children sympathized with Mrs. Ichimura and consoled her by saying, "We admire your perseverance." Half a year passed and still things did not change.

One day Yoshiyuki was called on again. He hung back as usual and stood bashfully at his chair. Mrs. Ichimura slapped him on the back and said sternly, "Go." Like a jumping jack, the boy sprang to his feet, walked to the teacher and bowed. Miss Kaoru Tomita, the teacher, said, "So you are now ready to begin." And so his lesson began. Of course Mrs. Ichimura was very happy. After the lesson, they skipped back home. Even the color of the sky seemed to change. The result was told to the father when he came home. He hugged the boy and said: "You are great. You made it!"

His sisters also congratulated him for his success. It was a small step but it was big. The boy now was making progress. But this incident was a good lesson for him. When he went to kindergarten and could not summon the courage to jump over a box or do some special thing, his mother would say, "Yoshiyuki, it's just like your violin. You made it and of course you can do other things."

And he did. The importance was the motivation. He needed courage for the first step to overcome timidity, reticence, or maybe just stubbornness. I think if we in our own lives have the courage to take the first step, we can accomplish a great many important things.

There is an old saying in China: It takes a year to raise grain, ten years for wood and a hundred years to make a man. Needless to say, education is not business, but we know it is the best investment in the world. Still financial problems do plague education.

Financial difficulties have hindered the development of the Talent Education movement very much. Even today we are in great debt for the money we borrowed for the construction of the Center in Matsumoto. The expenses of E.D.A. are handled mostly by donations from large companies or firms. But relying on donations only made the financial situation very fragile, and we thought it necessary to strengthen our financial status. Professor Tago, the Executive Director of E.D.A., proposed that we should publish books. Thus Goma Publishing Company was established, and the first book published was *Too Late in Kindergarten* by Mr. Ibuka. It became a best seller and was instrumental in introducing the idea of E.D.A. to the public.

One day in March 1971, I was having tea with Mr. Tomiji Yamazaki (president of Yamatane Security Inc. and also a director of E.D.A.) and Mr. Miyamoto on the top floor of the Hotel Okura. I noticed there were many buildings with numbers on them, like 19, 20, 21.

"Why do those buildings have numbers on them?" I inquired.

"Don't you know?" Mr. Yamazaki replied. "The owner of all those buildings is my friend Mr. Taikichiro Mori, who was once an economics professor. More than twenty years ago I advised him to go into the real estate business. At that time there were only a few office buildings, and as he owned a large tract of land in the center of Tokyo, he began building Mori Building No. 1. By the time Mori Building No. 1 was completed, he had accumulated enough funds from the tenants to build No. 2 and then No. 3; now No. 23 is under construction. He is a very successful man."

"I think I know Mr. Mori," I said slowly. "I think he lived in Kugenuma and he and his family were my patients. I remember treating his second son when he was a student at Tokyo University."

"Is that so! This is indeed a strange coincidence. I will arrange a meeting in the near future. Let's have him join our movement. He will be a great help."

So one evening Mr. Yamazaki held a party in a restaurant called Hamasaku. Mr. Mori and his son Mr. Minoru Mori, managing director of the company, were the guests. Mr. Ibuka and I sat at the same table.

"Oh it's you, Dr. Honda. I couldn't figure out who it was when Mr. Yamazaki told me that a medical doctor who was interested in education would be at the party. You were our family doctor almost twenty years ago." Yes, more than two decades had passed since we last met. Mr. Ibuka explained the purpose and ideals of E.D.A. As Mr. Mori was a professor and his son had graduated from an educational institution, they both understood the motive and philosophy easily.

"We are in need of a building to begin a class. We would appreciate it if you could rent us one of your buildings."

"That's not difficult. Near the Hotel Okura we have several buildings and you may use them free."

The meeting was a great success.

I READ ABOUT DR. DOMAN

One sunny afternoon I went to see the building. It was just the right size and I was overwhelmed with joy. Now we would have more space to expand our education.

That night after I returned home, I had an attack, another hemorrhage. It was like reactivating a volcano which I thought was dead. All summer I was in bed, suffering from illness and heat.

That spring Dr. Glenn Doman's new book, *How to Teach Your Baby to Read,* was translated and published in Japan. Reading the book carefully, I found that Dr. Doman's theory coincided with ours perfectly. What we were doing with normal children, he was doing with brain-damaged children, restoring them by stimulation. I was excited beyond expression. Here was a man in the United States who had been treating brain-damaged children, making them normal. Later some would even go to college. I understood his idea and philosophy perfectly and that night I wrote a long letter to him introducing our E.D.A. movement. I also sent him a booklet which I had written, titled "A Program for Early Development," and invited him to attend our concert in New York in the fall.

Several years ago Mrs. Chieko Akiyama, a famous columnist, told me about *Run Away, Little Girl,* a book she had introduced on radio. "Dr. Honda," she said, "it was the most moving book I ever read and I will send you a copy, so please read it."

The story was written by Marilyn Segal, mother of a brain-damaged girl.

One day when she and her child were in a restaurant, someone seeing the girl told Mrs. Segal of the Institutes for the Achievement of Human Potential which specialized in treating brain-damaged children. Up to this time she had visited many famous clinics and doctors but to no avail. What harm would there be in trying one more? The story tells of the wonderful cooperation of the whole family at Dr. Doman's institution in working to restore this girl.

Since reading the book the name of Dr. Glenn Doman stuck in my mind. Within a few weeks, I received an answer from Dr. Doman thanking me for my letter and booklet and expressing full understanding of our idea. I made up my mind then and there to visit his Institute.

In late August Mr. Ibuka called Junko and told her to use his villa in Karuizawa which is located in the cool mountain area where the air is clean. I hesitated, not wanting to trouble him, but he insisted that it was no trouble and that we should use the villa. I thanked him and decided to go. I was a little afraid to travel by train for three hours since my long rest. I walked slowly and felt dizzy at first, but Junko took my hand. We arrived safely in Karuizawa.

The next morning I took a five-minute walk. The lane in the pine groves was strewn with grass and the quiet of the country eased my mind and body. Within three or four days, I felt my strength coming back and I found I could walk nearly twenty minutes.

One afternoon we walked more than thirty minutes up the hill to find the villa of Mr. and Mrs. W. D. Cunningham. Before going I found the location on the map so I could trace the path. There was a road sign, so it was not difficult to follow the small pathway. Slowly the scene became familiar to me: it was the lane I had trod thirty-eight years ago. Then there was the big stone gate and marble bench just inside the gate. It was quiet and serene. We went up the hill to the front garden. I was expecting someone—maybe Miss Eloise Cun-

I Read About Dr. Doman 261

ningham—would be there for the summer. But everything was quiet and desolate. There in the front garden was a big tall fir tree. I remembered the sunny summer day when Mr. Cunningham sat on a chair under this tree reading his newspaper. Once Mrs. Cunningham gave me a picture of herself standing by his side smiling. The picture was vivid in my mind. The house was dark, the light shut off by the tall tree, and the garden was in the shade.

From the window I could see the large bare living room. Once there was a porch swing on which Mrs. Cunningham used to sit and talk with her friends. I thought I heard a voice and the echo of happy laughter. There was Mother Cunningham, smiling as usual, and stern Mr. Cunningham near her sitting in his chair. I thought I heard the voice of Yaguchi, my best friend. It could not be. He died long ago in the South Sea Islands. I went around the house, looking in the windows. It was vacant, and things that were left were dusty and faded. The kitchen and the dining room were dark and gloomy. Cobwebs were hanging from the ceilings. It was quiet, the silence deadly. The atmosphere was eerie and even in the daylight I felt a chill.

One aspect of the E.D.A. curriculum for newborn babies is to have them listen to good music. It should be repeated as often as possible and, though the baby will not understand the music, it will be absorbed and stored in the brain. When infants hear the same music, it seems they react and have a good feeling. The music was selected by Dr. Suzuki and especially arranged so that there is considerable repetition of each piece. The artists and orchestras were selected from the best possible. People are apt to think that music by symphony orchestras might make difficult listening, but to babies there is no difference between a lullaby, a children's song, and a concerto. It will be absorbed and stored in the brain cells.

Meanwhile the tour of 1971 was materializing; it was to begin in Stockholm, Sweden. I felt I must go. One day Dr. Suzuki called me and suggested that I not join the tour this year. A few days later Mr. Ibuka also called and suggested that it would be better for me to rest this year.

After thinking for some time, I decided I would not go, but instead would meet the group in New York and then visit Dr. Doman in Philadelphia. I saw the group off at Tokyo Airport and gave them advice for the tour. Veteran instructors like Mr. Hirose and Mr. Denda led the tour and Mr. Mochizuki joined them in Europe.

I had invited Dr. Doman to attend the concert on October 16, the opening day of Japan House in New York. Unfortunately on that day Mrs. Adelle Davis, a well-known writer, was to visit the Institute so he could not attend. Instead he asked me to come to Philadelphia and see his work. I asked Mr. Soffer to arrange the details and on October 13 flew straight to New York with Junko.

On the 15th we took the metroliner from Pennsylvania Station to Philadelphia. Mr. Dick McCommick was waiting for us at the station and drove us to the Institute. We drove through a park by a creek and within thirty minutes arrived at the Institute. There was a big stone gate on which was written:

The Institutes for the Achievement of Human Potential
8801 Stenton Ave., Philadelphia

I had imagined that the Institute was in the midst of the city; instead, it was located in a quiet residential section. As we passed the gate, I noticed a flowering bush, the name of which I did not know. "That's a dogwood. Do you have dogwood in Japan?" Mr. McCommick asked.

"No, it is the first time I've heard the name dogwood."

We passed a corner of a building and from the window I saw an elderly gentleman reading a book. "The gentleman is Dr. Raymond Dart. He is from the University of Johannesburg, South Africa. Formerly Dean of the Medical School, he is now retired and living here with us. He is a medical doctor and anthropologist. He's a very, very nice person and he's been to Japan many times."

I changed the subject. "Where do you get the funds to maintain the Institute?"

"Well, we have to have help, of course, and we have help from private foundations and individuals."

"Do you have help from the government?" I asked.

"No, no, none at all."

"But the government is interested?"

"Yes, the government is very much interested, but we prefer to keep the Institute as private as possible. When governments interfere, they sometimes mix things up. That new building there is our library. It's very lovely inside, but I don't want to keep you very long as Glenn is very anxious to see you. But I do want you to get a view of the Institute."

We walked through a lane to a building. It was the consultation room and many people were waiting with their children.

At the end of the corridor was a door and when Mr. McCommick knocked, a loud voice called ''Come in.'' There was Dr. Doman, with his bearded rosy, friendly, smiling face. He stood up as we entered and we shook hands warmly. After we were seated Dr. Doman began, "Will you have coffee or tea? We always offer Japanese guests coffee and offer tea to our Brazilian friends."

"Dr. Doman, the first time I heard about your Institute was when I read the book *Run Away, Little Girl* in the Japanese translation. It is a wonderful book. Many people have read it and have been encouraged by what those handicapped children can do."

He replied: "Yes, indeed, that's how we came to our conclusions. I don't know how I managed to remain ignorant so long of the work you are doing in Japan. But I knew of Dr. Suzuki for a long time. I knew he was teaching small children to play the violin and that he was doing so successfully. I have mentioned him in my lectures for more than ten years. Although I had no personal contact of any sort, I had heard of his work. Dr. Honda, I was most satisfied with the booklet you sent me. I agree with everything it says. I am persuaded there is no limit to what children can learn; they can learn anything we can present to them. Honestly, they can absorb. It is indeed we grown-ups who are retarded."

"That's right," I replied.

"It is sad, sir, very sad," he said. "Well, I am just so delighted that you have come, Dr. Honda. I would give almost anything to hear the children, but unhappily that is impossible. Adelle Davis, who is an American writer on nutrition and our dear friend, is lecturing tomorrow night also, and she is to be our house guest, so I must go to meet her and take her to my house. Last week I was in Ireland and I read about the children's appearance in the newspapers. I could have heard them there had I known early enough. Now I will also miss them in New York. It is my sadness, as everyone who hears the children is overwhelmed."

"Well," I said, "considering our method and philosophy, I don't think I can explain more than I have written in my book. It's poorly written, but now I have a feeling that since we have met in person, we understand each other perfectly and a deep friendship has developed. The reason is that we are both working for the happiness of the children of tomorrow. These children, by developing their abilities, not only mentally and physically but also spiritually, will learn to appreciate the beauty of nature and the happiness of other people. Unless we do this now, the world will stay the same for the next hundred years."

Dr. Doman's face flushed. He was clenching his fists. He perspired and I knew he was just as excited as I. "I agree sir," he said. "Yes, I absolutely agree. In the long, long history of the world, it seems too much a coincidence that in the same quarter of a century human beings should have discovered, on the one hand, the way to destroy all human beings, and at almost the same instant discovered the way perhaps to save all human beings, to teach them to be loving, more dignified and decent, and knowledgeable. If I were religious I might believe that God had said, "Put out your hands: here I give you weapons with which you may destroy all human beings, and here I give you a weapon with which you may save human beings. You may use whichever you like. I am sure, sir, that children who have the opportunity to learn at very early ages have the ability to acquire not only immense knowledge, but also to gain wisdom beyond that which any of us has ever known. I am not so much surprised by what you and I have learned as I am surprised that we did not learn it a thousand' years ago. Because, as you pointed out, language ability seems so obvious: children of every country learn whatever language they are exposed to. It amazes me. I understand you are a medical doctor."

"Yes, I am," I replied.

"I am sure the basis of your philosophy and ours is neurological. That is, that these characteristics are not inherited. This is quite clear, for by environment I could create any sort of human being. I have had the privilege of living with children almost everywhere in the world. I have lived with Eskimo children, with children in the heart of the Brazilian Xingu, who are very primitive, and I have lived with Bush children in Africa.

From our studies of brain-damaged children, we found that people tended to put too much emphasis on inheritance and too little emphasis on what occurs from conception onward. In our effort to discover why such children always fail, it became clear that we should compare brain-injured children not with other brain-injured children, but with normal children. If one is to compare a hurt person with a normal person, however, he must first know what normal is. We were astonished at how comparatively little attention has been paid to normal children.

"We therefore began our research. We spent approximately twenty years asking, What is a child? There was no one who had studied the culture of children of all nations. So we invested funds to study the children of the world. We have now concluded that at birth, in the neurological sense, all children are the same. By one year of age, they begin to manifest differences because of their environment, and by eight years of age they are almost hopelessly different from each other and probably will not change again. I am persuaded that if I were to take a newborn infant from the Xingu and bring him up in my home and, when he was eighteen years old send him to Columbia University, he would succeed. If he were to remain with the Xingu, he would have no conception of time nor written language, but he would be very good at shooting a fish under water with a bow and arrow, which I cannot do. On the other hand, I am also persuaded that if I took my son at birth to the Xingu and left him there, he would be very good at shooting fish under water and would have no conception of time. Now if this seems to be true—and I have a great deal of evidence to indicate that it is—then it behooves us to find out together what is the best in each of the cultures of the world, what is good and beautiful and dignified and stimulating from each culture, and to pass these things on to all children in the world. The idea that a child can absorb only one culture is very sad. It is strange to me that only a few people in the world know and understand this. It seems to me you have a duty to the children of the world, and I have a duty to the children of the world because we know that we need to do everything in our power to confirm each other's work.

"I have been attempting to solve the problem of brain-injured children for many many years. We began to see children who were paralyzed, speechless, whom we stimulated to walk, to talk, and then to read. We began to say here is a child who has severe brain injury, who used to be paralyzed, but now he walks, he talks, and behaves as everybody else does. Now the dead cells of his brain are obviously dead. Why can this child with millions and millions of dead cells behave as well as this child who has a normal brain? We could not answer this question. Then we observed children after the surgical procedure hemispherectomy. We saw a child still walk, talk with an I.Q. sometimes in the genius area, and we asked, How can this child who has only half a brain do everything that is done by the child who has a whole brain? Strangely enough, our work began to draw suspicion not to the brain-injured child but to the normal child, to question why the normal child does not perform better than the severely brain-injured child. In the end we had to say, obviously, well children are not as well as they should be. They should do better. For instance, if we amputate a man's leg and he runs just as well as a man with two legs, we should have to say there is something wrong with the man with two legs if he does not run better than the man with one leg. Then we began to see brain-damaged children who read at two years of age. Now if one sees a child who has been diagnosed as hopelessly brain injured and he can read at two years of age, one must say either it is good to be brain injured, which nobody believes, or well children are not as well as they should be.

In the United States we have a big problem. That side of the street is Philadelphia, this side is not Philadelphia. About two years ago the Philadelphia school system made a great confession. They said 25 percent of all children in the Philadelphia schools were unable to read—not children who did not go to school, but children who did go to school and did not succeed in reading or did not read at a normal level. Now on this side of the street, we have five hundred severely brain-injured children who can read; they are two years, three years and four years old. Now if normal children who are seven years old cannot read and very hurt children who are three years old can read, something is very, very wrong. And we must do something. Now after a lifetime spent studying stimulation and the vast power of stimulation, I know you would have understood the result instantly, maybe before you met me. First, the world has looked at brain growth and development as if it were static, an irrevocable fact; instead, it is a dynamic and ever changing process. It is not that you are assigned intelligence before you are born. It is not that! It's a process. This is a process which can be stopped as it is in severely brain-injured children. The brain-injured child who is chronologically twelve years old but who performs as a one-month-old child is not twelve years of age neurologically.

That child is neurologically one month old. Growth can be slowed, as it is in moderately brain-injured children: the eight-year-old child who performs like a child of four obviously is progressing at half speed. But most significant is that growth can be speeded up as Dr. Suzuki found out, as you found out. Neurological growth can be speeded up just as it can be slowed or stopped.

"Now, for the paralyzed, speechless, vegetable-like children who come here, all we do is give them increased visual, auditory, and tactile stimulation with increased frequency, intensity, and duration in recognition of the ordinary way in which the brain ordinarily develops. That's all we do. We take paralyzed, vegetable-like children, stimulate and restore them. We even send some of them to the university as normal, functioning, strong, intelligent, healthy children. Now, if we can do that with children who are considered vegetables, what can we do with the children of the world who are normal? I would not dare tell a mother what she should put into her child. I would not dare to say what is good taste or bad taste, because that is my judgment. But I do think I have an obligation to tell a mother that whatever she holds to be of value can be placed in her child as easily as nonsense, as easily as unimportant information. You know the primary job of the Institute is to treat brain-injured children, but my interest in life is in teaching well children."

On the train back to New York, I was thrilled, moved, excited to know that Dr. Doman was interested not only in restoring brain-damaged children but in the development of well normal children. His philosophy coincided perfectly with ours, and I made up my mind to cooperate with his Institute and at the earliest period invite him to Japan.

The next evening, October 16, the concert was held in the newly built Japan House. It was performed for the occasion of the opening. As the hall accommodated only 250, attendance was by invitation. The audience was mostly prominent guests, and of course the house was full. After the performance, Mr. Ibuka and Mr. Walker Buckner suggested that we should perform in a bigger hall so that many people could hear. They suggested Carnegie Hall and promised to underwrite the concert if it turned out to be in the red. I asked Mr. Soffer to reserve the hall for a Sunday the following October. Next morning the group left for Meadville, Pennsylvania. Dr. Daisuke Kamijo, who is a medical doctor and a director of Talent Education, came from Japan to tour with the group. We flew to Des Moines to visit Yuko's family and then to San Francisco, and back home via Hawaii. This was a most luxurious trip, so easy, no responsibility of any kind. We thoroughly enjoyed it and I was glad that I could repay Junko for her dedication during my illness.

WE ARE INVITED TO RIO DE JANEIRO

On the 9th of August, 1972 the Fifth Annual Meeting of the World Organization for Human Potential was held in Rio de Janeiro, Brazil. Junko and I were invited to participate in the conference so we left Japan on August 5. At the airport in Rio, Dr. Doman and Dr. Raymondo Veras, president of the organization, were waiting to welcome us. We took a taxi and drove to our hotel in Copacabana. I was surprised to see that the streets were crowded with vehicles and that the drivers drove much as they do in Japan. Considering the size of the country, which is twenty-three times that of Japan, with the population about the same, I thought it would be very quiet with little traffic. Evidently the people avoid the vast inland areas and crowd into the city. Copacabana is considered one of the most beautiful beaches in the world, and I agree that it is. Unlike in Japan, hotels are built near the beach just across a wide avenue. Dr. Doman explained that Brazil has no earthquakes, tidal waves, or typhoons. It has many natural resources, like oil and all kinds of minerals, such as gold, copper, and steel.

I was asked to give a speech about Talent Education on the last day of the conference. I had brought a tape of the national concert, but when I tried it at the hotel that morning, the sound had somehow disappeared completely from one side of the tape. But "The Swan," played by fifty cellists, was audible and I played it for the audience before my talk. People were very moved.

I began my lecture by telling about our experiences in Talent Education. We had been demonstrating the development of abilities in children through the violin for the past twenty-five years. Dr. Suzuki began developing the curriculum and taught it to the children. But the children progressed so quickly, he had to run as fast as he could to keep ahead of them. I explained the philosophy and the method of Talent Education. When I finished my lecture all got to their feet to applaud; it was the first time I had received a standing ovation. The next lecture was given by Professor Raymond Dart. Mrs. Adelle Davis, the nutrition expert, spoke on "How to Orient the Superior Child from Conception to Birth." All the lectures were very interesting.

Dr. Veras' son Carlos was the interpreter for many lectures. Dr. Doman told me how the Veras family became connected with the Institute. Dr. Veras was an otorhinologist in Rio de Janeiro. Carlos was his only son and when he was ten, he had an unfortunate accident; he dived into the sea where the water was too shallow, fractured his spine, and suffered brain damage. The family took him to New York to see the best doctors but to no avail. Mrs. Veras went to St. Patrick's Church on Fifth Avenue every day to pray for her son. One day a man observing her tearful prayers came up and asked her the reason. She told him her story. The man introduced her to the Institute and the family stayed there for two years. Dr. Veras, seeing his son recovering, made up his mind to start a similar institute in Rio. He began his clinic in an old building, but now they had enough funds to build a center which was opened in August. Carlos still needs a wheelchair, but he was graduated from medical school and became an M.D. Now this institute is the center in South America for the treatment of brain-damaged and injured children and is having good results. Dr. Veras told me that he began treating children with Down's syndrome, which is supposed to be hereditary and difficult to cure, and is having good results. On the last evening a formal party was held in the big ballroom. All the men wore tuxedos and the women, evening dresses. It was a colorful party. Junko had brought her kimono for this event and it attracted much admiration.

During the banquet all those attending were introduced. Those who represented their countries made short speeches. But as the hall was big and no microphone available (and besides they spoke Spanish, Portuguese, or English), no one could understand all the content of the speeches.

When I was introduced I stood up and said, "I have met most of you for the first time and I love you all. My wife will sing a Japanese song called 'My First Love.'" Junko was surprised as we had not talked about this before. But she stood up and sang beautifully. People were very impressed, and I thought music is after all the most eloquent language.

After dinner we moved to the next room for the ceremony. The two persons in the world who had contributed most for the benefit of children in the past year were to receive awards from the organization. During rehearsal, which took place in the morning, Dr. Doman told me that the candidates were Mrs. Hazel Doman and Miss Gretchen Kerr of the Institute. I knew these two ladies had been devoting all their energy for children and were more than worthy to receive the award.

In fact, I couldn't understand the meaning of the ceremony or how it was to proceed. Compared to the merry atmosphere of the party, it was solemn and men talked with dignity. The preamble was read in four languages: English, Portuguese, Spanish, and Japanese which I read. The name of the first recipient was read by Dr. Robert Doman, the secretary. It was Mr. Walter Burke. When his name was called, he blushed, evidently not expecting to be called. Mr. Burke, as general secretary of the American Steel Workers Union, had cooperated with the Institute in many ways and all people nodded their heads in assent. "Next will be Mrs. Doman." I whispered to Junko, "She seems very calm." For a moment silence fell on the whole group. Dr. Robert Doman for the second time began reading: "The International Forum for Neurological Organization does accord itself the honor of presenting to," here he paused, cleared his throat and continued, "to Dr. Masaaki Honda, M.D., the statuette with pedestal as the highest honor it may bestow."

I was surprised, stunned. I never expected, even dreamt I would receive such an award. Dr. Doman continued to read:

We cite him then—

A man of medicine who saw beyond the physical ills of his patients, who caught the vision of the quintessential promise of all mankind, the bright hope in the infinite potential of children, who became enraptured with the dream of the day the promise would be fulfilled and a new superior order of man might then successfully govern himself and the material world.

He spoke his word and was ignored. He elaborated his wisdom and it fell upon deaf ears. He showed the way and was resisted.

He was obliged to fight on, a quiet man who manifested courage and determination, and who persevered until others joined with him to pursue his noble cause. His strength of purpose inspired powerful allies. Now, in the full tide of struggle, the blazing light of victory looms.

As with all true honors that men sincerely bestow on other men, the value of which may be measured only in the hearts of those who have chosen to bestow the honor, Masaaki Honda, M.D., the recipient, may not hereby the right reserve to feel personal ownership of this honor, for who owns symbols?

Nor, on the contrary, is he accorded the right of disclaiming the honor so sincerely conferred, for who may disclaim honor for many other men?

He is instead herewith decreed to be its permanent custodian as the symbol of the many men it honors.

And were it not intended to be so, he still would hold it so, for only to such men is honor due. He is the symbol of the symbol.

We who have banded together cannot welcome him to our company but must instead be worthy of his flame.

Presented on the twelfth day of August in the year of Our Lord nineteen hundred and seventy-two.

Robert J. Doman M.D.   Raymondo Veras
(Signed)   (Signed)
Secretary   President

My name was called again and I slowly walked to the front. The heavy bronze statuette with pedestal was handed to me by Dr. Robert Doman. I addressed the audience: "Ladies and Gentlemen, I personally think I do not deserve this honor. It was presented to me on behalf of Dr. Suzuki, Mr. Ibuka, and thousands of children and their parents who have devoted all their time and love for children. This movement I am convinced will in the future be one of the keys to solve the problems of the world." A feeling of gratitude surged up in me—to be understood and appreciated for the work I had done.

It had always been my pleasure to devote my time, energy, and money to spreading the ideals of Talent Education. I have never regretted for a moment the work I undertook. Nonetheless, to be honored not by my country or my people but by a world-wide organization was more than I ever expected. I felt tears welling up and Junko, who sat by my side, put a handkerchief to her eyes also.

After the conference in Rio, we traveled to Brasilia and Manaus. Rio can be thought of as a city in its prime of life, Brasilia a city of tomorrow still in its youth, and Manaus a city of the past. We cruised down the River Negro where it intersected with the Amazon. The color, temperature, and speed of both rivers are different. So the great quantity of water gushed, whirled, and then mixed and became one to flow down thousands of miles to the Atlantic. It was like the meeting of two different nations, different in color and customs but once mixed they become one and mighty.

I had visited Colombia more than thirty years ago. At that time I had the impression that the country was dirty and uncivilized. But when we visited Bogota again, I found that my impression was wrong. Bogota is called the Athens of South America and for good reason. In our life we often make mistakes in judging places and people too quickly. We must acknowledge that time changes everything on earth; what we know of a certain person is only a very small part compared to his whole life.

Once I entered an office in Tokyo and I saw hanging on the wall an Indian prayer: "Great Spirit, grant that I may not criticize my neighbor, until I have walked a mile in his moccasins." Shakespeare expressed this sentiment in other words: "Give every man thine ear, but few thy voice; take each man's censure, but reserve thy judgment." I always speak these lines to myself whenever I feel like criticizing a person.

There were many things of interest in Bogota, like an underground cathedral made of salt, but the museum was the most interesting. In it was a special room. We were ordered to wait at the entrance. The lights were out and it was very dark. The usher told us to move five steps forward; we shuffled in the dark. Then suddenly the lights were turned on. It was a dazzling sight. A big glass display case which flanked us on three sides was full of pure gold ornaments. The size ranged from very tiny rings to large necklaces, bracelets, and other ornaments. These objects were made by Indians long before Columbus discovered America. Looking at the glittering gold ornaments, I imagined that these must have been very precious to the owner, and probably only a chief of the highest rank could possess such treasures.

The experience of traveling two weeks with Americans was my first such experience and I enjoyed it very much. The trip, however, was not always pleasant. The hotel in Manaus was not very well equipped. Mosquitoes feasted on our legs as we dined on the terrace. Once the electricity went out, and we had to carry our luggage down to the ground floor because the elevator was out of order. Everyone suffered the inconveniences without complaint.

The plane to Bogota was very late in arriving at Manaus. People ate, drank, read books, and utilized the leisure time to relax. When we arrived in Bogota, it was late at night and very cold. As we had just left a tropical climate we were wearing only thin clothes. There was shivering, but no grumbling. Customs took a lot of time, but no one complained. The last two days we had a real vacation in Caracas, Venezuela.

I had a chance to speak with Mr. and Mrs. Daniel Melcher in the cool lobby of the Sheraton Hotel. "There are many books in this world, too many. It is difficult even to read the best literature. My profession is to introduce these good books to the public. They need a guide just as sailors do who look for a lighthouse in the dark." Mr. Melcher talked softly. I agree. We always need a guide in this dark world.

Indeed this trip was a wonderful experience and I learned much from my friends.

MOTHER INVESTIGATION TEAM

We thought it important to study the results of babies who are provided with a good environment from the day of their birth. For this study, we decided to select mothers who were in their eighth month of pregnancy and would have time to prepare before giving birth. We reported our plan in the Asahi Newspaper, the largest in Japan, and more than 1500 mothers applied. They were requested to write their views and philosophy of child rearing and accordingly fifteen mothers were selected. These mothers were selected for two reasons, their ability to write a report and their proximity to the Center. We met for the first time in the Center and all came with their babies inside themselves. It was an orientation to prepare them for the arrival of their babies.

Five months later they all came with their babies in their arms. We had distributed the first record in the music curriculum to each home. It was Mozart's "Eine Kleine Nachtmusik." We did not expect instant results, but were mainly interested in how the babies were responding. These children were the first born and naturally the parents were very cooperative. I looked at each mother's face as she spoke and noticed that her eyes lit up. While waiting their turn some looked homely, but when they began speaking they looked beautiful. I thought these were indeed beautiful mothers, full of love for their children.

One mother reported that after three months, she took her baby out for a walk on a beautiful spring day, when suddenly a melody from "Eine Kleine Nachtmusik" came floating through the air. It was from the loudspeaker of a nearby grammar school. The baby stopped moving, cocked her ears and then looked up at her mother as if to say, "I know that music, I have been listening to that melody since I was born."

Most of the reports were similar. Now the babies are two and a half years old and they are ready to receive instruction in violin and other fields. The results have to wait, maybe for two or three years, even for five or ten years, but the program has been engendered in the children so we are expecting good results.

THE 1972 TOUR

The 1972 tour began September 28. This was the longest and most strenuous tour and many unexpected things happened. We flew from Tokyo straight to London, touching down at Moscow for refueling. Our friend Dr. Stephen Moore was waiting for us at the London airport. As he had a letter from the Minister of the Home Office, we were allowed to pass without any other customs inspection.

Our first night was spent in Hitchin on the outskirts of London. Mr. and Mrs. Jean Solder had prepared a nice hot supper for us. But as we had been served on the plane and the children were very tired, they took only hot soup and retreated to their beds. I sat before the fire and talked till late in the night with Mr. Solder. The fire flickered, casting shadows on the wall. It was cozy and warm, a big English home.

"This house and estate were given to us by a wealthy widow. She willed it to us, and we have enough room to accommodate students who want to stay, and a hall to have small concerts. The garden is big enough for the children to run around and I am sure they will enjoy it tomorrow. We received a grant for the Talent Education movement from Gulbenkian Foundation and Leverhulm Trust for which we are very grateful. It will be used to study more about this movement and also to cover teacher training." Listening, I was glad that the seed we had sown in Portugal sprouted in England in the form of a grant from Gulbenkian.

After midnight I woke up shivering. It was cold, very cold, and I put all my coats over the blanket. But still I shivered. It was an unpleasant sensation, and I knew the chills came as a result of catching cold. Next morning I found I had a high fever. I bit my tongue—of all times to be sick, at this moment far away from home and at the beginning of the tour!

The day was arranged so that the children would all go to London for sightseeing and give a short concert with a high school orchestra. But I knew I could not accompany them. I put on my clothes and went down to the dining room to tell the instructors I could not go. Then I went back to bed and slept till evening.

The next morning my temperature went down and I was feeling better. It was a beautiful Sunday, a whole day's rest for us all. I heard a chapel bell ringing in the distance and everything was quiet. In the afternoon I took a walk in the town but the streets were deserted, all the shops closed. People were probably reading or resting in their homes.

The five-day tour from Southampton to Manchester began on Monday. We all got on a chartered bus and off we drove through the countryside through fields, lanes, and small villages. Compared to the big prairie in the United States, the scenery is on a smaller scale but picturesque.

The concert was held at eight that evening and nearly three thousand people filled the big Guildhall. The program began with Presto and Largo from the Vivaldi Concerto in A Minor and was followed by the Eccles Sonata in G Minor. As this was the first performance, I was concerned about the results. But at the end when the audience gave the children a standing ovation, I knew we had succeeded.

Mr. Peter Davis, music advisor to the Southampton School of Education, shook my hand and exclaimed: "I have been in this city for ten years, but this is the first time I have seen a standing ovation given to either professional or amateur musicians. Miss Coke has been here longer than I and she also said it was the first standing ovation."

In Stafford we had a very interesting unofficial concert which I can never forget. Mr. John Taylor, music advisor to the School of Education, was waiting for us at the entrance to the city. He took us to the Stafford Girls High School for lunch. The principal of the school sat at my table, and I asked her if she could attend the concert that evening. She replied that as all the teachers were to have a meeting that night, they would be unable to go. I thought for a moment and then suggested to the instructors that the children give a special concert for them in the school after lunch. We moved to a large teachers' lounge, facing the grounds, and after tuning their violins, the children began playing a concerto by Vivaldi. Looking outside, I saw girls running from all directions on the playground to see this performance. Of course, the windows were too small for them and, observing their eager faces, I thought of having an outdoor concert. There was a suitable place for a concert right outside the building. It was a beautiful day, the sun shining brightly and a soft breeze flowing. The concert was as beautiful as the day, the children playing under the blue sky and the girls with their golden hair fluttering in the wind listening to the concert.

The last concert in England was held in Manchester and the New Century Hall was filled with an audience of two thousand. The people in England were very understanding and friendly, and I knew that the movement had taken root in the soil of that fair country.

Dr. Stephen Moore gave me the following report:

1 In allowing the country to see and hear the results of Dr. Suzuki's outstanding contribution to music as education, The Schools Music Association has been instrumental in rendering a most valuable service to the progress of music education in the country. In days to come it may be looked back on as being an outstanding event and a major contribution not only to music but to education as a whole.

2 Dr. Suzuki's philosophy in educating children under five could well change our whole outlook on Nursery School Education, and to focus attention on the 2- to 5-year-old age range as being one of the most important in a child's life.

3 The children who came this year included two six-year-olds who were able to play from memory both solo parts of the Bach Concerto for 2 Violins and the Vivaldi Violin Concerto (solo part) in A Minor, and many other pieces. It was not a case of just playing through the music; they knew it absolutely and their technique and intonation were excellent. These two children were two of many hundreds who might have come and who could have played to the same standard.

4 Although thousands of children are now receiving lessons in the violin and other instruments, and also in other subjects than music, the whole concept has still to be recognised in Japan by the State, which is contrary to the official backing music in schools receives in this country under the State.

5 As a result of the visits, the Rural Music Schools Association has obtained a £27,000 grant from the Gulbenkian Foundation and Leverhulm Trust in order to go fully into the methods and to cover teacher

training. One course for teachers took place in July of this year at Hitchin under Dr. Alfred Garson, a personal friend of Dr. Suzuki, who has taught the method very successfully for many years in Canada. Two years previously he gave two lectures on the method for The Schools Music Association prior to the first visit to England in 1970 of the Talent Education tour. Lecturers from U.S.A. who are now experts on the method may be visiting England in 1973. Progress has been made in that country, and this year over 200 American children played with the Japanese children at Carnegie Hall, New York.

6 The object of the visits has been to allow as many teachers and other interested persons to hear and see the results of the teaching in Japan, and the very high standards demonstrated have been far in advance of any standards dreamed about in this country for children of comparable ages. If these standards can be equalled in the future, as it is hoped will be the case, then the whole standard of school and youth orchestras and eventually even of professional orchestras will soar.

7 Hundreds of young violin players have now had the opportunity to hear the playing of the Japanese children as well as adults, and places visited include London, Birmingham, Bristol, Manchester, Winsford (Cheshire—twice), Southampton, Stafford, and Ayr in Scotland. In October 1973 visits will include Leeds and Carlisle and possibly Jersey with a second visit to Southampton and to Scotland. [Visits to Jersey, Leeds, and Carlisle did take place, and also visits to Darlington and the London borough of Newham, but the visits for a second time to Southampton and Scotland could not be arranged.]

8 After 1973 there may be a pause with annual visits, when concentration upon teacher training will be the major factor. It is very much hoped that at least one

teacher can be sent to Japan to study the methods on the spot.

We crossed the Atlantic on BOAC airlines and rested a night in New York City. Next day we arrived in Ithaca fully refreshed, and I am glad they took my advice to schedule one night of rest after a long flight.

After a performance at Ithaca College, Mr. Sanford Reuning, director of the Talent Education Institute, presented us with a 1/3 size old violin. He said, "After having known Talent Education, my conception of life has changed completely. We are in trouble financially, but compared to what we have received spiritually, this is nothing. To show our gratitude, I would like to present this violin made by Giovanni Vandelli in 1827 to the Talent Education Institute in Japan." I thanked him from my heart for the violin and for his thought.

I was ashamed to admit that I did not know there was also a city of London in Canada. We were invited to play at the University of Western Ontario and Mr. Paul Green and Mr. Tsuyohi Tsutsumi were waiting for us at the airport. Mr. Tsutsumi began his musical career on the violin but changed to the cello, and after studying under Professor Janos Starker at Indiana University was hired to teach at the University of Western Ontario. His home city is also Fujisawa, and I had known him since he was a boy. I was surprised to see many buses loaded with small children arriving at the school. I asked one of the boys where they came from. He replied simply, "New York." They had traveled across the border to hear the children play. Mr. Tsutsumi told me after the concert that this was the first time the hall was full since it was constructed.

The concert at Carnegie Hall was planned the year before, just after the performance at Japan House. It was proposed by Mr. Ibuka and Mr. Buckner who promised to underwrite it. The Carnegie Hall concert was held on October 15, a Sunday afternoon.

Miss Louise Behrend took the responsibility for the American children who in the latter part of the program joined the Japanese children. At the beginning of the second part, I went up on the stage and addressed the audience of nearly three thousand. "Ladies and gentlemen, when I first came to the United States with Dr. Suzuki to demonstrate his ideas, the people in your country said, 'It's the Japanese mother who can cooperate and teach children. We American mothers are too busy in our daily life and have no time to spare.' But if I had told them that eight years later, more than 180 American children would join our children to play in Carnegie Hall, they would have said, 'You are either a liar or a dreamer.'

"Today is a very important day in the history of Talent Education. What the people supposed to be a dream has been realized. On the ceiling of this hall, I see many lights in a circle. To me it is symbolic of the children of the world. If they all took hands and made a ring like this, the world of tomorrow would be much better." Observing American and Japanese children play together, many people wiped their eyes.

In Lynchburg, Virginia, a concert was held in the high school auditorium. A strange thing happened when the children were playing Allegro by Fiocco, a very fast piece of music. A spider as big as a man's thumb came down to the floor. The children kept on playing as if nothing had happened. I asked Akiko after the concert if she had noticed the spider, and she just smiled and said "Yes."

We had never had much trouble with flights during the past nine tours but this year was different. We left Bemidji, Minnesota, a little past six in the morning. Fog had settled over the city and the clerk hinted to me that the flight might be cancelled. I felt something cold grasp my heart but luckily the plane came and we started for Stevens Point via Minneapolis. On arrival in Minneapolis, we checked in for Stevens Point, and as there was a four-hour wait before the plane was to leave, we had a nice long rest in the lobby feeding the children hot dogs and cake. When I went to the counter to confirm the flight, they told me that due to heavy fog in Stevens Point, all flights had been cancelled. Mr. Nobuo Takahashi accompanied us from New York instead of Mr. Mochizuki, so I asked him to inquire if a bus to Stevens Point was available. He returned and told me that the agent had phoned various companies, but as this was Saturday afternoon and a big football game was being played in the city, all buses were chartered and none was available. The workshop was to be held at 3:00 p.m. and a concert at 8:00 p.m. We could postpone the workshop but not the concert. I knew thousands of people would be traveling hundreds of miles to be there. We had to make it by all means. I went to the North Central counter and told the agent how necessary it was for us to be in Stevens Point that night. I asked him to call all the other bus companies, which he did and at last found a bus. The trip took a little over four hours and we arrived in Stevens Point at dusk. Mr. Jack Cohan, Miss Margery Aber, and our hosts were waiting for us at the University of Wisconsin. My host was Judge Robert Jenkins and he drove me to his home by the river. When I crossed the threshold of his home exhausted, Mrs. Jenkins was waiting for me at the door and with a warm smile she said, "Welcome, Dr. Honda, we are honored to welcome you in our home." When I heard these words, I felt all my fatigue and weariness disappear. Here I was invited to stay with real friends.

That day was Yumi Higuchi's seventh birthday. During the intermission of the concert, Miss Aber led the audience in singing "Happy Birthday" while Yumi stood alone on the stage.

Next afternoon we had a workshop at the University and it rained heavily from morning to night. I looked out from my host's home to the river below flowing with a great quantity of muddy water. A boat was pulled up on the landing and heavy rain was falling on the bulwark. Perceiving my anxiety, Judge Jenkins came with the newspaper in hand. "The forecast says you will have good weather tomorrow," he said.

That evening Mrs. Jenkins arranged a party inviting Dean and Mrs. Fritschel of the University and Miss Margery Aber. After dinner I had time to talk with Miss Aber. "Miss Aber, I pay my deep respects for your work and your courage. When I heard your plan for summer school three years ago in Madison, I was a little concerned about the results. It was, of course, not the workshop but finances that concerned me. You were asking the cream of this country to help instruct and offered to pay their round trip expenses as well as salary. If there were not sufficient numbers of applicants you would have been in the red. But after all it was a great success. You have proved that summer school can be operated successfully in this country. Also the instructors have had a chance to discuss the present status of Talent Education and talk about what should be done in the future. From this discussion they have established the organization, Suzuki Association of the Americas. You are the person who motivated this, and I think will be a great power in the future."

"Yes," she replied. "Since I first visited Japan in '67 with the tour to study Talent Education, my views on the field of music changed, and I thought I would dedicate my energy to spread the movement. It was your daughter Yuko who taught me the philosophy of your movement. I happened to sit by her in the bus and she told me that there was no competition, only encouragement and the spirit to help each other. I never knew such an idea existed in music. It was like a beam of light."

I was moved and my respect for her became deeper. It was an unforgettable night.

Finale

THE BEGINNING OF A NEW WORLD

April 16, 1961, was a big day for Talent Education. Pablo Casals was coming to Bunkyo Hall in Tokyo to hear the children play. About 400 children within the Tokyo district assembled to participate. Teachers and children were excited to have the great artist, to whom they had so often listened on records, come to hear them play. The excitement reached its peak when Mr. Casals, after hearing the children play, came up on the stage and gave the following message with tears in his eyes. "Ladies and gentlemen: I assist in one of the most moving scenes that one can see. What we are contemplating has much more importance than it seems. I don't think that in any country in the world we could see such spirit of fraternity, of cordiality at its utmost.

"I feel in every moment that I have had the privilege of living in this country the superiority of desire for the highest things in life. And how wonderful to see that grown-up people think so much of the smallest like these as to teach them to begin with noble feelings, with noble deeds. And one of these is music.

"To train them to music, to make them understand that music is not only sound to have to dance or to have small pleasure but such a high thing in life that perhaps it's music that will save the world.

"Now I not only congratulate you the teachers, the grown-up people, but I want to speak my whole admiration, my whole respect and my heartiest congratulations. And another thing that I am happy to say in this moment is that Japanese are great people and Japan is not only great by deeds in industry, in science, in the arts but Japan is, I would say the heart of the hearts and this is what humanity needs first, first, first."

After translating these words from the tape, I read them over and over and was deeply moved. But at that time I could not grasp the meaning of his words "Music will save the world." Since then I have visited many cities in the United States, met many people for the first time, received their hospitality, talked with them. And though at the time our communication was brief and many I might never meet again, the friendship and understanding created through music will always be cherished in my heart. Now I understand the words "Perhaps it's music that will save the world."

Dr. Robert Morris, president of the University of Plano in Texas, came to Rio de Janeiro to join the conference in 1972. I had a chance to talk with him in Brasilia. Dr. Morris' son William was brain injured and was restored after receiving treatment from Dr. Doman.

To Dr. Morris just restoring William was not enough. He must be accepted in society the same as any youth. Therefore, he needed an opportunity to graduate from a college or university. There are a number of boys and girls who though restored do not have a chance to go to college. So he bought a hundred acres of land on the outskirts of Dallas, resigned his presidency of the University of Dallas and established the University of Plano. The objective of the school is to give orientation to the students, to raise them to the level of normal students, and then send them to the university. Besides brain-damaged youths, there are many other youths who have potential, but because of the obstacles they have encountered have failed to develop their abilities. These will tend to have an inferiority complex which often leads to juvenile delinquency. So Dr. Morris' school offers an opportunity to these students to reach a standard that will allow them to complete a university course successfully. This is indeed a wonderful testimony, and I could not but pay deep respect to his work. He came to Japan on March 26, just missing the concert, but we discussed many things. Dr. Glenn Doman told me that Mr. John D. Goodell had been taking movies of children of the world. We emphasize that all babies are the same at birth. Within a year they will change much, and in ten years they are hopelessly changed from each other. It is the environment that is the cause of these changes. People are apt to think they have to see to believe. But it is impossible for us all to travel to far countries to see all the children of the world. Mr. Goodell has gone to twenty-six countries, including the Kalahari desert in Africa and the jungles of Brazil, to take the pictures. It took him four years and the film is almost completed. Dr. Doman told him that, without adding the children of Talent Education in Japan, it would not be complete.

In March 1973, Mr. Goodell cabled me asking if it was vital that he shoot the National Concert. I cabled back, "It is vital." He arrived on the evening of March 24, just two days before the concert. I asked him his motive for making the film. His answer was, "I was a technical director in a U.S. industry and designed a teaching machine. Then I became interested in education. I thought that the best way to communicate with people at large is through motion pictures."

It is the children of the world who will solve the future problems, because we don't know how. So somehow we must give children the opportunity to be better people. Whenever a baby is born, be it in the Kalahari desert or in the jungles of Brazil or in the U.S. or Japan, it is the beginning. So the title of his film is: "The Beginning."

I absolutely agree with him. My past life, the history of Talent Education, and the National Concert which will be held today is The Beginning. The Beginning of a New World.

Masaaki Honda, November 1975

John Kendall and Dr. Honda

National Concert in Tokyo

David Oistrakh
conducting the
National Concert, 1967

Introducing an
American participant
at the National Concert

Small performers,
Tokyo National Concert

Kazuyo Kageyama

At the National Concert:
(*left to right*)
Princess Chichibu, The Empress,
Crown Prince and Princess

Poster in front of
Philharmonic Hall, New York,
announcing concert

Boat tour around Manhattan

With Eugene Ormandy
on stage of
the Academy of Music,
Philadelphia

On campus,
Florida Southern College

Performance inside
the Washington Cathedral

Playing en route

Arriving in London

At a school in England

Queen Elizabeth Hall
London, 1971 tour

Yehudi Menuhin
plays the Bach Double
with Yasuko Fukada